THE SIMPLE DOLLAR

Vice President, Publisher: Tim Moore
Associate Publisher and Director of Marketing: Amy Neidlinger
Executive Editor: Jim Boyd
Editorial Assistant: Pamela Boland
Development Editor: Russ Hall
Operations Manager: Gina Kanouse
Senior Marketing Manager: Julie Phifer
Publicity Manager: Laura Czaja
Assistant Marketing Manager: Megan Colvin
Cover Designer: Alan Clements
Managing Editor: Kristy Hart
Project Editor: Andy Beaster
Copy Editor: Water Crest Publishing, Inc.
Proofreader: Jennifer Gallant
Indexer: Publishing Works, Inc.
Senior Compositor: Gloria Schurick
Manufacturing Buyer: Dan Uhrig

FT Press offers excellent discounts on this book when ordered in quantity for bulk purchases or special sales. For more information, please contact U.S. Corporate and Government Sales, 1-800-382-3419, corpsales@pearsontechgroup.com. For sales outside the U.S., please contact International Sales at international@pearson.com.

Printed in the United States of America

First Printing June 2010

ISBN-10: 0-13-705425-4
ISBN-13: 978-0-13-705425-1

Pearson Education LTD.
Pearson Education Australia PTY, Limited.
Pearson Education Singapore, Pte. Ltd.
Pearson Education North Asia, Ltd.
Pearson Education Canada, Ltd.
Pearson Educación de Mexico, S.A. de C.V.
Pearson Education—Japan
Pearson Education Malaysia, Pte. Ltd.

Library of Congress Cataloging-in-Publication Data

Hamm, Trent.
   The simple dollar : how one man wiped out his debts and achieved the life of his dreams / Trent Hamm.
      p. cm.
   ISBN 978-0-13-705425-1 (pbk. : alk. paper) 1. Consumer credit. 2. Debtor and creditor. 3. Finance, Personal. I. Title.
   HG3755.H237 2010
   332.024'02—dc22
                                                    2010005204

THE SIMPLE DOLLAR

How One Man Wiped Out His Debts and Achieved the Life of His Dreams

Trent Hamm

*To Randy Byrn, who not only
taught me how to write but
made me believe I could*

Contents

Acknowledgments

A book like this doesn't get written without a ton of help from a mountain of sources, both expected and unexpected. Here's a big list of these people.

First of all, I'd like to thank Randy Byrn, my high school English teacher, for his constant insistence that I had the ability to write and his similarly dogged attitude that any writing can always be improved. Even more than a decade later, I still turn to a faithful grammar handbook when the correct usage escapes me, and the usage of a strong note-taking procedure was fundamental in making this book possible. Even after many, many revisions, I fully expect him to find at least twenty five huge errors I made in this book—in fact, he'll probably send me a copy with them marked in red pen.

An enormous thanks to Kristen Cross, Daniel Koontz, Matthew Jabs, Catherine Krikorian, Victoria Rosin, Amanda Schuler, Kerry Taylor, and John Warfield, who all took time out of their busy schedules to share their personal experiences with me, answer my questions, and elaborate on even the simplest of points.

Ideas and suggestions came from countless wise sources: Philip Brewer, Erin Doland, Jonathan Fields, Seth Godin, Christopher Guillebeau, Brett McKay, J.D. Roth, Gretchen Rubin, Ramit Sethi, Pamela Slim, Glen Stansberry, and Gina Trapani.

This book was written while listening to a wide variety of music, but a few albums were played over and over again. Special thanks to Neko Case, Old Crow Medicine Show, The Duhks, Bruce Springsteen, Modest

Mouse, Nellie McKay, Laura Cantrell, Johnny Cash, Apples in Stereo, Feist, AC/DC, The Sugarcubes, Bob Dylan, The Smiths, Morrissey, A Fine Frenzy, U2, Gillian Welch, Peter Gabriel, The Blind Boys of Alabama, The Decemberists, Belle & Sebastian, and The Roots. Time and again, your music was able to help me get in the right mindset for writing, even when it seemed like I was miles away from the right words.

A deep thanks to Jim Boyd of Pearson Education, who advocated powerfully for this book and made it possible to turn the ideas in my head into the printed words you now hold.

I would be remiss if I did not mention my abundantly humorous and insightful pastor, Heidi Williams. Faith and writing are both incredibly challenging struggles, and Heidi has an impeccable knack for giving me advice when I most need it. This book would have never been finished without some prayer, some meditation, and some long nights searching for guidance, and I'm lucky to have found the answers I needed along the way.

Last but not least, I'd like to thank my wife Sarah for her infinite patience and love during the process of writing this book, as well as Joseph and Kathryn for their constant ability to give Dad a big emotional boost right when he needed it the most. I love you guys.

About the Author

Trent Hamm transformed his life, escaping both massive consumer debt *and* work he couldn't stand. He began sharing the lessons he learned through his website, The Simple Dollar (www.thesimpledollar.com), which has quickly grown into one of the nation's most popular personal finance sites, attracting more than 600,000 visitors every month.

He is the author of *365 Ways to Live Cheap: Your Everyday Guide to Saving Money,* and writes articles that are regularly syndicated to hundreds of small newspapers and newsletters.

Introduction

On April 20, 2006, when my son was roughly six months old, I realized that we didn't have enough money to pay our bills. It was shocking and incredibly painful. Although I had come to some valuable realizations already, the fact that we didn't have enough money to make ends meet, and we had tens of thousands of dollars in credit card debt, student loan debt, car loans, and a bunch of financed furniture and equipment in our home, meant that something had to change. Now.

I buried myself in personal finance books, coupling them with the philosophy and economics books I had already been reading. Over the next few months, I started to take some radical steps to fix our financial state.

More importantly, I began to realize that this entire experience was one that other people were struggling with. How can a person balance all the aspects of modern life on a limited income? How can we find personal and professional happiness in an increasingly complex world where real wages for most of us haven't changed in decades?

So, in October 2006, I started TheSimpleDollar.com on my own with no fanfare to share these experiences. Within two months, I had 100,000 visitors. Today, The Simple Dollar has nearly a million visitors a month and tens of thousands more who receive articles by email.

Along the way, I've had conversations with thousands of people who were struggling with questions like these in their own lives. I've heard countless stories of people digging through the challenging connections between their money, their happiness, their daily choices, and their mission in life.

I began to live my life as a laboratory for these ideas in many ways, and I shared these experiences with my readers. I tried countless methods of reducing my spending. I quit my job and devoted myself to writing full time, a truly scary endeavor. I bought a home, and then wondered if it was the right move after all. I had a second child.

And along the way, I learned some surprising lessons about our modern lives. Many of the rules that we use to live our lives are broken. They were written down many years ago to describe a way of living that no longer exists. Our grandparents couldn't imagine the ability to share information via the Internet, the power of communication from nearly anywhere via cell phone, the ability to sell one's ideas and products anywhere—and buy them from anywhere—thanks to globalization.

Those are the realities of life today, and they're rewriting more than just the rules of how we make friends and do business.

The most valuable investment today is not in the form of a dollar, but in the form of a relationship. All the income we need can come from a large set of healthy relationships.

Debt is a prison of our own choosing, and we're enticed to enter that prison by the availability of a variety and quality of goods unimaginable fifty years ago.

Life is far more unpredictable than most of us think, and it gets more unpredictable all the time—and almost all planning ignores that key fact.

Saving for your child's undergraduate education is almost useless because the value of a bachelor's degree—and the methods we are using to get there—are changing radically.

Being a reliable employee is a path to the unemployment line—we've entered a new era where an employee-employer relationship is an exchange of a new kind of value.

Overspecialization is a dangerous trap. The route to the top relies on a Swiss army knife of transferable skills, regardless of your career path.

The American dream of a nice home of your own is just one card in a rigged game of three-card monte—and you have to pay a desperate price to play. Instead, there's a much smarter way to find a place to live.

If these ideas intrigue you, keep reading. I'll touch upon these ideas and many others—and share in detail how they work in my own life and in the lives of many other people—as we talk about change.

I'm going to start, though, with an area that hits home to far too many people and keeps them from even thinking about moving on and fulfilling their dreams.

Chapter 1

Prison Made of Plastic

I sat at the kitchen table flipping through the mail, seeing bill after bill after bill. I tore open a couple of them immediately, wanting to see the terrible news in its full glory. I began to calculate what I could afford to pay and what I could not, I began to quickly realize that the pile of bills I just received not only wouldn't be covered by the current balance of my checking account, but that my next paycheck would not cover them either—and that was if I spent absolutely nothing on food, gasoline, or anything else. I sat there completely stunned for a moment; then I got up and went into my son's room, closed the door behind me, and sat down in the rocking chair across from his crib. He was so tiny lying there, less than six months old, and sleeping so peacefully there without a worry in the world. As I watched him lie there, gently breathing, emotions poured through me. Guilt. Shame. Embarrassment. Pain. I was failing this wonderful little boy, this child who had already brought incalculable joy into my life. He relied on me for everything, and because of my poor decision-making and my selfishness, I was letting him down. I closed my eyes and didn't realize at first that I was crying, almost uncontrollably. My wife came in and put her arm around me. Eventually my sobbing woke up my son, who also began to cry. Sarah held us both.

April 2006

Let's make no bones about it: High-interest debt is a prison of your own making. Financial writer Michael Mihalik puts it quite simply: "Debt is slavery."[1]

Debt increases your risk while at the same time decreasing your opportunities. If you accumulate debt, an unexpected negative event in your life has much more impact than if you were debt free. Similarly, debt often causes you to pass up positive opportunities in your life, such as a job offer or an incredible bargain on a car.

I believe deeply in a debt-free lifestyle. The only additional debt you should ever incur is a home mortgage and, if you do have a mortgage, it should be paid off as quickly as possible. The greatest personal freedom you can have occurs when your monthly bills are as low as possible, and there's no better way to accomplish that goal than to get rid of your debts—all of them.

It sounds like an impossible goal. I know that when I was stuck in an overspending lifestyle, it seemed impossible for me, as well. When I finally realized that I needed to make a change, I still didn't believe it was really possible.

1   Michael Mihalik, Debt Is Slavery. Page 23. ISBN: 9780978545703.

Then, in the course of about three years, we paid off $21,000 in credit card debt, $2,600 in additional consumer debt, $6,600 in car loans, and $17,000 in student loans. Along the way, our financial status became so secure that I was able to walk away from my full-time job and follow my dream of being a full-time writer, giving me an incredibly flexible schedule and much more time to spend with my children.

To put it simply, three years of focused debt repayment *completely changed our lives.* I have a new career. I have a new home. I have a much more stable marriage. I'm no longer scared at night about our financial position. I no longer dread getting the mail.

Debt was a prison, and we escaped.

How exactly did we do this? Here's a step-by-step guide describing exactly how we managed to extract ourselves from this precarious debt situation and put our lives in a whole new place.

Get Everyone on Board

We've all heard the horror stories. One spouse secretly racks up $20,000 in credit card debt, while the other one saves and scrimps. One partner talks about the large amount of money in the bank, while in truth there's not much saved at all. Married couples fight— and even separate—because one partner spends with reckless abandon while the other partner is constantly cleaning up the mess and working to keep the couple above water.

In each of these cases, the same problem rears its ugly head: The people in the household are on different pages with regard to the plan for long-term financial security. To put it simply, **if you and your partner are not in agreement with your long-term plans, actions on behalf of those long-term plans are useless.**

The best opening step in this journey is to simply sit down with your partner and do two things. First, identify the big goals that you have in common. Where do you want to be in five years? Do you want to have children? Do you want to have a nicer home? Do you want to have a different career? Figure out what you both want out of life. From there, look at your financial state—your debts and your income level. What needs to change for those dreams to come true? Don't get bogged down in the specifics at this point—instead, the point is to recognize whether or not you're both open to making changes in your life to achieve the dreams you share.

Remember, **actions speak louder than words.** Quite often, people will give lip service to the initiative of their partner, but won't make any real change to their own behavior. If this happens, there is a much deeper trust issue in your relationship, one that will require a lot of communication—and perhaps some counseling—to solve. You will not find financial, personal, or career success until you address it.

If you find yourself in this type of situation, move your focus from fixing your finances to fixing your relationship. Take some time to carefully evaluate the entire state of your relationship. Communicate calmly with your partner—don't let emotions run the day. Seek counseling and build a relationship based on trust where you both feel safe expressing your viewpoints and are able to work through disagreements in a rational and healthy fashion.

Without that, you will not be able to work together for a brighter future.

Reduce Your Interest Rates

If you're ready to make changes, and your partner is on board as well, you're already ahead of the game. The next step is to minimize the amount you pay each year in interest on your debts. After all, the less money you lose to your debtors without actually reducing your debt, the better.

The first step is to simply make a list of every debt you owe. On that list, record several pieces of information for each debt: the name of the person or company you owe money to, how much money you still owe, what the interest rate on that debt is, your most recent monthly payment amount, your account number, and the telephone number of the person or business you owe.

Next, move through that list of debtors and call each one. Explain your situation—you're attempting to set up a debt repayment plan because you're worried about your financial future—and request a reduction in the interest rate of your debt. If the first person you talk to won't do this, request to speak to their supervisor and repeat your case.

Some people argue against this approach because there is some risk that the business may reduce your credit limit or close your account. To that argument, I say, "Who cares?" After all, your goal here is to *repay the debt*, not to merely free up some room so that you can charge it up again.

Once you've directly reduced your interest rates, it's time to look at indirect methods. Set up a meeting with a representative of your local credit union and see whether or not they have a loan package that will enable you to consolidate some of those debts. Consider transferring balances from high-interest credit cards to lower-interest ones (this can usually be done with a phone call to the company holding your lower-interest card).

One suggestion: Do *not* borrow money from family or friends to pay off high-interest debts. Borrowing money from people you love puts a completely new dynamic on the relationship, adding a lender-borrower relationship to the mix. Now, ask yourself, do you love the businesses you owe money to? Do you enjoy the bills they send you, requesting money? Is that a dynamic you want to add to your relationship with your friend or loved one, where they're trying to decide how to ask you to start repaying that debt, while you're feeling resentment when they ask you for repayment? Don't mix loved ones and debts—they just don't mix.

At this point, you've made some significant progress toward minimizing the amount you're going to pay in interest. Your monthly minimum payments should be lower than before as well. Now comes the hard part—buckling down and paying off the debts.

A Plan for Debt Repayment

The next step is to assemble a debt repayment plan, which is far easier than it sounds. Remember the list of debts you made before, when you were attempting to reduce your rates? Make it again with all the debts you have now and their current interest rates. This is the backbone of your debt repayment plan.

There are two common ways to build this plan. One method is to pay off the debts in order of their balance, from smallest to largest. This is often referred to as the "debt snowball" and is popularized by personal finance pundits such as Dave Ramsey. The advantage of this plan is that it lets you feel the thrill of victory over debt as soon as possible, since the easiest debt to pay off is the one with the lowest balance.

On the other hand, the method that minimizes the total amount of dollars you'll pay out is to pay off the debts in order of their interest rates, from largest to smallest. The largest interest rate debts are the ones that are eating up more of your money, so paying them off first means that you'll end up, over the long run, paying less in interest. However, this plan can sometimes leave you with long periods without the thrill of eliminating a debt—it's psychologically more challenging.

Whichever route you choose, set up your debt repayment plan by listing the debts in that order. Then, each month, make the minimum payment on each debt except for the top one. For that top debt, *throw everything you can at it*. You should strive to make at least a *triple* payment on that bill at the top of your list at a minimum. Set a goal for each month—how much can you consistently pay on that bill? Treat *that* amount as the minimum payment on that top bill.

When you manage to pay off a bill, cross that bill off the top of your list and celebrate a little! Then get down to business on the next bill. Add the payment you were consistently making on the previous bill to the minimum payment on this new top bill—that's your new minimum payment! Strive to make it each month.

The question many people ask is *how can I possibly make more than the minimum payments when I was not really making them before?* You'll have to make some choices along the way. Those choices, however, are often less painful than people initially think they will be. Stay tuned—Chapter 8, "Frugality as Framework," will explain all about it.

Get a Rope

Our living room, now an eBay shipping center, was littered with packages, small boxes, brown paper, and labels. Our previously-overstuffed DVD rack lay largely empty, and our video game consoles were as bare. Sarah peeked around the corner and admired the chaos. "Are you sure this is really worth it?" She nodded toward my trading card binder, which formerly housed an enormous collection of sports cards and gaming cards, but now was nearly empty. I looked up at her. "According to my math, once we sell and ship out all of this stuff, your car will be paid off and our MBNA credit card will be paid off next month." She looked at me for a moment just to make sure I wasn't joking. She opened her mouth to say something, but then just burst into a big smile.

June 2006

Over the years, I've had the chance to talk to many readers who felt they were drowning in their debt. They were simply overwhelmed with the amounts they owed, and it felt hopeless. Even after coming up with a debt repayment plan and ensuring that their interest rates were low, they still felt as though they were climbing Mount Everest without a rope.

To those people, I say, "Get a rope." What do I mean by that? What I mean is, give yourself a big boost on your debt repayment plan right out of the gate.

Go through your home, room by room, with a discriminating eye. Look for things that you don't use—or rarely use. Start with your closets, your junk-collecting areas, and your collections. Go through these items and ask yourself, honestly, if these items are adding genuine value to your life—or if they're just representing memories that you hold in your heart and your head, regardless of what items are filling your closet.

I'll use myself as an example. Once upon a time, I avidly played several trading card games, and I played with enough skill to amass a large collection of these. Yet, as time went on, I found that I really wasn't enjoying this enormous collection I had amassed. I'd look at them on occasion, but mostly I just enjoyed spending time with friends. My cards would go untouched for months, but I kept them because of the memories.

I realized, though, that the memories come from within me, not from collected items that I barely looked at. I might get a smile from the memories brought about by looking at them on occasion, but I could get that same good feeling from meeting and chatting with an old friend or keeping tabs with those friends on message boards or on Facebook. It was the camaraderie and the stories that I enjoyed, not a closet full of stuff.

So, I spent a week going through that collection. I sorted it, determined the items that had significant individual value, and sold almost all of them.

I applied the same philosophy to our DVD collection and our book collection and our video game collection. We sold stuff on eBay, at consignment shops, at used stores, and directly to people. Just like that, some of our debts went up in smoke, and we suddenly felt in control of our situation for the first time in a long time.

Try this approach with the items you possess. The unwanted, unnecessary purchases of your past can often serve as a wonderful rope to help pull you up to a new place in your life.

Snowflaking

What would you do if you found a $50 bill lying in the street? Would you go off and spend it on something frivolous? Or would you quietly stick it in your pocket, knowing that it has the power to push you a little bit further toward your dreams of debt freedom?

Many people would choose the former strategy, arguing that it's *just* fifty dollars. That type of attitude is exactly the type of attitude that leads to a lack of control over one's life. If you spend every dollar you find, you're completely at the mercy of the unexpected in life, as great opportunities will pass you by and bad situations will bring you to your knees.

The alternate strategy is to allow yourself money with which to have fun each month, but when extra money comes in, treat it as a way to get ahead with your long-term plans. This strategy is often referred to as *snowflaking*, perhaps in reference to the "debt snowball" concept.

These "snowflakes"—the little money you find here and there in your life—are applied to your debt repayment plans, helping you to make a little bit more of a payment each month. That $50 bill found in the parking lot becomes an extra $50 on your next debt payment, perhaps giving you just enough to pay off that debt a month earlier than expected.

There are many ways to snowflake. Recycle aluminum cans once every few months and apply that money toward your debts. Ride public transportation once a week and apply the $3 you saved in gas toward your debt repayment plan. Keep all the change and small bills you accumulate in a jar; then cash that in twice a year and use that amount to whack away at your debt. You can even go big with this and start a part-time job solely for debt repayment—a big snowflake, indeed.

The goal is simple—just use the little opportunities life gives you to get rid of that debt faster, which opens the door to even bigger opportunities.

Five Steps for Today

If you remember one thing about debt repayment, it's this: The reason to pay down and eliminate your debts is that it opens up a great deal of personal freedom in your life—freedom to change careers, freedom to try new things, and freedom to take advantage of opportunities. These freedoms are essential to the ideas covered in the rest of this book.

Debt is the opposite of freedom—it reduces your opportunities and leaves you with a sense that your life is out of your control. You *can't* lose your job. You *can't* make a career change. You *can't* move to a different city. You *can't* say no when your boss demands more overtime.

Break Free

Here are five steps you can take today to get started on repaying your debt:

1. **Schedule a talk with your partner or spouse.** None of this matters if you're not on the same page and working toward the same goals. During this talk, allow things to be an open book—no hiding secret plans, no hiding financial mistakes. Instead, strive to find out your real financial state and discover the goals that you have in common.
2. **Make a list of all your debts.** Simply cataloging all of one's debts goes a long way toward making the situation real and tangible. This will likely involve digging through statements, checking websites, and perhaps making a phone call or two.

3. **Think about the stuff you own that's unneces-sary.** Ask yourself if you really use some of the items you have or if you keep them around sole-ly for sentimental reasons. If it's for sentiment, ask yourself if the memories exist in that item or if they exist in your heart.

4. **Make a list of the things you hope to accomplish in life.** What five big things do you hope for in your life over the next five years? Once you've got those down on paper, ask yourself what needs to happen for those things to be achieved. You'll likely find that these things you dream of are much, much easier to accomplish if you eliminate your debts.

5. **Recognize that it's not hopeless.** Many people feel overwhelmed by their debt load—I know I cer-tainly did for a number of years. It's not hope-less—nothing ever is. Just stop, take a deep breath, and start looking through your entire life situation with a careful eye. You might just be surprised at what you'll find.

Chapter 2

What's Missing?

I watch out the window as my wife and my son drive away with her parents, and I hate every second of it. It's hard not to see the disappointment on all of their faces as, yet again, I have to turn away an invitation to focus on my work. Several hours later, my wife wakes me up. A half-eaten burrito has congealed on my plate, and I have fallen asleep at the keyboard. As I stagger into our bedroom, my wife tells me that our son had strung together a sentence for the first time at dinner. I peek into his room and see him asleep. I have missed yet another moment—the type of moment I had sworn I would never miss in my child's life. Was work all I was really living for?

September 2006

All of us have a story to tell, a story distinct from every other story in the world. I could talk at length about my own story—and I share snapshots of it throughout this book—and perhaps you see things in those snapshots that you recognize in your own life.

For some of us, that distinct story has taken us to a negative place—painful experiences in your past, physical ailments, and other conditions.

Every negative in your life is a positive. Perhaps you went through an experience in your life so horrible that you're afraid to mention it. Yet here you are today, still walking forward, reading this book, and figuring out where to go next. Your story has power—the ability to bring about positive change in others, no matter what their background.

Here's my own truth. I was born with an inactive thyroid and legal blindness in my right eye. When I was four years old, I started having excruciating earaches, which culminated in five different head surgeries, removal of a tumor, and complete deafness in my left ear. As you might imagine, I didn't fit in real well in junior high with scars on the left side of my head and eyes that would jump around sometimes.

It would be very easy for me to be ashamed of these things and to hide them. I'm not ashamed, and I certainly don't hide. They're just part of who I am. Sure, sometimes I can't hear people who sit on my left side, I can have difficulty seeing at times when I overwork my good eye, and I can gain ten pounds from simply sitting near cookies.

These "problems" don't mean that I can't do something. They mean I *can*. I've figured out how to overcome these things and keep moving forward in my life, doing the things I want to do. I can't change the things that have happened to me, but I sure can use the things they have taught me and move forward from here.

If you've gone through something difficult and are still here reading this book, that's not something to be ashamed of. That's something to be *proud* of. You have the strength of character to survive obstacles that the people around you can scarcely imagine, and your story has the potential to inspire others. Don't be ashamed—be proud of who you are, the good and the bad.

If you find this to be a difficult struggle, ask for help with it. Talk to your friends, or seek out a therapist who can walk you through things.

Just remember, you're sitting here right now. You've made it to this point. That means you're strong.

What Do We Really Need?

Quite often, people assume that if you're rich, you must be happy. In truth, the idea that riches bring happiness is an optical illusion, an artifact of our natural competitive nature.

Daniel Gilbert, professor of psychology at Harvard University and author of Stumbling on Happiness, put it succinctly in a talk in 2004: "[A]fter basic needs are met, there isn't much 'marginal utility' to increased wealth. In other words, the difference between a guy who makes $15,000 and a guy who makes $40,000 is much bigger than the difference between the guy who makes $100,000 and the guy who makes $1,000,000. [...] [O]nce basic needs are met, further wealth doesn't seem to predict further happiness. So the relationship between money and happiness is complicated, and definitely not linear. If it were linear, then billionaires would

18   *The Simple Dollar*

be a thousand times happier than millionaires, who would be a hundred times happier than professors. That clearly isn't the case. On the other hand, social relationships are a powerful predictor of happiness—much more so than money is."[1]

Gretchen Rubin, author of *The Happiness Project*, points to several other key factors for happiness. "Long, deep relationships contribute mightily to happiness. When people move around a lot, it becomes more challenging to have these kinds of relationships. Feeling out of control is a big happiness drag, and if people feel out of control because of the economy, or because of job or family pressures, that makes it harder to be happy. People also are happier when they have a certain amount of fun in their lives—absence of pain isn't enough, though it's a good start! It's easier to feel happy when you're feeling energetic, so doing things that contribute to energy—having fun, getting exercise, going outside, getting enough sleep—will make it easier to feel happy."[2]

In short, happiness doesn't revolve around financial success. Instead, it revolves around simple elements that we can all foster in our lives: building positive relationships with other people, cultivating low-pressure situations and minimizing high-pressure ones, and improving our personal energy level all contribute heavily to a personal sense of happiness. These things together also produce financial and career health as

1   From "Affective Forecasting, or, The Big Wombassa." Speech by Daniel Gilbert, retrieved in video form on July 23, 2009 from http://www.edge.org/3rd_culture/gilbert03/gilbert_index.html.

2   Personal interview.

well. Throughout the rest of this book, we'll cultivate these ideas, see how they contribute both to personal happiness and personal financial growth, and also identify how they reinforce each other to build a happier life without constantly chasing the riches that bring a mythical happiness.

> "Daddy! Up the escalator!" Joseph shouts at me. He is anxious to get to the second floor of the Science Center so we can build dams and fly paper airplanes together. My son and I are spending the day together visiting the Science Center of Iowa, where we blow bubbles using Hula Hoops, make paper rockets, and fire them across the room. We laugh. We play. The stress of work and money were far from my mind. The difficult choices of cutting my spending drastically, changing my career, and dealing with a lower income were all secondary to the freedom that had made this moment possible. Happiness has come at last.

May 2009

Five Steps Toward Happiness

Finding happiness in the modern world can be difficult. Our lives contain a mix of happiness and toxicity, and untangling that Gordian knot can be a real challenge. Here are five simple ways you can take control of your life and put yourself on a sustainably happier path. Doing this will set the foundation for taking on more difficult challenges and living your dreams:

1. **Make a list of the things that make you happy.** Don't include the things that are *supposed* to make you happy—the things you think should make you happy but don't truly fulfill you. Instead, just watch your life for the things that really bring about happiness and make you feel good. Keep a notebook with you and jot down everything that brings you significant happiness over the course of a week. Walk through your home and the places you regularly visit and look for things that bring happiness.

2. **At the same time, make a list of the things that make you unhappy.** Again, pay attention to your true feelings. Things that you believe should make you happy are sometimes the things that are leading toward unhappiness. Keep this list for a week.

3. **Go through your list of things that make you unhappy and build a to-do list from it.** For each item, think of an action you can take to eliminate the source of that unhappiness. Perhaps you're made unhappy by a strained relationship—why not make a phone call to make it better? If someone at work is making you unhappy, resolve to find ways to avoid that person or perhaps pledge to face this person head-on. If possessions make you unhappy, pledge to sell them. If aspects of yourself make you unhappy, look into what it would take to change them—an exercise plan, a dietary change, or a set of coursework, perhaps.

4. **Let a month pass; then trim down the happiness list to the two to five things that fill you with the most happiness.** They might be things, people, or activities—whatever they are, these are the things that filled you with happiness in the moment *and* fill you with happiness on later reflection. These things point straight toward the core of what makes you happy.

5. **Spend a week cultivating that happiness.** Invest your energy in activities that revolve around the happiness. Avoid spending money or energy on activities and things that aren't on that short list of things that make you happy. This might mean that you turn off the television for a week (because it leaves you indifferent) and instead play with your children every evening (because you feel happy when you do this). Engage in activities that are known to bring happiness along the way, such as moderate exercise and positive relationships with others. Then, after that week, reflect on whether the week was significantly more fulfilling than the way you normally spend your time.

In the end, the message is simple: *Be yourself.* Quite often, unhappiness comes from the areas where we're restricting our true selves for some reason, and happiness arrives when we let our true self shine through.

Chapter 3

A Visit from the Black Swan

My wife and I went into the bathroom together and studied the pregnancy test. An unmistakable line appeared, indicating a positive result. There was a child inside of her, one that was going to arrive in several months, whether we were ready or not. We celebrated that night. I had a glass of wine, while she chose not to "because of the baby," of course. And then it hit me. Just like that, everything was changing. I thought, I can't afford this! My life as I knew it was no more.

February 2005

Life hands you unexpected things all the time. Your car breaks down. You or your spouse get pregnant unexpectedly. A new person enters the picture and sweeps you off your feet. You get into an accident. An old college friend looks you up and asks you to throw in with his new startup. A loved one suddenly passes away. You get sick. Your spouse tells you that the marriage is over and walks out the door. You're handed a pink slip. A lot happens.

Sometimes those events are positive. You get a great new job. A child comes along at the exact point when you're emotionally ready for it. You fall in love and move clear across the country to follow that passion.

Your life is populated by unexpected events—things that can overwhelm you when they happen. One of the most amazing natural gifts as human beings is that you're able to take these unexpected events, process them for a while, figure out some kind of plan to deal with them, and before long, that completely unexpected event becomes a normal part of your life. You deal with it.

Here's the problem: You may be able to adjust emotionally, but you're often completely unprepared financially for those unexpected events.

A new lover invites you to move to Toronto. Is it the right thing to do? You can tap your friends for advice—and often that's incredibly useful—but the unexpected act puts you on unstable financial ground.

If that college friend pops out of nowhere and asks you to join that startup, can you? Will you be able to offer anything valuable to make the startup succeed? Do you have the resources to truly chase that opportunity in front of you? Can you handle what life throws at you?

Our Lives Are More Random Than We Think

Most of us see our lives as fairly predictable. We fill our days with similar activities and, for many of us, a life routine different than the one we have now is something that's an almost-forgotten memory.

In Nassim Nicholas Taleb's book, *The Black Swan*, which discusses unpredictable events and how we handle them, he identifies this part of human nature as the narrative fallacy. "The narrative fallacy addresses our limited ability to look at sequences without weaving an explanation into them, or, equivalently, forcing a logical link, an *arrow of relationship*, upon them. Explanations bind facts together. They make them all the more easily remembered; they help them *make more sense*. Where this propensity can go wrong is when it increases our *impression of understanding*."[1]

To put it simply, our lives are chock full of random events of all kinds, but our minds, to make some sense of our lives, attempt to construct a story that makes it all make sense. The problem with this is that quite often, random events don't make any sense at all—they just happen.

That's why, when we look back at the past, we see something very orderly. We've created a very nice story that explains all the unexpected things that have happened to us. We come up with explanations for events that simply happen as a matter of chance.

Because of this, we often believe that our lives are less random than they actually are, and we fail to prepare for the unexpected events that are coming in the future. Our long-term plans, after all, rarely account for falling head over heels in love after a chance encounter, an offer to join a hot startup, or a serious car accident. But these things happen all the time.

1   Nassim Nicholas Taleb, The Black Swan. Pages 43–44. ISBN: 98-1-4000-6351-2.

Unprepared for the Good

Surprisingly often, the unexpected events in our lives are positive ones. We run into an old friend. A former coworker contacts us with an intriguing professional opportunity. We bump into someone interesting and find ourselves with a date. We're swept off our feet by an exciting new interest. We see a box of valuable vintage video games at a yard sale. A challenging new project comes up at work—it involves a big risk but a huge reward. Unexpected positive events happen constantly—and they cause tremors throughout our lives.

However, without some preparation, we're unable to take advantage of these opportunities. We can't make a radical career shift because we have too many bills and not enough cash in the bank. We can't take advantage of that incredible bargain because we're running on empty due to living paycheck to paycheck. We're afraid to jump on the challenging new project because it risks failure, which would deplete the bonus we "need."

As a result, we lose out on those opportunities. We grow less confident and more tied to the routine of our life today—one that we're unhappy with in some ways. We look for ways to soothe that unhappiness. Marketing is always there to give us suggestions on how to make it better with some of our hard-earned dollars that, in the end, makes the problem even worse.

The solution is simple: Keep a big, healthy emergency fund in the bank. With each paycheck, contribute a portion of it directly to a savings account for the unexpected opportunities that come along in life. Such an emergency fund prepares us to take risks and jump on board life-changing opportunities.

Daniel Koontz of Bloomingdale, NJ, a financial services worker and author of *The Casual Kitchen*, migrated from paycheck to paycheck living to an emergency fund that covered *two years* of living expenses. "After I had reached this goal, which took a couple of years of disciplined saving, I began to think of my responsibilities and opportunities at work as totally divorced from my compensation. I no longer 'needed' my next paycheck, or for that matter, the next two years of paychecks. I started to feel more confident at work, I no longer had any fear of losing my job, and as a result, I began taking on higher-profile projects at work, and later, making decisive and aggressive job changes to further my career. I never would have guessed that saving two years' worth of dough would provide such significant nonfinancial benefits."[2]

Unprepared for the Bad

On the flipside of good opportunities are unfortunate situations—ones where something unexpected happens to your life and drains your finances. A job loss. An unexpected death of a loved one. A serious car problem. An unexpected irregular bill.

Much as with unexpected good things, the modern world has made the unexpected bad things more frequent. The well-documented breakdown in long-term relationships with employers, the advent of globalization, and the rapid developments in communications have made job turnover far more rapid than before.

2 Personal interview.

Our reliance on more services has opened us up to more crises due to the failures of such services, like a cell phone cutting out at a key moment or a flight canceled due to bad weather.

In short, as the world gets more complex, we're exposed to more bad events as well as good events. We are simply more exposed to large-scale phenomena than our parents were.

Just as with opportunities, the best protection against unexpected negative situations is an emergency fund. Cash regularly saved from a paycheck and put into a safe and reasonably easy to access place (like a savings account) ensures that such disasters do not destroy our long-term plans and dreams.

Kerry Taylor, an organic farmer from Vernon, British Columbia and author of SquawkFox.com and *397 Ways to Save Money*, experienced the value of an emergency fund when she required emergency knee surgery: "My emergency fund saved my butt when I needed knee surgery. Over the course of five years, I saved $125 a month and slowly grew my emergency fund to $7,500. This money became my lifeline when I faced a possible diagnosis of cancer and had to take time off work for various tests and a surgery. When my tests were clear, I was relieved to be healthy and not have debt, thanks to my emergency savings."[3]

Kristen Cross, a stay-at-home mother in rural Maryland, shares a similar story: "My husband found out at the end of March [2009] that his company was outsourcing the entire IT department where he works

---

3   Personal interview.

and that he'd be laid off in about 90 days. Naturally, we were a little bit freaked out at first, but we had a decent amount of savings, and while he was still employed, we worked really, really hard at padding that fund some more. We saved everything we could, cut back even more (and that's saying something because we're pretty frugal...we spend about $80/week to feed our family of six). We also calculated how much money we'd need to live off of each month if my husband didn't manage to find a new job before his old one ran out. We could squeeze by on about $2400 a month, and we've managed to save up about $12,000 in our emergency fund. Mercifully, my husband just found a new job, so we won't have to actually use our emergency fund, at least for now. But I can't even really put into words how wonderful it was to know that we could survive for a fairly decent amount of time without having to incur debt. It really gave us a 'we'll be all right' feeling in the midst of an unsettling situation."[4]

Sources of Personal Risk

It's clear that the modern world increases the chance of random events having a strong impact on our life, even if we don't see them in hindsight. However, we exacerbate the problem constantly by the day-to-day choices we make, putting ourselves even more at risk of missing out on great opportunities and falling flat when crises come our way. Here are five major avenues of personal risk that we invite into our life:

4   Personal interview.

- **Credit card and other consumer debt.** A credit card can be a very powerful tool for facilitating routine purchases, but it has a dangerous side. Credit cards detach you from the money itself and make it incredibly easy to spend more than you think, leaving you with escalating debt. That debt manifests itself as another monthly required payment, which adds risk to your life because it increases the danger from job loss. The solution? Pay off that debt as rapidly as possible (see Chapter 7, "Minding the Gap," for help).

- **Car loans and leases.** Yes, many people *need* a car for their career, but they choose to buy a car that exceeds their needs without the cash to pay for that *want*. That car loan (or lease) becomes a personal risk—yet another required monthly payment that keeps you from jumping on opportunities and hamstrings you when a crisis occurs. The solution? Drive a string of low-end used cars until you can afford to pay cash for the car you want.

- **Mortgages.** A mortgage is the least problematic form of debt you can have, as it gives you shelter and does build equity over time (albeit at a slower rate than real estate charlatans might tell you). However, it does include the same risk as other forms of debt. The solution? If you're going to live in an area for less than five years, rent your housing. If you don't have a 20% down payment, rent your housing. If you're still in the game, break out the calculator and compare the amount of money you'd be paying in mortgage interest versus the amount you'd be paying in rent. For more details, see Chapter 8, "Frugality as Framework."

- **Monolithic careers.** A monolithic career is one where your skills are limited to the career you're currently in. If you lose your job, your skill set doesn't leave you with many career options. The traditional mindset has been that if you have skills that others don't have, you'll always have a job— but in the era of globalization, there's a lot more competition out there for your job, and there's more opportunity for people with your skill set to be living halfway around the world and willing to work your job for much less. The solution? Diversify your skills. Build your social network. Start a side business in an area you're passionate about. For more ideas, see Chapter 9, "Cultivating People and Opportunities," and Chapter 10, "The New Career Rules."

- **Poor health choices.** A few simple dietary and exercise choices can help everyone, regardless of their personal shape. Moving toward a healthy body shape and a basic level of physical fitness improves your career opportunities and reduces your health risks. Have a quick chat with your doctor during your next checkup and see what he or she recommends. Some good rules of thumb: Eat mostly plants and move around actively for an hour each day.

Minimizing your risk in these areas reduces the chances that life can derail you and maximizes the chances that you can jump on board a great opportunity.

Maximizing Luck

In the movie *The Incredibles*, Edna Mole sums up the role of luck in our lives beautifully and succinctly: "Luck favors the prepared, dah-link."

Luck has very little to do with a four-leaf clover in your pocket. Instead, luck is simply finding ways to take maximum advantage of the numerous random positive events in your life, as well as opening yourself up to more possible random events, from noticing a great sale to having a powerful idea. Being prepared for these positive events in advance helps you cultivate these opportunities into a beautiful garden:

- **Keep a notebook or voice recorder with you at all times.** Whenever you have a useful idea or spot a useful piece of information, record it as soon as you can; then review those notes once a day or so. Quite often, little positive events—like a good idea or a valuable piece of data—slip through our memories without being utilized, causing a useful random event to go completely to waste.

- **Keep a healthy but reasonable amount of cash with you at all times.** Cash is often the quick answer to many opportunities that present themselves to us. We stumble upon a going-out-of-business sale that has nice shirts for $1 each. We bump into a friend who is scavenging for taxi fare. We find an amazing deal on a particularly valuable collectible at a yard sale. Cash in your pocket turns these potential missed opportunities into money in the bank.

- **Be aware of market values in areas of personal passion.** If you're passionate about a certain area, keep up-to-date with the market value of items in that field. For example, I still keep up with the prices of video games (especially vintage ones), trading cards, and comic books. Thus, if I'm ever at a yard sale or a small-town "junk" shop, I might be able to turn a huge profit because I know what such things are worth. This doesn't take much additional effort if you're already passionate about that area.

- **Shop at places where extreme bargains can be found.** Instead of shopping for new clothes at the expensive shops, start your journey at a second-hand shop or a Goodwill store. You might find exactly what you're looking for for just a few dollars instead of the high prices found elsewhere.

The final key is perhaps the most important: *Build lots of positive relationships and minimize negative ones.* Chapter 5, "Running to Stand Still," and Chapter 9 are largely devoted to the roles that relationships fill in our personal, professional, and financial lives.

The Need for Reliability

Another key component of battling randomness is enforcing order in our lives where we can by simply reducing the opportunities for random events to derail our plans.

The clearest expression of this is to automate as many payments as you can, including your savings for an emergency fund. If such savings and payments go off without requiring your personal interaction, it's harder for unexpected events to alter your plans. This ensures that your emergency fund is there when you need it and isn't altered by an impromptu moment or by forgetfulness.

Another clear expression of reliability comes from strong, cultivated relationships with other people. When times are tough, we have a much easier time getting through when we can rely on powerful relationships with others around us.

Reliability also comes in the form of careful purchasing. By taking appropriate time and care in advance of a significant purchase, you can avoid unreliable products and instead enjoy a lower rate of unexpected mishaps due to the malfunction of the things you own. If you buy a reliable car, you have a lesser likelihood of being late for work due to car trouble. If you buy a reliable water heater, your basement has a lower likelihood of flooding.

In each of these cases, choosing the more reliable option reduces the opportunity for random negative events in our lives or reduces the negative impact such events can have. This results in a more secure, more reliable you.

Preparing Yourself

Here are five key steps for getting started on maximizing the impact of positive luck on your life—and minimizing the impact of negative luck:

1. **Start an automatic emergency savings account.** Contact your bank and schedule a weekly automatic transfer from your checking account to your savings account. Start with a small amount so that you don't derail your life; then gradually increase the amount until you reach a comfortable level. Remember, there is no real upper limit on this account—just leave the automatic transfer in place no matter what happens. Murphy's Law seems to dictate that the unexpected events happen in bunches, so the more money you have, the more prepared you are to protect yourself and take advantage of opportunities.

2. **Seek out—and utilize—online banking.** Banks that allow you to manage your finances from any Internet-connected computer and also allow you to schedule payments in advance go a long way toward reducing the impact that unexpected events can have in your life. If your bank does not offer this feature, seek a bank that does—advice for switching banks can be found in Chapter 12, "Managing the Gap."

3. **Take simple steps to prepare yourself for the unexpected.** Start carrying a notebook with you and jot down ideas and things that come to mind; then review them later in the day. Keep a reasonable amount of cash with you as well. If you're job hunting, carry a resume with you at all times.

4. **Make a strong long-term goal of eliminating your debt.** Debt does nothing more than increase the effect of negative random events and decrease the effect of positive random events, so get rid of it.

Start a strong debt repayment plan (see Chapter 6, "With or Without You") focused on short-term goals that lead to bigger ones.

5. **Devote energy to cultivating relationships and finding community in your life.** Relationships are a powerful barrier against the unforeseen, as they can provide support and resources for those times when you most need the help. See Chapters 5 and 9 for more information.

Chapter 4

The Power of Goals in a Random World

I slit open the envelope, a tiny ray of hope stirring, and then saw the standard phrases on the form. A rejection. Even though I had gotten them often enough, each one landed like a punch low in my stomach. Inside I sat down in front of the computer. I had spent three years writing that novel, and now my finger hovered over the Delete button, ready to do away with all that work of many long nights at the library researching, typing, editing, building characters and plot lines, and tying them together in interesting ways, I had finished the novel. I had achieved my great goal. Or so I thought. I wasn't prepared for what came next. For several months, I attempted to get someone—anyone—in the publishing industry interested in the book I had written. Instead, I had a pile of rejection letters. My finger hovered over that Delete button—and in that instant, I made my decision.

November 1999

It's easy to be resistant to the idea of setting goals. It requires introspection, commitment, and facing your fears. Yet, without clear, written goals with discrete follow-ups, it is *substantially* harder to achieve significant gains in life. Without them, it's likely nothing will change in your life.

A recent study by Dr. Gail Matthews of Dominican University of California compared the goal completion of individuals who did not set personal goals, individuals who wrote down their personal goals but did not follow up on them, and individuals who wrote down personal goals and coupled them with progress reports on a regular basis. Simply writing down the goals resulted in a 42% increase in achieved goals, and written progress reports resulted in a 78% increase in achieved goals.[1] To put it simply, **people who wrote down their goals and followed up on them achieved substantially more, leaving those without written goals behind.**

Matthew Jabs, an IT manager in Lansing, Michigan, discovered the profound power of written goals in his life. "Historically I had always been a man of no specifically set goals. I was never sure exactly why or how I developed and maintained this aversion to [them]. I just couldn't find the time, didn't place enough value in achievement, or maybe just didn't want to be bothered."

---

1   http://www.dominican.edu/academics/artssciences/natbehealth/psych/faculty/fulltime/gailmatthews/researchsummary2.pdf retrieved on July 22, 2009.

He goes on: "Setting goals was not something I regularly purposed to avoid, but rather I had always been a "fly-by-the-seat-of-my-pants" type of guy who just didn't find it commonly necessary to assimilate goals into my life."

So what happened? Simply put, Jabs was inspired by Lao-Tzu's well-known quote, "The journey of a thousand miles begins with a single step."

Jabs explains: "[T]he quote combines the wonder and excitement of travel and discovery with accomplishing established tasks in life. Since first reading that quote [...] I have been able to set up a working, living, family budget. I have been able to increase my ability to read and finish books. I have been able to lose nearly 40 pounds. I have been able to grow more and more self-reliant. I have been able to change my eating habits to include predominately healthy, local, organic foods. I am closer with my wife and I am closer with my God."[2]

The Changing Value of Long-Term Goals

In my hand, I held an offer letter. It detailed a job that would pay me $43,000 a year straight out of college, something almost beyond the dreams of someone who grew up poor and went to college without any real direction. My goal for the last several years had been to finish college with a degree, find a simple job where I wouldn't have to focus on the work with my mental energy, and make myself become a successful writer.

2   Personal interview.

The unexpected, though, sometimes happens. I found myself exploring other areas, digging into deep analysis of genetic data. It was an area I found to be exciting—I loved the chase of digging through a new problem, applying an unusual model, and burying myself in deep intellectual challenge. This offer letter held that promise. But it also promised responsibility and a lot of work, something that seemed to seal off the dreams of writing that I had held onto for years. Was this a trade I was willing to make? Undoubtedly, it was an opportunity that I needed to try. After some hesitation and a bit of reflection on writing dreams that seemed to be going nowhere, I closed my eyes and signed on the dotted line. And with that signature, my long-term vision for my life lurched in a new direction.

April 2002

It's easy to be resistant to the idea of setting goals. It requires introspection, commitment, and facing your fears. Yet, without clear, written goals with discrete follow-ups, it is *substantially* harder to achieve significant gains in life. Without them, it's likely nothing will change in your life.

There's a big problem with such goal setting, though. As we discussed in Chapter 2, our lives are more chaotic than we realize. Events constantly happen in our lives, changing the terms of the game and often altering the goals we reach for.

To put it simply, the grand life-long plans that might have guided earlier generations no longer works. The world is changing so rapidly that in five years, your life will likely be substantially different than it is now due to events you cannot foresee.

So why set long-term goals at all? To put it simply, **long-term goals put short-term goals in an appropriate context.** A long-term goal is often just a sequence of short-term goals leading toward a greater good. Long-term goals add a powerful transformative sense to short-term goals—going on four runs in a week won't change your life, but committing to going from being a couch potato to running a marathon in two years certainly can change your life. Short-term goals become the stepping stones to getting there.

A good long-term goal is audacious and life changing. It seems beyond your realistic grasp, but the thought of reaching it makes your heart soar. It matches perfectly with the things you hold most dear in your life. Are you ready to reach for it?

Timothy Ferriss puts long-term goals in excellent context in his book, *The 4-Hour Workweek*. He writes, "Having an unusually large goal is an adrenaline infusion that provides the endurance to overcome the inevitable trials and tribulations that go along with any goal. Realistic goals, goals restricted to the average ambition level, are uninspiring and will only fuel you through the first or second problem, at which point you'll throw in the towel. If the potential payoff is only mediocre or average, so is your effort."[3]

An important note: Accumulation of money is not an audacious goal. A Scrooge McDuck-esque swimming pool filled with gold coins is the most ordinary of goals.

3   Timothy Ferriss, The 4-Hour Workweek. Page 50. ISBN 978-0-307-35313-9.

That's not to say money accumulation is not part of an audacious goal, but it's the application of that money toward something in line with your personal values that makes it audacious. Becoming a millionaire may be a big goal, but the great things you're able to do when you make it there are the truly exciting things, the ones that will keep you up at night working toward it.

The Power of Self-Reliance

Long-term goals push you in directions that can transform your life. You want something very different than what you have now, and a long-term goal simply states what you want to change. You're a couch potato and you want to not be one, so you set a goal of running a marathon. You're in poor financial shape but you want to be financially self-reliant, so you set a goal of being completely debt free and with a large emergency fund. Your career is going nowhere, so you set a goal of switching to a new career. The idea of starving children sickens you to your core, so you resolve to reach financial independence so you can spend your life's energy doing something about it.

Short-term goals make those long-term goals possible. You want to run a marathon, but you're woefully out of shape, so you set a goal of five one-hour walks this week. You want to be debt free, so you make it your goal to cut your unnecessary spending to $20 this week and funnel the rest into your largest debt. You want to start a new career, so you set a goal this week of talking to someone in that career path to see what it takes to get there. You want to tackle global hunger with all your might, so you throw that energy into getting yourself to a point where you can devote yourself to the problem.

Short-term goals often have another benefit: *They make you more self-reliant and move you closer to success in other areas.* Your marathon training causes you to start losing weight and get some color in your skin, making you look more presentable at work and in social situations and thus improving your confidence. Your debt reduction causes you to have fewer monthly bills, enabling you to broaden your horizons and look for opportunities elsewhere, as with Daniel Koontz and his two-year emergency fund. Your search for a new career pushes you to communicate with different people—improving your communication skills—and take classes that push your mind in new directions.

Communication skills, time management skills, information management skills, improved personal health, better appearance, leadership, and creativity are all things that you often pick up while working on short-term goals. These skills and attributes are the most valuable of all—they're *transferable*, meaning they help you in your daily life and in any career path you choose.

Transferable skills can also be considered part of a personal emergency fund, a topic described in the previous chapter. If you have a strong set of transferable skills—the ability to communicate, the ability to lead, good health, leadership skills, and so on—these make it possible to maximize *any* opportunity that comes your way—and navigate any challenge that life gives you.

When I launched my website, TheSimpleDollar.com, in November 2006, my goal was to reach people who were interested in transforming their own lives and finances (a long-term goal). I knew that the best way to do this was to talk about my own experiences in detail—and frequently, so I set up a series of short-term goals that required me to write on a daily basis about my challenge to find happiness and financial stability. Writing a substantial amount every day certainly helped me achieve my goal—attracting people who are interested in talking about these things—but it had a secondary benefit of improving my communication skills and my time management skills. Regardless of where I go in life, I can take these learned skills with me.

The Key: Short-Term Goals

It was three in the morning, but the story in my mind was fighting to escape, keeping me awake and at the keyboard. My hands drummed over the keys, throwing words on the screen, giving birth to a tale about a corrupt security guard on a riverboat. The character was alive inside my mind, a desperate man trying to cover his tracks. When he met his climactic end, I rested my hands for a moment and let my weary eyes read through the five thousand words I had just typed. It was good—perhaps the best thing I had ever written. I had been pushing myself for months to spend time in the evenings writing a short story a week, and I could finally see it paying off. For the first time in a long time, I actually saw myself as a writer, not as someone who just dabbled in the written word. And it felt quite good.

January 2005

It's easy to be resistant to the idea of setting goals. It requires introspection, commitment, and facing your fears. Yet, without clear, written goals with discrete follow-ups, it is *substantially* harder to achieve significant gains in life. Without them, it's likely nothing will change in your life.

The real power for changing your life comes from short-term goals set within a really big, audacious goal. A good short-term goal pushes you toward something amazing in your future while also contributing a useful transferable skill or attribute to your life, which will stick with you if the circumstances of your life change.

What makes a powerful short-term goal? First, *it's clear.* There's no ambiguity about whether you've achieved it or not. Usually, this means using a numerical metric, such as "I'll take four thirty-minute walks this week" or "I'll only spend $20 on unnecessary things this week."

Second, *it fits in the context of a big, audacious goal.* If you achieve your short-term goal, it actually helps with a larger goal in your life. Your exercise moves you a bit closer to that marathon. Your reduction in spending moves you closer to financial freedom.

Third, *it contributes to something transferable.* If you achieve the goal, either your product or something gained along the way is helpful to you in a broader scale. Your exercise slightly improves your physical shape and appearance. Your reduction in spending teaches you self-discipline and gives you financial freedom no matter what you might do.

Five Steps Toward Your Dreams

How can you apply this to your own life? Here's a simple five-step framework to make one of your dreams come true while improving your other opportunities along the way:

1. **Imagine what your life would be like if there were no obstacles.** Where would you live? What would you do with your time? Who would you spend your time with? What would your home be like? Focus on what *you* want—what things would truly fulfill you the most?

2. **Select one specific element of that vision.** Perhaps it's your physical shape. Perhaps it's your work. Maybe it's your relationships with the people around you. Perhaps it's a talent you have. It might be an experience you've enjoyed. Maybe it's your home and the place you live. Look for the *one* thing that fills you with the deepest joy when you consider it. Describe it specifically, and write it down. That is your audacious long-term goal.

3. **Reflect on some of the steps you would have to take to accomplish that goal.** What would you have to do to get there? It's likely that many of these steps seem very difficult. If a step seems insurmountable to you, break it down some more. Keep breaking steps into pieces until the first step seems as though it's reachable within a month or so if you really push yourself. That is your short-term goal.

4. **Keep that short-term goal front and center for the next month.** Write it down every single day. Detail something you did every single day to make that short-term goal a reality. Put reminders of this goal all over the place—your bedside table, your computer monitor, your rearview mirror. Whenever you take an action of any type, ask yourself if that action is helping you reach your goal. Is buying this unnecessary thing really helping me reach my goal? Is sitting on the couch vegetating really helping me reach my goal?

5. **When you reach your goal, revel in the feeling of pure success.** Then go back to your long-term goal and look at your new state in comparison to it. What's the next step? Can it be broken down into another short-term goal that will really push you over the next month? Keep repeating this process, and you'll walk, step-by-step, toward whatever your big dream is.

Chapter 5

Running to Stand Still

Was I actually seriously considering working part-time fast food hours to save enough money for Christmas gifts, simply because it was September and I had less money than I had at the start of the year? For someone making just shy of $50,000 a year, was this really going to help make ends meet, or was it to continue to fund a lifestyle that exceeded what I brought in? I thought about it. Then I lifted my pen and started to fill out the application.

September 2004

I wound up not taking that nonsensical fast food job. I simply didn't go to the interview. But the point is still obvious. I was running in place. I didn't have enough money.

How could this possibly happen? I held a college degree and had a full-time salaried position that earned me over $45,000 a year. On top of that, my wife also held a full-time position. At the time, we were living in an apartment and didn't have any children.

I thought I was just doing something a little bit wrong and that my future self would take care of it. After all, my friends seemed to have many of the same trappings of lifestyle that I had.

What I didn't realize is that many of my friends were in worse financial situations that I was. A few of them were well on their way to eventual personal bankruptcy, and others are still mired in an enormous pile of debt.

All of them were trapped in jobs that were incredibly mentally and emotionally demanding. They were tied to work that never left them—a laptop or Blackberry always at their sides, a cell phone ringing regularly with new things to handle via text and phone calls, a schedule that never seemed to have room for anything more than occasionally collapsing in an exhausted heap.

They, like myself, were running in place. For all the effort we were putting forth in our lives, we were not making any progress toward the things we had always dreamed about. Our kingdoms for a flat panel television, indeed.

The Changing Nature of Income

Life was much simpler for my parents. When I was young, my mother stayed at home and handled the multitude of household chores while my father worked outside the home, alternating between factory work and small-scale commercial fishing. One income was enough, and even then, my father always seemed to have plenty of time to spend with me, teaching me how to garden, how to ride a bike, how to throw a baseball, and all of those other classic elements of fatherhood.

Today, this simply wouldn't work. According to the Bureau of Labor Statistics, the average full-time worker in the United States works more than eight hours a day.[1] Not per weekday—every day, including weekends and holidays. That's over fifty six hours per week, on average. In married households, both partners are often working. This leaves less and less time for household chores, leisure time, parenting, and adequate rest.

To put it simply, work is more demanding and more intrusive into our personal lives than ever before.

At the same time that work hours are increasing, our *real wage* is decreasing. Real wage simply refers to the income of the average American adjusted for inflation—after all, a dollar today doesn't buy what it did thirty years ago. The Labor Research Association reports that the real wage of the average American *dropped 8.2% from 1964 to 2004*.[2]

Over that same period, people have begun to pay for services that were once nonexistent that are now considered standard. Cell phones, cable bills, and Internet access are all new additions to the bills of an average household. In addition, the real costs (again, adjusted for inflation) of housing and higher education have risen substantially over the past forty years.

In short, we work more and get less for our efforts.

---

1   http://www.bls.gov/news.release/atus.t04.htm.

2   http://www.workinglife.org/wiki/Wages+and+Benefits%3A+Real+Wages+%281964-2004%29.

Your True Hourly Wage

Quite often, people comfort themselves from these harsh realities by admiring their annual salary. "I'm bringing home $40,000 a year, so I'm doing fine," goes the logic. For a long time, I was guilty of the same thinking.

However, the truth is that your salary is a very poor indicator of how much money you're actually earning and able to spend. In many cases, that $40,000 a year job is actually bringing home *less than minimum wage* when you break it down to the amount actually earned per hour.

In the book *Your Money or Your Life*, Joe Dominguez and Vicki Robin encourage people to calculate their true hourly wage. The calculation itself is simple—divide how much you earn in a year by the number of hours you work in a year.[3]

But when you dig a little deeper, the amount you earn in a year is quite a bit less than you think. How much fuel and auto maintenance do you purchase for your commute—or perhaps you have a car solely for the purpose of getting to work? Do you buy clothes specifically for work? Do you go out for meals and drinks and other events with coworkers mostly for work purposes and foot the bill yourself? Do you eat out for lunch when you could otherwise eat leftovers at home? Do you buy "escape entertaiment"—go out to movies, buy DVDs, take trips, ride your motorcycle, and so forth—to take the edge off of your stress? Do you pay taxes at a level higher than others simply because of your

3   Joe Dominguez, Vicki Robin, and Monique Tilford, Your Money or Your Life. Page 56. ISBN: 978-0-14-311576-2.

higher income? All of these costs over a year should be deducted from your annual salary.

What about the hours spent on business trips? What about the time spent going to work-related social events? What about the time dropped every day on your commute? What about the time you burn working from home—or even thinking about your stressful job? Don't forget the time shopping for work-related items, such as work clothes. What about the phone calls and other interrupting communications that your job inserts into your life? What about the time you spend each evening vegetating as you "unwind" from your stressful day? All of this time should be added on to the time you actually spend at work.

When you calculate your hourly wage with the adjusted salary divided by the adjusted time commitments, your true income level can be really shocking.

My $45,000-a-year job actually earned me just slightly over minimum wage when the true costs were used.

The Things We Sacrifice

I sat in a hotel room, listening to my son Joseph shout loudly over the phone. He was enjoying his dinner. For the first time, Sarah had given him a spoon and allowed him to feed himself, and he was having tremendous fun. There was baby food all over his face, according to Sarah, and I could hear his shouts over the phone. Earlier that day, he had taken his first few tentative steps in our living room. Sarah said she tried to get the camera out to take some video of this moment, but he had already fallen to the floor and resorted back to crawling. When I hung up the phone, I tool a long shower and tried not to think about the key moments in his life I was missing.

January 2007

Quite often, as our salaries go up, so do our responsibilities. We're working from home in the evenings and sometimes running into work to take care of things. We go on business trips, falling asleep in an uncomfortable bed to the noise of the news on the hotel television.

These responsibilities take away from the very things that we're working for. We work long evenings and go on business trips so that we can afford a nice home, one that we don't have the time to enjoy. We get second jobs to provide for our children—but our children are home with a babysitter.

Whenever we choose to work, we sacrifice other things: time with our loved ones, time for our hobbies and passions, time to help others, and time for ourselves. The solution for reclaiming that time is simple: Reduce our material needs and cut down strongly on our material wants. Our reward for that choice is not misery—it's a much richer life, full of the time we need to be involved in the things most important to us.

Do you live to work, or do you work to live?

Your Future Self Isn't Reliable

The ease with which you can borrow money to buy the things you want may make it seem as though you really can have your cake and eat it, too. With a flourish of the credit card, it often seems as though you can have the things you want today, while your "future self" will deal with the bills.

But, as you saw earlier, our lives are more random than we think. By the time your "future self" gets around to paying off those credit card bills, your job could be downsized, rendering you unable to pay our bills at all and *desperate* to find more work. On the other hand, a friend might offer you an amazing job— your *dream* job—at his new small business, but you can't take that risk because of your big pile of bills.

Your future self isn't reliable. The challenges and opportunities you'll have in six months are likely ones you can't see right now. However, every time you buy something frivolous and wasteful, the one thing you do ensure is that your future self will have fewer options. Your future self will be in complete panic mode during any downsizing. Your future self will have to watch your dream job float on by.

The life you dream of is just around the corner. It's up to you whether or not you'll be able to take advantage of it.

The Power of Today

How can you be sure that you'll be able to take advantage of the opportunities you'll have tomorrow? The answer is simple: Live a better life today.

Instead of upgrading your television, hold off for a while and pay off your debts first. A great opportunity might come along in the meantime.

Instead of eating out every night, start preparing a few meals at home. You might discover that it's actually easy, or fun, to cook at home—and suddenly your credit card bills become lighter.

Instead of stopping at Starbucks, make your own pot of coffee. Take the $5 you save each day and put it in the bank. At the end of the year, you've got $1,800 in cash—enough for a nice car down payment.

Instead of going shopping with your friends, invite them over and go through your closet, trading items with your friends. You have a fresh new wardrobe and several fun evenings without racking up bills.

The choices you make today have profound effects on your life tomorrow. The more you spend today, the more restricted your choices tomorrow. The less you spend today, the more choices you have tomorrow—a new career, a new relationship, a new life. Every time you choose to spend frivolously today, you shut off some of the great opportunities life has in store for you.

Five Steps for Breaking Out

Here are five simple things you can start doing immediately to stop running to stand still and start running to move forward:

1. **Issue yourself a thirty-day challenge to cut all non-essential spending in your life.** For one month, if it's not a requirement in your life, don't spend money on it. Buying food to prepare at home is fine—eating out is not. Hanging out with friends is fine—spending money while shopping

with friends is not. See if you can make it thirty days with this type of perspective. As you're going along, ask yourself if you really do miss the things you're going without. You'll find that, indeed, you do miss some of them—but many of them will surprisingly fade into the woodwork. At the end of the thirty days, just bring back the things you genuinely missed.

2. **Make a list of the responsibilities in your life that you feel you're overlooking.** Perhaps it's your marriage. Maybe it's your children. Other possibilities might be your religious or spiritual life, your friendships, your charities, your home, or your health. You'll soon see that you have more things on your plate than you have time for, and you might feel guilty or disheartened. Don't be. Go through each of these items and address them head on. Find ways to combine these things— perhaps start an exercise program *with* your kids or take the whole family to a charity activity once a month.

3. **Calculate your true hourly wage.** As mentioned previously, your true hourly wage is the income you bring in each year *minus* the extra costs associated with your job (the cost of gas, car maintenance, wardrobe, food, and so on) divided by the number of hours worked *plus* the extra hours devoted to work-related activities (the commute, traveling, work-related dinners and social events, and so on). That resulting number might just shock you—you might just find that your exhausting job isn't really earning you as much as

you thought it was and that a much easier job might earn you nearly as much while also giving you other opportunities and benefits that will improve your life (getting a degree or a certification, flexible scheduling, more interesting work).

4. **Find ways to minimize the extra time and financial costs of your job.** Start a carpool or try public transportation. Move toward a more adaptable work wardrobe (if you need to, leap ahead and see Chapter 8, "Frugality as Framework," for more details on this idea). Ask about flexible work hours or telecommuting opportunities. Order salads when you go out for work-related dinners—if you're still hungry, eat at home afterward. A few simple routine changes can reduce the costs of your job quite a bit, both in terms of time and finance.

5. **Unwind with mindless tasks, not vegetation.** One of the most powerful changes I made in my own life was simply filling my after-work "unwind" time with mindless tasks instead of pure vegetation. Rather than flopping in front of the television for a half an hour after work to unwind, I'd just turn on the radio quite loudly and engage in some of the mindless activities that need to be accomplished. I'd sort the mail, clean the refrigerator, empty the dishwasher, mow the lawn instead of hiring someone to do it for me, and so on. When I was finished, I'd feel even more refreshed than if I had just vegetated for that half an hour, plus I now had an extra half an hour to spend on an activity genuinely important to me— my children, my friends, or my hobbies.

Chapter 6

With or Without You

When I walked out of the room that day, I knew I would never return. For four years, I had been heavily involved with a technical community that promoted the use of open source software. When I first joined, the community was a huge personal boon for me. I built several strong friendships, received tons of valuable advice and suggestions, was given a lot of used computer equipment, and found myself with new potential career opportunities. I participated in nearly every event the group held and eventually wound up being elected president of the group. But the group had dissolved into a bitter war over how to organize ourselves: Should we remain an informal gathering of people with the president largely making most of the decisions, or should we become a more formal group with missions and aims? The bitterness of the argument drove people away, including many of the people I cared the most about. When my term ended, I no longer felt the same sense of community. I walked away from the group, but I kept my dignity and a handful of great friends.

August 2001

The economist Adam Smith identified enlightened self-interest, which he described as the "invisible hand," as the most powerful force in the world. In his words, "by directing that industry in such a manner as its produce may be of the greatest value, he intends only his own gain; and he is in this, as in many other cases, led by an invisible hand to promote an end which was no part of his intention. Nor is it always the worse for the society that it was no part of it."[1]

Smith's message was simple: Our greatest successes occur when we work in our own self-interest while simultaneously bringing about positive change in the broader world. Think of Thomas Edison working in his laboratory on the light bulb—his motivation may have been income, but the light bulb brought about tremendous positive change in the world.

Our natural human need for community fits into this equation. We participate in communities with our own self-interest in mind—we *need* connection with other people, and we often desire the wisdom and other resources possessed by others. Yet, by participating in communities in a positive fashion, we get the connections and wisdom and resources we covet while simultaneously improving the lives of others in the community—and often in the broader world. **Participation in a community is perhaps the most valuable thing we can do as people—the value we put in is amplified and returned to us.**

1   Adam Smith, The Wealth of Nations.

One particular example of the power of community that I've been involved with in the past is the online community of game documenters—the people who write detailed FAQs and walkthroughs for complex video games. Within this community, people invest hundreds of hours writing extremely detailed documentation, explaining every trick and puzzle to be found within a video game *without compensation*. Over the years, I've contributed documentation to this community several times, simply because I get value from these documents myself and I feel it's worthwhile to give back.

In 2007, Andy Oram of O'Reilly Media surveyed participants in online game documentation and asked them why they invest so much time in this without compensation.[2] Overwhelmingly, the reason people contribute this time is a sense of *community*—a group of people with similar values and interests who share their knowledge and resources freely for the benefit of all. Countless friendships have been built and connections have been made through this process, benefiting the lives of these documenters.

The Broadening of Community

In their paper "Sense of community: A definition and theory," David W. McMillan and David M. Chavis provide a very thorough definition of a community: "The first element is membership. Membership is the feeling of belonging or of sharing a sense of personal relatedness. The second element is influence, a sense of mattering, of

---

2   http://onlamp.com/pub/a/onlamp/2007/06/14/why-do-people-write-free-
    documentation-results-of-a-survey.html.

making a difference to a group and of the group mattering to its members. The third element is reinforcement:
integration and fulfillment of needs. This is the feeling
that members' needs will be met by the resources received
through their membership in the group. The last element
is shared emotional connection, the commitment and
belief that members have shared and will share history,
common places, time together, and similar experiences."[3]

This clearly describes the type of community many
of us seek to participate in, in which like-minded people
engage each other and share thoughts and resources
openly and without prejudice, creating a shared emotional connection.

In the past, such communities were often found in
our local physical area. Without pervasive communication tools like the Internet and cellular phones, we were
often connected with the people around us simply by
the fact that we lived near each other.

Although this community continues to exist, communications tools have made countless other communities possible, ones based on common interests and other
factors but without the physical closeness of a local
community.

Both types of communities have some advantages
and some disadvantages. The local community is
stronger in a physical, tangible sense, whereas a distributed community is stronger in terms of shared information and ideas. The distributed community tends to
offer better support in times of stability, whereas the

---

3   McMillan, D.W. and D.M. Chavis. "Sense of community: A definition and
     theory." Journal of Community Psychology, 14 (1986): 6–23.

local community often provides more support in unstable times (like natural disasters and personal crises).

While it's easy to see the benefits of each type of community, it's similarly easy to see the problems as well. Having such a multitude of communities available to us means that we often neglect other communities. Quite often, this means that we have a weaker connection to our local, physical community. We no longer know our neighbors as well, but we do know someone across the country that shares an interest with us. This creates a sense of disconnect, as people no longer enjoy the deep connections with the people physically around them as previous generations had.

Both types of communities are valuable, and we suffer when we miss out on the advantages in our lives provided by either type.

The "*Tragedy of the Commons*"

As many of us know, there is a dark side to community. It occurs when the tension between self-interest and the greater needs of the community break in the wrong direction. Unenlightened self-interest takes hold, and an individual, in an effort to maximize the value he personally receives in the short term, devours the resources of the community and effectively damages or destroys it.

In his 1968 paper, "The Tragedy of the Commons," Garrett Hardin describes this phenomenon well:

> "Picture a pasture open to all. It is to be expected that each herdsman will try to keep as many cattle as possible on the commons. Such an arrangement may

work reasonably satisfactorily for centuries because tribal wars, poaching, and disease keep the numbers of both man and beast well below the carrying capacity of the land. Finally, however, comes the day of reckoning, that is, the day when the long-desired goal of social stability becomes a reality. At this point, the inherent logic of the commons remorselessly generates tragedy.

"As a rational being, each herdsman seeks to maximize his gain. Explicitly or implicitly, more or less consciously, he asks, "What is the utility *to me* of adding one more animal to my herd?" This utility has one negative and one positive component.

"1) The positive component is a function of the increment of one animal. Since the herdsman receives all the proceeds from the sale of the additional animal, the positive utility is nearly +1.

"2) The negative component is a function of the additional overgrazing created by one more animal. Since, however, the effects of overgrazing are shared by all the herdsmen, the negative utility for any particular decision-making herdsman is only a fraction of -1.

"Adding together the component partial utilities, the rational herdsman concludes that the only sensible course for him to pursue is to add another animal to his herd. And another; and another. . . . But this is the conclusion reached by each and every rational herdsman sharing a commons. Therein is the tragedy. Each man is locked into a system that compels him to increase his herd without limit—in a world that is limited. Ruin is the destination toward which all men rush, each pursuing his own best interest in a society that believes in the freedom of the commons. Freedom in a commons brings ruin to all."[4]

The tragedy of the commons pops up quite often. People join committees with the purpose of steering their work in a direction to just benefit a few. Trolls invade online communities to get a shred of personal enjoyment from the destruction of a prosperous group. Individuals will make plans for a group of people that will only be enjoyed by a few members of the group. *Un*-enlightened self-interest is a danger to any community.

How do we overcome this? It's vital to keep in mind that every positive community has only a certain lifespan—no community is permanent. It's also vital to remember what communities are actually composed of.

The Value of a Relationship

I spent the afternoon cleaning out my desk and talking with my coworkers. It was my final day at my "nine to five" job. I was leaving to spend more time with my children, to write, and to figure out what came next for me. As I took a final look over the documentation I left behind, I realized that I wouldn't miss the work at all. I had been doing repetitive and unengaging maintenance tasks for years without the creative work that had really lit my fire during the early years of the job. I would miss

4   Garrett Hardin, "The Tragedy of the Commons," Science, Vol. 162, No. 3859 (December 13, 1968), pp. 1243–1248.

the people. I walked across the hall and spent a good hour chatting with Darwin about nothing much at all, realizing I wouldn't be able to do that again. I walked through the office and said my goodbyes to lots of different people. As I walked out with a box of belongings under my arm, I glanced back over my shoulder. There stood Darwin, a person I had worked with since day one at that job and had become a true friend, looking at me out of the window of his office. He grinned and I grinned back. My job might be over and that community might be changing without me in it, but I would still keep the relationships I had built.

March 2008

In the end, a community is made up of a bunch of interconnected relationships. You know a certain group of people, and some of those people know each other. The little clusters of people who know each other and have things in common is a community—you share things, have common values, and help each other.

It is those individual relationships, built up over time, that are the fundamental source of value in our modern world. They provide material assistance, emotional help, and countless ideas. They boost you when times are good and support you when times are tough. They help you get your foot in the door and they give you a helping hand when you need it. A collection of solid relationships with people that inhabit a wide variety of communities is *the* strongest foundation for long-term success today, because social capital pays dividends in ways that dollars can never reach.

Finding a community is easy—all you have to do is identify people with something in common. Do they live near each other? Do they share a common interest? Do they share common beliefs?

Building a community is much more difficult. It requires building strong relationships with a number of people with common interests or other attributes, and then fostering relationships between them. Together, these relationships form a strong safety net for everyone involved—a mutual community of support that can provide far more value than you put into it.

We'll dig into the power of relationships deeper in Chapter 9, "Cultivating People and Opportunities," but it's vital to recognize that a community—a sense of belonging—relies on a bedrock of individual relationships, and it's up to you to bring forth the investment of time and energy to build these relationships.

Social Intelligence

For many of us, being part of a community can be difficult. It requires some very strong initiative to get our foot in the door—an overpowering common interest. More transient connections are often hard to make; as Simon and Garfunkel once put it, "I've built walls, a fortress deep and mighty, that none may penetrate / I have no need of friendship; friendship causes pain / Its laughter and its loving I disdain." It's often easier to not speak up and to be alone.

For others, such outward connection is much easier. They are blessed with gifts that make communication and relationship building intuitive and natural.

Daniel Goleman, in his book *Social Intelligence*, argues that much like some people have a higher IQ, others have a high social intelligence, meaning that they're able to be successful in many situations. He defines social intelligence as being a combination of a multitude of factors, many of which are learnable.[5] Let's look at these eight factors in detail:

1. **Primal empathy.** Goleman defines primal empathy as "feeling with others; sensing non-verbal emotional signals." Pay attention to how others act, not just the words they share. This skill is incredibly difficult in written communications— it's the reason that written sarcasm often utterly fails and is perceived as an insult.

2. **Attunement.** In Goleman's words, attunement is "listening with full receptivity; attuing to a person." Listen to a person's words without interjecting your own, and attempt to understand what they're saying. Put yourself in their shoes for a moment and make a conscious effort to see the situation as they do.

3. **Empathic accuracy.** Defined as "understanding another person's thoughts, feelings, and intentions," this often means that you need to obtain a deeper understanding of who the person is before sharing more challenging or intimate thoughts. The more you understand a person, the easier it is to put yourself in his position and understand where he is coming from.

---

5   Daniel Goleman, *Social Intelligence.* Page 84. ISBN: 978-0-553-38449-9.

4. **Social cognition.** Described as "knowing how the social world works," this refers to understanding that relationships are varied and complex.
5. **Synchrony.** Goleman defines this as "interacting smoothly at the nonverbal level." Do the body motions of people in conversation signify interest in each other and pleasure with the situation?
6. **Self-presentation.** Are we "presenting ourselves effectively"? Hygiene and cleanliness are a big part of this, as is an appropriate level of clothing.
7. **Influence.** "Shaping the outcome of social interactions" means offering your own opinions and guiding the conversation in useful directions.
8. **Concern.** Goleman describes concern as "caring about others' needs and acting accordingly." If someone needs assistance or help, you step up to the plate and offer what you can.

In the end, the keys to social intelligence revolve around appearing presentable, listening to what others have to say, expressing concern for and interest in their thoughts, offering useful help when appropriate, and shaping the conversation with our own contributions, all of which can be learned with practice if they do not already come naturally to you.

Our church's constitution was in shambles. It needed dozens of changes in order to satisfy the requirements set down by the bishop—and perhaps to retain our 501(c)(3) status. The task looked monumental. It would require dozens of emails and lots of phone calls and long hours of rewriting. No one wanted to step up and do it, but it needed to be done. I raised my hand. "I'll give it my best shot," I said. People applauded. Several people slapped me on the back. I was helping, I felt energized and ready.

July 2008

Getting Started

Being involved in a community is perhaps the most valuable thing you can do with your time—it will return ideas and resources and connections far beyond the value that you put in. Here are five steps for getting started:

1. **Get to know the people around you.** Make an effort to start a conversation with each of your physical neighbors—the people who actually live near you. Find out who they are, what they do, and what their interests are. If you know of something useful locally, share it—if you have a need for something local, ask for it. If you feel a rapport starting, suggest doing something together, perhaps sharing a meal with all of your neighbors.

2. **Take the passions you identified in Chapter 2, "What's Missing," and locate communities centered around them, both online and offline.** Use Google as a starting point and seek out places where people congregate in relation to your interests. If you have friends that share passions with you, ask them about communities.

3. **Dip a toe into each of these communities.** Listen to what's being said. Offer up information and resources you have to help. Keep in mind the nature of social intelligence as you get involved. You'll find that some communities "click" for you and others do not—that's normal.

4. **Get involved in communities that "click" with you.** Give heavily of yourself at first by putting in effort to add to the value of the community. Contribute ideas and materials to the group and see what others do with it. As you grow, don't be afraid to ask for help from these communities— if you're a giving member, you'll be amazed to find how much help is out there.

5. **Use communities to help each other.** The real value comes when you see opportunities for one community to benefit another community and you can make that connection. Let's say you're passionate about woodworking and you're involved in a woodworking community. One of your coworkers asks for a recommendation of a local woodworker. By combining your foothold in both communities, you increase the value of each one—and increase your own value in each community.

Chapter 7

Minding the Gap

I recall the rush of excitement as I held my first real-world paycheck in my hand. After taxes and savings, it amounted to $1,300 and a whirlwind of products and possibilities paraded through my mind—a new television for the living room, a small "celebration" spree at the bookstore, and picking up a couple DVDs I'd been eyeing. I needed a new hard drive for my computer, and it'd be awesome to take Sarah out for a great dinner. Oh sure, I had some bills to pay, but once those were out of the way, it was time to have some fun. I knew there was something else I should be doing with that money. Our wedding and honeymoon were less than a year away, and there was a nebulous dream about owning a house of our own. But that was tomorrow. Time to play today.

July 2002

It would be easy for me to look back and say I regret the hundreds of thousands of dollars that I blew through during the third decade of my life.

I don't, though, at least not in a general sense. My memories of those years are filled with a lot of peak experiences that I wouldn't trade away at any price.

What I do regret is how much I *wasted* on the ordinary experiences and things that didn't really add much at all to my life. I bought so many things without thinking about them at all along the way. I threw down $20 bills over and over again on quick experiences that, in the end, didn't really add a thing to my life. It was mindless, thoughtless spending—the type of things that brings a really quick rush when you do them, but fills you with regret later when you realize your wallet is empty.

I don't begrudge a dime that I spent on the great things. I begrudge the money I wasted on the lesser things.

Spending Less Than You Earn

When your paycheck comes in, you have to spend a certain portion of it on your required bills—energy, communications, housing, basic food, transportation, clothing, insurance, and other areas. In essence, these cover your physiological needs: nutrition, safety, and so on.

Most people have a substantial surplus left over after that—and, unsurprisingly, they spend it. The U.S. Bureau of Labor Statistics reports that in 2009, the average American family spends $2,816 on entertainment, $2,668 on dining out, $808 on a nebulous category of "miscellaneous expenses," $588 on personal care products, $457 on alcoholic beverages, and $323 on tobacco and supplies. This doesn't include the large portion of automobile expenses spent on luxury automobiles, thousands spent on luxury apparel, and the portion of housing expenses spent on excessive homes. With an average family post-tax income of only $49,638, it's easy to see that a sizable percentage of our income is spent on non-essentials.[1]

I'll be the last person to tell you that you should just cut all of that non-essential spending and live a stoic existence, subsisting on grass and living in a shack with only a deck of cards for entertainment.

Instead, my argument is simple, a refrain I heard over and over again on the London Underground while on our honeymoon. *Mind the gap*.

Mind the Gap

The gap is simply the difference between your income and your required bills—the money left over when you've taken care of the bare essentials.

As the preceding statistics show, individuals spend the vast majority of their "gap" on non-essential items: entertainment, dining out, alcohol, luxury apparel, luxury automobiles, extra housing, and other such expenses.

The "gap" is also the source of our savings for the future (like the emergency fund discussed in Chapter 2, "What's Missing"), for debt repayment, and for other financial goals.

---

1   Consumer Expenditures. U.S. Department of Labor. U.S. Bureau of Labor Statistics. April 2009.

"Minding the gap" doesn't mean dropping all of your fun expenses and putting it all in the bank. Instead, it simply means stepping back and looking at your core values for a moment before you bust out the plastic.

Remember that picture of your ideal future that you sketched out in Chapter 3, "A Visit from the Black Swan?" The aspects of that picture—the people you're with, the things you have, the career you have, the activities you're involved with—details what your core values are. That picture is quite reachable.

Your "gap" is your key to get there—or merely a continuation of the tired path you're already on.

Whenever you have an opportunity to spend some of that "gap" money, you have a choice: You can spend it on the things that truly matter to you—the pieces of that wonderful picture of your future—or on things that don't matter (or matter substantially less).

It's much like that photograph that Marty McFly holds of his future family in *Back to the Future*. When Lorraine or George make a poor choice—even if it looks good in the moment—that wonderful future family begins to disappear just a little. When they finally choose to grab hold of the truly good thing right in front of them, that future picture fills itself in, clear as can be.

Wants and Needs

Modern life muddies the waters quite a bit when it comes to smart choices with our "gap." Marketers and social influences prey on that gap. The resultant confusion ends with us feeling as if we "need" something that's just a short-term want, planted by a clever marketing message.

Amanda Schuler, a human resources worker from Omaha, NE, struggled with distinguishing wants versus needs in a car purchase: "I totaled an almost brand-new Toyota Camry. Even though I received a sizable check from my insurance settlement, I still had to go out and get a new car. As I began my car shopping, I started getting swept away by all of the bells and whistles, and the salespeople sure talked a great pitch. Instead of purchasing, I walked away. While I was at home that evening, I called my dad, and he reminded me of 'wants versus needs.' I wanted a brand-new sports car, but could I afford the payments? Absolutely not."[2]

What's the solution to this problem? *Time.* Whenever you're about to make an impulsive buy, put it back on the shelf and resolve that you'll buy it in thirty days if you still want it. Most of the time, you won't even *remember* the item in thirty days, let alone still want it. If your mind keeps returning to the item during that waiting period, ask yourself why. Does it help you accomplish your big life goals? Does it add significant meaning to your life? If you're still convinced of the value of the purchase, bargain-hunt for it. Spend some time looking for the best deal on it. Dig up coupon codes and do some comparison shopping.

Upon hearing this solution, many people reject it, immediately assuming that it means an end to all spontaneity. Again, there's a simple solution: Put a $20 bill

2   Personal interview.

in your pocket (or on PayPal) once a week and use that for your most spontaneous urges. When you find something you want to spontaneously buy or experience, go right ahead. But when that $20 is gone, don't immediately replenish it. Wait until Friday, then put another $20 in your pocket.

The Frugalist and the Capitalist

It doesn't take much thinking to realize that the most effective way to get ahead is to make that gap as large as possible. There are two distinct schools of thought on how to go about that.

The frugalist argues that the most effective way to increase the size of your gap is to reduce your expenses. How can you trim your regular bills, particularly in a way that minimizes your time investment and doesn't reduce your quality of life in other areas? The frugalist's advantage is that these tactics are virtually guaranteed to work. They *will* increase your gap by some amount.

The capitalist, on the other hand, argues that the best way to increase the gap is to increase and diversify your income. How can you maximize your financial returns without raising your expenditures as much? The capitalist looks for the home run—six months of work opens the door to a raise or a new job that vastly increases income (and thus vastly increases the size of one's gap), but it doesn't *guarantee* a job.

There's a frugalist and a capitalist inside all of us, and the balance largely rests on our personality type. In the end, the balance usually shifts on the basis of the other passions of the person—an individual highly interested in home improvement or in cooking is much more likely to be a frugalist, whereas a person who loves networking or is thoroughly passionate about his career is more likely to lean toward the capitalist side of the equation.

The key, as always, is to use the tactics from both sides that work for you and don't detract from your big goals.

Budgeting

Almost every personal finance book you read will have several pages on how to set up a budget. They'll give you forms to fill out, templates to follow, and press you into the idea that this budget will solve all of your problems.

It won't.

That's not to say that a budget isn't a useful tool. It truly can be for many people, particularly those with analytic minds.

However, a budget is often saddled with much more than it can ever live up to. A budget *can* help you identify areas where you overspend, and it *can* help you find areas where you can cut spending.

The big problem is that a typical personal budget assumes a very orderly life, and as we discussed in Chapter 2, our lives are more disorderly than ever. An old-fashioned household budget, fastidiously followed every month, is a twentieth-century tool in a twenty-first century world. It doesn't account for the onslaught of opportunities and problems thrust into our lives every day.

A much better answer comes from recognizing that most of our money management problems come from our own decision making and that the multitude of online tools make it very easy to manage our money in ways never even conceived of two decades ago.

Five Steps Toward Minding the Gap

Here's a five-pronged solution for minding your own gap:

1. **Automate your savings and payments.** Choose a bank (see Chapter 12, "Managing the Gap," for more details on selecting a good bank) that allows you to do online bill pay and schedule automatic transfers into a savings account from your checking account. Schedule as many of your bills as you can and also schedule an automatic weekly transfer into your savings account. Choose a realistic starting amount, one that gives you plenty of breathing room—why not $25? This amount is effectively the start of your emergency fund, as discussed in Chapter 2, and it will grow into the source of your financial freedom.

2. **Reduce your footprint.** Dig deep into tactics for reducing your spending and jump headfirst into the ones that offer a healthy bang for the buck and don't go against your core personal values and goals. Chapters 7, "Minding the Gap," and 8, "Frugality as Framework," offer a great deal of guidance in this area.

3. **Increase and diversify your income.** Look for effective, simple ways to bring in more income, whether from your primary career or from other avenues of income. Chapter 10, "The New Career Rules," offers a lot of help for both dimensions.

4. **Refactor.** If you find sustainable ways to increase your income or decrease your expenses, include that change in your automatic savings. If you manage to cut your energy bill by $25 per month and can see that consistently in your energy bill, bump up your automatic savings by $5 a week. If you get a raise and it results in an extra $50 every two weeks, add $20 to your automatic savings each week. A success in increasing your gap simply means that you're closer than before to your dreams.

5. **Conserve the difference.** What often happens when people execute the first two steps is that they discover there's still a leftover in their checking account at the end of the pay period. They immediately think of this money as "mad money"—money that's "off the books" that they can do with as they please without any real consequence to their plans. Instead, *sweep the excess into savings or into another specific goal* and forget about it. Don't let the balance of your checking account tempt you into purchases that don't support your big goals in life and leave you feeling empty.

Chapter 8

Frugality as Framework

We had to wait for twenty-five minutes for the waiter to bring our meal, and after that, bring our bill, where we would pay $30. Why were we here? We could be having a nice dinner with conversation at home. The pasta dish we had both ordered could be made in fifteen minutes in our kitchen, and Joseph could be sleeping comfortably in his crib. I realized that what I cared about was a nice meal and dinner conversation with my wife, not the experience of paying someone else to prepare the food for us. The part I valued and loved could be found at our own dining room table at a much cheaper price.

May 2006

Benjamin Franklin once said, "Watch the pennies and the dollars will take care of themselves."[1] That quote is often used as a call to arms to pinch pennies, but simply whipping out the scissors to clip coupons misses much of the point of what Franklin was saying. His argument is, quite simply, to be mindful of how you spend your

---

1   Benjamin Franklin, "Poor Richard's Almanac."

money. If you're alert enough to be mindful of your small expenditures, keeping track of your large ones comes easily and naturally.

The Difference Between Frugal and Cheap

In *Lifestyle of the Tight and Frugal: Theory and Measurement*, John Lastovica defines frugality as the practice of acquiring goods and services in a restrained manner and resourcefully using already owned economic goods and services to achieve a longer-term goal.[2] In other words, whenever frugal people spend money, they are conscious of the fact that their resources (time, money, mental energy, physical energy, and so forth) are limited, and they'd prefer to invest those resources in something in line with their core values.

So, what differentiates that from a cheap person? Cheap people focus on nothing but retaining money for themselves, regardless of what their personal values might be. Frugal people, on the other hand, are happy to spend money on something in line with their personal values, but outside of those values, they seek to minimize their use of time, money, and energy.

A great example of this is in the purchase of a car. A cheap person will go for the car with the lowest sticker price, period. A frugal person will figure out what they want out of a car and how much they value it, and then do a bit of research to find the best "bang for the buck" for that set of values.

---

2   John L. Lastovicka, Lance A. Bettencourt, Renee Shaw Hughner, Ronald J. Kuntze, "Lifestyle of the Tight and Frugal: Theory and Measurement," *The Journal of Consumer Research*, Vol. 26, No. 1. (June 1999), pp. 85–98.

Frugality as a Framework for Freedom

Many people associate frugality with sacrifice: You have to give things up. They hear stories about having to give up lattes or giving up eating out or giving up nights on the town, and it sounds incredibly tedious.

A more appropriate view is that frugality is an exchange: **You're trading the things you don't value for things that you do value.**

It all comes back to your core values. You have a handful of things that you personally value. Spending money on those things is completely normal and healthy—it reaffirms the things you care most about.

Outside of this exist many things that we might care about a small amount, and other things we don't care about at all. These are the areas where it's fine to deeply cut spending.

It's easier to see this with an example. You're part of a small circle of friends that you value very much—those friendships are one of the core values in your life. Those friends go out to dinner together all the time. You don't particularly value the dinner, but you *do* value the friendships.

Many people would just shrug it off and keep going out with friends, spending money on something that they don't really value to maintain something they do value.

A frugal person will find a new solution: Why not learn how to cook at home and invite them over for dinner? This might inspire others to host additional dinners or convince some of them to come over with ingredients and help you prepare other dinners. You still get the value of dining with friends (with perhaps the additional value of cooking with friends) without the constant cost of dining out.

If you can then redirect that saved money into another aspect of your life that you value—say, perhaps, saving for a down payment—your life as a whole improves. You don't sacrifice anything that you truly value while also improving an additional area that you value.

John Warfield, a quality control chemist from Des Moines, IA, puts it well: "I take the long view. Is there anything I really need today, be it extra excitement, gizmos, food, drugs, sex, rock and roll, or so on? I'm not afraid to spend an extra buck to try a new restaurant or a few hundred to jump out of a plane. But I don't need to do those things every day or every week. The financial security of tomorrow is more important to me than a large high-definition television."[3]

Instead of spending money on relatively frivolous things now, he steps back and looks at his core values—and he values security. A short-term rush might be fun once in a while, but financial security brings real lasting value to his life, enabling him to make powerful choices later on.

The rest of this chapter is filled with suggestions for trimming your spending. As you read them, keep your core values in mind and *don't follow* the suggestions that damage those core values. Instead, focus on the ones that don't interfere with your key values at all and

3   Personal interview.

recognize that the money you save by trying these things will actually improve those key values.

What's Essential?

Whenever I give a talk about my experiences and personal finance philosophy, I usually show a slide that depicts nothing more than a bucket of soapy-looking liquid. This usually elicits a raised eyebrow or two from the crowd, and several more eyebrows shoot up when I tell them that this bucket contains homemade laundry soap.

You see, I make my own laundry soap out of borax, washing soda, a bar of soap, and water—all available at your local grocery store. A single bucket takes me about ten minutes to make and has enough soap for fifty loads of laundry. Here's the kicker—I save about eighteen cents per load as compared to the brand of laundry detergent I previously used.

That adds up over time. In a household of four, we do an average of a load and a half of laundry a day. Over a full year, my laundry detergent choice saves us $100.

The laundry detergent is not what's important here. The important idea is simple—just go through your life, determine the things that are important and the things that aren't, and find every way you can to cut back on the things that aren't important.

To me, laundry soap isn't important. As long as my clothes are clean, I don't care what kind of soap I throw in there. So, I cut back as sharply as I could. I tried a homemade recipe that pledged to be the cheapest option—and I found that it did the job up to my standards. That's what I use now.

When you start applying this litmus test to everything in your life, you begin to find lots of areas to cut back. You start trying generic products. You start trying to make things yourself. You trim out expensive non-essentials.

Here are three examples from my own life:

1. I used to drink three or four sodas a day. It was expensive, plus it wasn't exactly good for my health. Since I mostly just drank them whenever I was thirsty, I started substituting bottled water for the sodas, with no real drawbacks. This saved a bit, but the real savings came into effect when I just got a handful of sturdy water bottles and started cleaning and refilling them myself. The upkeep cost of four sodas a day basically went away.

2. Clothes aren't an important issue in my life—as long as they fit well and aren't terribly worn, I'm happy with them. I used to just replace clothes by shopping at a big and tall men's store, but I substituted that choice by starting my shopping trip at a few local thrift stores. I would often find barely-worn shirts that fit me well for just a tiny fraction of the price. Sure, I might not have a choice of patterns or prints, but such issues really aren't essential in my life.

3. I've been an avid reader since I was a child, and I carried this wonderful hobby with me into adulthood. Because I read (and still read) two or

three books a week, I would often head to the bookstore twice a week and pick out a new title or two each time I visited—and that really added up. What I began to realize, though, is that what I truly enjoyed wasn't buying books, but reading them. So, I began to use my local library, and today I purchase only the occasional book, supplementing them with a well-worn library card. After all, my passion is reading, not buying.

Graham Miller, an independent advisor from Glasgow, Scotland, points to another area of concern. "Clutter and accumulating things is self perpetuating and leads to unhappiness. I was asked to declutter a room in my house and see how I felt," Graham says. "Before I got this advice, I had a house full of clutter (DVDs, video games, books) and very little money in the bank. I had a lot of things, but I was ultimately unfulfilled and unsatisfied. I would buy something to add to the clutter for the initial rush. This wore off, often within hours, and I would be back at square one. Needless to say, I spent a huge amount of money."[4] The accumulation of things in itself can lead to unhappiness—a point I'll touch on again later in the book.

Take the time to look at *everything* you spend money on in your life. Ask yourself if that spending is essential to your life—or even truly important. **If it *is* important, leave it alone. If it's not, cut it sharply**—find every way you can to trim every cent from your spending. Eventually, you find that you actually have enough money to cover everything important to you *and* have

4   Personal interview.

money to pay down your debts or to save for the future. The only things you've given up are the things that aren't essential to you.

The Peak-End Rule and Life Experiences

We were supposed to be packing for the move, but I had stumbled across an old photo album, buried in the nether regions of the guest room closet. It was filled with photographs of our 2004 trip to Seattle and British Columbia with my wife's sisters, parents, and grandfather. My memories mostly revolved around a beautiful day spent at the Butchert Botanical Gardens and a lazy evening spent camping near Mount Rainier. Rather than admiring the things we did, the expensive hotel, or the pricey meals, I got the most joy out of looking at the pictures of people. The smiles that come when people who love each other and spend time together are worth far more than any money frittered away—something to think about before a next trip.

June 2007

In his book *Objective Happiness*, Daniel Kahneman describes the peak-end rule, which states that we judge our past experiences based on our strongest emotional response (the peak, which can be positive or negative) and on how it finishes (again, either positive or negative).[5]

5   Kahneman, D. (1999). "Objective Happiness." In Kahneman, D., Diener, E., and Schwarz, N. (eds.). *Well-Being: The Foundations of Hedonic Psychology.* New York: Russel Sage, pp. 3–25.

It's easy to see this at work. Imagine your last family vacation. What do you remember? Your first thoughts will be either a positive or negative overall feeling, along with a specific memory or two (the peak experiences of the trip). Most of the rest of the vacation will be fuzzy and disordered.

If you keep the peak-end rule in mind when you plan major events or trips, it's easy to plan to maximize the positive memories and minimize the cost. Figure out the two or three *big* things you want to see or do on the trip (the peak experiences); then minimize the cost of the other elements (the fuzzy parts you won't remember). Stay in an inexpensive hotel—or even camp out in a tent. Prepare your own simple meals instead of eating out all the time. Focus primarily on events and attractions that are free, excepting the small number of things you *really* want to enjoy.

You'll still get the peak memorable experiences, but you drastically reduce your expenses, enabling you to focus on other goals with your dollars.

Overvaluing Routine Experiences

During my early professional years, I made a daily habit out of stopping at a local coffee shop. I'd pick up a bagel, a newspaper, and a cup of overly sweet coffee and retreat to a back table, where I'd browse through the pages, sip my sweet beverage, and nibble away at my breakfast.

I started doing it because I really enjoyed going to coffee shops when I was in college and going to this one felt a bit nostalgic. I'd remember long evenings playing checkers with my friends, arguing about some frivolous point or another, and generally avoiding the studying that needed to be done.

After a while, the morning cup and bagel became so routine that I didn't believe I could possibly live without it. I *needed* it.

When our finances hit rock bottom, I took a hard look at the money I was spending, and I couldn't help but notice that $7 was disappearing, day in and day out, at that coffee shop. $35 a week, $140 a month.... $1,680 a year is a lot of money.

So I challenged myself to cut back to just a day or two a week, expecting that it would be very difficult. What I found, though, is that the change was surprisingly easy—the hard part, if there was one, was breaking the caffeine addiction. Before long, I was stopping at the coffee shop once a month at the most.

What changed? For one, I realized I was overvaluing my routine. Humans are creatures of routine—yes, even for those of us who seem to thrive on spontaneity. Most of our days are filled with many of the same activities as other days—a similar amount of sleep, a similar meal pattern, and other such actions. This routine is fairly comforting—it makes us feel in charge of our lives. Thus, we often overvalue that routine in our heads, since it makes us feel *normal* about what goes on in a day.

In truth, a daily routine is surprisingly malleable. Most of the time, it only takes a single month of daily repetition to establish a new routine as a normal behavior. By simply pledging to use a different morning routine every day for a month, the desire to go to the coffee shop each morning slipped away quite easily.

Another major factor that made this routine easy to shed is that I realized that the part of the coffee shop I valued was nostalgic. I enjoyed that fleeting sense that I was still in touch with the earlier experiences that I valued so much. In truth, though, that experience lived on inside of me and with the relationships with people in my life. By putting time into re-establishing those relationships and simply enjoying my memories, I found the real value of those coffee shop visits without throwing down $7 a day.

A third factor is that, by visiting the coffee shop each day, the visits no longer seemed special and enjoyable. Instead, they seemed ordinary. Visits to that coffee shop were no longer a treat—they were just part of my morning routine, carried on without much conscious thought or pleasure.

Today, I visit a coffee shop perhaps once every two or three months. Those visits are quite enjoyable, as I'm able to enjoy the specialness of the moment. It feels like a real treat instead of just another tired routine. Yet, in the mornings when I used to stop at the coffee shop, I no longer feel the need. I have the great memories of my younger years and strong relationships with the people I care about from those days. Instead, I have a new morning routine, one that keeps my wallet in my pocket and my future clearly in mind.

What routines do you hold to without question? Do you have daily money leaks in your life that seem almost unchangeable? Step back for a moment and ask yourself *why* you're spending this money each day. Are you getting personal value each day out of this routine? Or are you merely running on nostalgia and dreams? Is there perhaps a better routine you could utilize—like working on relationships with others instead of spending money?

If you genuinely find value in a routine, by all means, keep that routine. Some routines do make our lives better. However, I've found that the things that we often consider to be beyond question are often the things that are hurting us the most and are the very things that we truly benefit from changing.

Frugality and Food

One constant regular drain on our wallet comes in the form of food. We are constantly bombarded with food options: dining out, fast food, convenient boxed meals, and so on. With this wide variety of choices—and with many of them being really convenient—it's not surprising that we often overspend on our food options.

One important thing to remember when it comes to food choices and saving money is that *unhealthy foods have a big long-term cost that you don't see on the sticker price.* The food on the dollar menu at your local fast food restaurant might seem like a bargain right now, but if you factor in the long-term health costs of regularly eating such food, it's not. Unhealthy food adversely affects your health, reduces your energy level (which affects your career and your personal activity choices), adversely affects your appearance (also affecting your career and your interpersonal relationships), and, often, doesn't save you money at all.

In terms of balancing food flavor, quality, personal health, and cost, I find the simple advice of food writer Michael Pollan to be a very useful rule of thumb. In his pro-eating manifesto, *In Defense of Food*, Pollan encourages people to "Eat food. Not too much. Mostly plants."[6] In that, he encourages people to stick to raw ingredients—the ones found in the produce section and the meat counter of your store—have slightly smaller portions, and to increase their vegetable intake. Each of these choices not only reduces the long-term health cost of food, but often decreases the *immediate* sticker price of food as well.

Here are ten steps toward reducing the overall cost of food in your life without reducing the taste of it:

1. **Learn to cook for yourself.** Many people—my sister-in-law, Vicky, included—argue that cooking meals from scratch is too challenging and takes too much time when compared to other convenient food options. In truth, most food options you prepare yourself are actually surprisingly fast— often faster than the time one spends waiting at a restaurant. In terms of skill, yes, it does take some time to learn how to cook properly. The best way to learn, though, is not to start off tackling coq au vin or something else that's difficult and time consuming. Start with scrambled eggs or chili—dishes that are very simple to prepare in their basic form. Pick up a cookbook that teaches technique along with the recipes—Mark Bittman's *How to Cook*

6   *In Defense of Food*, Michael Pollan. Cover. ISBN: 978-1-59420-145-5.

Everything and Irma Rombauer's *Joy of Cooking* are two great options for this. With even a little practice, you'll find that making a meal for yourself at home isn't all that time-consuming—and, quite often, the flavors are such that you'll never want to return to convenience foods.

2. **Prepare a meal plan and a grocery list each week.** At our home, Saturday morning usually finds one of us making a list of the meals we intend to eat over the next week, digging through the cupboards to make sure we have all the ingredients, and then making a list of those items we don't have. This simple process takes about twenty minutes and usually results in a surprisingly short grocery list. At the grocery store, we earn those twenty minutes back by shopping for much less time—instead of wandering from aisle to aisle trying to decide what to get, we just follow that short list. The money we save by avoiding tons of impulse buys is substantial and, in the end, it doesn't take us any extra time.

3. **Use a simple price list strategy to figure out which store to shop at.** One common technique for minimizing grocery costs is the price list. First popularized by Amy Dacyczyn in her *Tightwad Gazette* newsletter, a price list is merely a listing of the cost of most of your commonly-purchased items at several different stores. So, for example, you might have a gallon of milk in your price book—next to it, you'd find the price of that gallon at several different stores. This way, you could use that price book to plan which store (or

stores) to shop at for groceries that week, minimizing your cost.

Today, with stores constantly shifting food prices and the selection seemingly changing on a daily basis, a price book doesn't work as well. Instead, I've substituted what I call a "price list"—a much simpler method of doing the same thing.

For a few weeks out of each year, I'll shop at several different local grocery stores. At each store, I'll get the price of the 25 items I buy most frequently—bread, milk, eggs, lettuce, and so on. I just do this as part of my weekly shopping trip. After visiting several stores, I go home and add up the cost of the 25 items from each store, giving myself a total cost of buying all those items from each of the local stores. Whichever store has the cheapest total wins my business for the next year or so.

This simple method helps me to always dig out what the least-expensive store in the area is. Because I update the list annually, I can also keep track of changes in pricing policies of different stores and also identify whether or not a new store is worth shopping at. Doing this once a year saves me about $15 a week in groceries, according to my figures.

4. **Use the weekly fliers.** Many grocery store chains distribute fliers in local newspapers and on their websites describing the special deals the store is offering this week. Use these fliers to your advantage. Each week, as you begin to plan your meals,

download the flier from your store of choice and use the discounted fresh items—meats and vegetables—as the core of the meals you plan for the week. This way, your grocery list will naturally be full of the items already on sale that week.

5. **Prepare meals in advance and freeze them.** For many busy families—my own included—preparing a meal from scratch every single night is difficult. Evenings are often scheduled to the gills, leaving only a short window of opportunity to get a meal on the table. Our solution is simple. On the nights when we have plenty of time to prepare a meal, we partially prepare a second or third or fourth copy of that meal, bringing it to the point that it's ready to be tossed in the oven. Then, we freeze that prepared meal (or group of meals). If an evening is going to be busy, we get the meal out the night before to allow it to thaw; then we put it in the oven as soon as we get home. Presto—a homemade meal made of inexpensive ingredients ready to go as quickly as we need it.

6. **Prepare convenience foods in advance and freeze them.** The flip side of this idea for me happens in the morning when I've got an appointment to make. I'm rushing around, trying to get out the door, but I also know how important it is to get a good breakfast inside of me. In the past, I would compromise and stop for some fast food, but that would really add up over time. So I began to apply the same principles as the advance

meal preparation and made myself an enormous batch of breakfast burritos in advance. Filled with beans, eggs, and salsa, they're quite tasty—and easy to prepare, too. All I do is grab a frozen one, wrap a paper towel around it, defrost it for two minutes, cook it for another two minutes, and go! One can do the same thing with lunch burritos, sandwiches, and other similar convenience foods. It's convenient, as healthy as you want to make it, and really inexpensive.

7. **Chain meals together.** During the summer, our grill gets a lot of use. I'm constantly grilling vegetables, chicken breasts, steaks, and other such items. Yet, if you took a look at our grill, you'd probably be shocked at the amount of food on it. Whenever I cook anything that could be used as a major ingredient in another dish, I make sure to cook plenty of it. This serves two big advantages. First, it allows us to buy that major ingredient in bulk, thus saving us money. Second, having that key ingredient already cooked and ready to go saves us time in preparing a homemade meal later. So, for example, I might take advantage of a "buy two, get one free" deal on chicken breasts at our preferred grocery store and then cook them all at once, saving the cooked breasts for other dishes (like chicken soup or chicken stew or a salad).

8. **Don't fear leftovers.** Every second or third night, we have a "leftover" night at our home. Our dinner just consists of whatever remains from the dishes served the previous few nights, plus a new

side dish or two if it seems necessary. Why do this? Food left uneaten is money thrown away. Besides, it's incredibly easy to add new flavor to leftovers. Just spice it up a bit with fresh ground pepper, salt, or Italian herbs and spices. Another avenue is to simply reconstitute it into a new meal—take a leftover hamburger, break it into small pieces, add some Italian seasoning and some tomato sauce, and you have an incredibly easy meaty pasta sauce.

9. **Select recipes full of inexpensive staple ingredients.** Beans and rice are two of my favorite foods. They serve as the backbone for almost any type of cuisine, can be flavored in infinite ways, and are incredibly inexpensive. Focus on making recipes that utilize beans, rice, vegetables in season in your area, and any vegetables you can easily grow. Using such inexpensive ingredients as the backbone of your meal makes the entire meal incredibly inexpensive while still being delicious.

10. **Break the soda addiction.** One final food suggestion: if you find yourself drinking soda daily (or more frequently), break the addiction. Train yourself to replace your sodas with water you bottle yourself. If you want more flavor, add a splash of lemon juice or whatever fruit juice you prefer to the water. Not only will this directly eliminate the surprisingly significant daily cost of soda (it can easily add up to $1,000 a year), but it's one of the easiest things people can do to get their weight under control and their health in a better place.

Trimming Your Utility Bills

Another area where we all spend money—and where it's often easy to trim a lot of spending without affecting our quality of life one whit—is with our utility bills. Energy, communication, and cable bills add up to a significant amount of money each month.

Install a programmable thermostat. A programmable thermostat is a simple device that allows you to schedule rises and falls in the temperature of your home. For example, if you have a programmable thermostat, you can have the air conditioning turn off automatically from ten at night to five in the morning each day (when you're asleep), as well as from nine in the morning to five in the evening each weekday (when you're at work). The end result is that your air conditioner runs less, significantly reducing your summer energy bill, and the same effect occurs during the winter with your furnace.

Air seal your home. Heat constantly leaks into your home (during the summer) and out of your home (during the winter), costing you on your energy bill. Air sealing your home simply means that you locate the worst air leaks in your home—meaning the places where the most heat is lost or gained—and block those leaks using caulking and weatherstripping. This can be done in a weekend afternoon or two and can reduce your heating and cooling bills by as much as 20%.

Improve your insulation. A well-insulated home can drastically reduce energy costs in both the winter and summer seasons. Many homes are under-insulated, as recommended insulation guidelines have gone up significantly over the past twenty years. Add into that situation the fact that many homes are under-insulated when constructed and you have a perfect recipe for energy loss in your home. Consider a do-it-yourself home energy audit to find out your current insulation levels and determine whether an upgrade might save you significantly on your energy bills.

Look into pay-as-you-go phones or Internet telephony. For many phone users, standard plans are simply overkill for their usage. For a domestic phone line, look into an Internet-based telephone solution like Skype, which offers unlimited long distance calling, a number of your own, and voicemail for $2.99 a month (plus the initial cost of an inexpensive phone). If your cell phone use is limited, look into pay-as-you-go phones, many of which offer all the basic services you need without a required monthly bill.

Eliminate your cable bill entirely. The Internet provides an abundance of free access to television programming, and for a very small fee, services such as Netflix offer on-demand, commercial-free access to television programming and films. If you're looking for an idle entertainment fix, you can get all you'll ever need through the broadband Internet connection you probably already have.

Housing and Transportation

More than half of the annual income of the typical American family is spent on housing and transportation—51.7%, in fact.[7] With housing and transportation filling such a large role in our financial life, it's easy to see how a few clever choices in this area can make an enormous difference in our bottom line.

Rent. Unless you (a) plan to live in the area you're at for more than five years, (b) have more than 20% of your down payment saved, (c) relish the idea of investing a hundred hours of year in home maintenance, and (d) prefer to handle your own plumbing and electrical problems instead of calling a landlord, renting is almost always a better financial and personal deal for, well, everyone.

What about home equity? During the first few years of a home mortgage, more than 80% of your mortgage payment goes directly toward paying the interest on that mortgage. Add into that the financial and time costs of maintaining a home versus maintaining an apartment and, in most cases, renting really is the better option.

This, of course, assumes that you'll do something responsible with the money you save by renting. For renting to truly be a financial boon, you have to be saving or investing a substantial amount each month, either toward a home down payment or some other equally important financial goal (like seed money for a small business).

If you've already made up your mind to buy for other reasons, rely on the lessons of the past decade. If

7   The average American family spends 34.1% of their income on housing and 17.6% on transportation, according to *Consumer Expenditures* (U.S. Department of Labor, U.S. Bureau of Labor Statistics, April 2009).

the housing bubble of the late 2000s taught us anything at all, it's that no one wins when you borrow more money than you can afford. Avoid the pitfall that caused so many people to be evicted from their homes—rent until you have 20% of the total cost of the home in the bank and your credit is strong enough to get a low fixed rate mortgage with payments below 28% of your household income.

Live small—even downsize. The best home to live in is one where you actually have a real use for every room in the house—unused space is incredibly expensive to buy and maintain. Instead of buying a house that exceeds your needs, focus on finding one that meets your needs. If you have rooms in your house that go unused for weeks, you might want to consider downsizing into a home that offers all the livable space you actually use and smaller payments to boot.

Rent out spare space in your home. Another option, if downsizing doesn't work in your area, is to rent out the unused space in your home. Convert your basement into an apartment and rent it to a quiet college student, a recent college graduate with a fresh new job, or a married couple that's new to town. This directly increases your income and likely increases the resale value of your home.

Buy cars solely for reliability and fuel efficiency. When you boil it down to the core, a car's purpose is to get you from point A to point B as inexpensively and efficiently as possible. Comfort? Cars cannot match the comfort of home, so you often end up paying a huge premium to sit in slightly less miserable conditions for an hour or two a day. Instead, focus on bang for the buck—what will get you where you need to go with the least amount of money spent? Generally, used cars offer far more bang for the buck than new cars.

Use public transportation. Another option—if it's available to you—is to simply get rid of your car and its associated expenses and use public transportation. Public transportation passes in most large cities are incredible bargains—they get you where you need to go throughout the city without the hassle and cost of owning a car and paying for parking. If you live in the suburbs, look into commuting by train into the city if you need to, or at the very least, look into forming a car pool.

Maintain what you have. Careful maintenance of your home and automobile can greatly extend the life of each and also reduce the amount of costly repairs that are required. Follow the maintenance schedule in your car's manual to the letter—if you're buying a used car and can't certify what needs to be done, get a trusted mechanic to evaluate what maintenance should be done. With your home, develop a home maintenance checklist and follow it carefully each month—such checklists are easy to find on the Internet.

Get Clever with Your Entertainment

Entertainment is the trickiest part of a family's budget. Some entertainment spending is great—it can be the source of quite a lot of personal and social enjoyment. However, entertainment spending is often misdirected into buying things instead of having experiences.

Discover the library. If you're into reading, watching films, or listening to music, the library is an incredible free warehouse to fill your entertainment needs. Many public libraries have extensive DVD and CD archives, as well as an enormous collection of books, often including bestsellers. Many libraries now have an online reservation system, making it easy for you to reserve exactly what you want from the convenience of home. In some rural areas, the library will even deliver materials to you via the postal service. The question you should ask yourself is this: Do I enjoy reading or do I enjoy spending money on books? Do I enjoy watching films or do I enjoy spending money on DVDs? The answer will often point you straight to the library.

Have a "media swap." Invite some friends over and allow them to simply borrow a large portion of your DVD or CD or book collection. A few weeks later, have them reciprocate, allowing you to borrow a large portion of their collection. This gives both of you an enormous source of free entertainment—and often, because it's entertainment picked by your friends, it will already match your tastes quite well.

Get to know the community calendar. Most cities have a thriving free cultural life, with concerts, festivals, and other events going on regularly throughout the year. Locate your community's event calendar and see if any events are of interest to you; similarly, check the event calendar of nearby towns and cities as well.

Join a club. This ties directly into developing a sense of community, but clubs and organizations also fulfill a role for socializing and entertainment at a very low cost. Look at options in your community that match your interests—book clubs run by the local library, gaming clubs, volunteer and service groups, a church, and so on.

The Five Fundamental Rules of Frugality

I regularly give talks to various groups on personal finance and my own experiences with debt recovery and talk with people about their own debt recovery journeys. At these events, I always find that people equate frugality with some form of misery—they either see it as being cheap or see it as putting themselves through misery. I argue that it's neither—that instead it's joyful and life-affirming. I boil down the entire discussion on frugality to five simple rules. If you keep these five rules in mind when you evaluate your spending, you'll always find happiness and freedom, both now and in the future:

1. ***Don't* give up the things you love.** Yes, it's always worthwhile to give any lifestyle change a trial run—don't just assume you can't live without something until you give it a shot. However, if you find that a money-saving choice really is making you miserable, *don't* be miserable. Bring that element back into your life. If you are constantly making choices that genuinely bring you down, you're going to hate what you're doing and, eventually, you're going to rebound in a very financially painful way.

2. **Find inexpensive ways to enjoy the things important to you.** We're all passionate about certain things, and for some of us, those passions often translate very easily into spending money and

buying things. Strive to dig into what your passion really is and ask yourself if that passion really is met by pulling out your wallet. For example, if you're as passionate about reading as I am, you know how tempting a bookstore can be. But ask yourself this: Are you passionate about reading and enjoying books, or are you a book hoarder who likes to overstuff his or her shelves? If it's the reading you're passionate about, find less-expensive ways to fuel the hobby. One great way to start is at your local library.

3. **Cut back *hard* on the things that matter less.** If you're not entirely defined by the clothes you wear, give thrift shops a shot. If your self-identity isn't ruled by the brand of window washer you use, try using vinegar out of a spray bottle. If preparing gourmet meals that take all afternoon isn't at the center of your emotional life, stick with just a few high-quality kitchen implements and forget the rest. If something's not a central value in your life, don't invest even a dime more into it than you possibly can. Seek stuff that works well for the lowest possible cost and move on with life.

4. **Never go shopping without knowing exactly what you want.** If you ever walk into a store without a plan, it's highly likely you're going to walk out the door with something you didn't intend to buy—which means it's something you didn't need. That something you didn't need sacrifices part of your future, because it's money that's not going toward paying off your debt or

building your dream home or freeing you up to have the career of your dreams. Every time you enter a store, know *exactly* why you're there and, if it's not to buy a specific item, *don't* walk out with an item. Sure, you might find something you like there, but if you do....

5. **Use the thirty-day rule for any unplanned purchase.** If you find something you'd really like to have and you're trying to talk yourself into it, stop for a second. Jot down what that item is on a piece of paper, and then leave the store. Give yourself thirty days to think about that item. See if you can't find it for a lower price elsewhere. Ask yourself if you honestly need or even really want this item. At the end of the thirty days, if you still truly want the item, pull the trigger on it using the best deal you've found. That way, even if you do decide you need this impulse buy, you're not spending as much as you would have to begin with.

Chapter 9

Cultivating People and Opportunities

It was 5:30 in the morning and, finally, the project was finished. I sent my boss an email letting him know it ready to go for his demonstration later that day. My boss hadn't asked for such effort. He knew that I was a college student just working in his lab and that I had a very full class load. However, I knew that he was about to demonstrate the project to a group of very important associates and that the more feature-rich the project was, the more likely the project would impress them—and reflect well on my boss. So I dug in. While he took a red-eye flight, I added features and polished up details. And now it was complete. A week later, when he had returned from the trip, he gave me a small gift, shook my hand, and said, "Thank you. I owe you one."

November 1998

Sextus the Pythagorean once said, "What you wish your neighbors to be to you, such be also to them."[1] Jesus of Nazareth said, "Do unto others as you would have them do unto you."[2] Robert D. Putnam, in his book *Bowling Alone*, spells it out in detail: "Even more valuable, however, is a norm of *generalized reciprocity*: I'll do this for you without expecting anything specific back from you, in the confident expectation that someone else will do something for me down the road."[3] In other words, it's all about the *golden rule*—the idea that by giving to the community at large and individuals in specific, you will be treated with the same type of value in return.

Our lives are filled with relationships and communities—some cultivated and some uncultivated, some positive and some negative. Shifting the balance toward more positive, stronger relationships through your own positive actions lets the golden rule work in your favor instead of against you. It fosters positive communities, enables you to connect with more people, and provides more resources and help when you need them.

Negative Relationships

I had just lost eighty dollars in about ten minutes at a no-limit-hold-'em poker table, and I had had enough. I had gone to the casino with a few friends who

1   Kersey Graves, "The World's Sixteen Crucified Saviors," p. 308, published in 1875.

2   Luke 6:31, NIV translation.

3   Robert D. Putnam, *Bowling Alone*, pp. 20–21. ISBN: 0-684-83283-6.

seemed to be spending every dime they had as fast as it came in. For a while, keeping up with them had been a lot of fun. Now I sat in a daze, realizing that the payment for our electric bill had just disappeared. These guys didn't really care, and instead, they were encouraging me—quite loudly—to drop another $60 on the table and keep playing with them. It was an expensive game. It had been an expensive game for years. And I was really wishing for the game to end.

August 2005

During much of my early professional career, I hung out with a group of guys who spent money like it was water. They were constantly buying gadgets, dropping an ever-escalating amount of money on games, and indulging in all kinds of different expensive activities. One night, it might be an all-night gaming session. Another night, it might end up with an expensive game of poker. We might stop by a bar, or go to a driving range. There was always something going on that would cause money to slip through one's fingers like water.

What made the situation worse is that, if a person chose not to participate, they were goaded and belittled by the rest of the group. Taunts were delivered and names were called until you "manned up" and dropped your money on something wholly unnecessary.

Most of the conversation in the group was extremely negative as well. Insults were constantly hurled at anyone not a part of the group. Negative stories about other people were pretty much the lingua franca of our circle. Often, we would cut each other down, as a well-placed insult usually elicited high fives from the other members of the group.

On one level, it was fun. I could just relax and let out all of the angst inside of me built up while trying to plow forward in a challenging career. Yet, I began to realize that this black hole of money and negative feelings was changing me as well. It was causing me to generally feel more negative about everything. It was causing me to spend money without really caring about the future.

Eventually, I walked away from this circle of people. I just stopped hanging out with them. Instead, I started spending evenings at home with my wife and infant son. I started seeking out new relationships in my life and rebuilding old ones.

Take a look at the people around you—the people you choose to spend your time with. Are the conversations with them positive or negative? Do you spread gossip and relish in the crumbling lives of others? Or do you support each other and encourage success and positive results? Do your friends constantly engage in activities that drain your pocketbook? Or are your friends truly happy with an afternoon just hanging out at each others' homes?

I'm not suggesting at all that you should end your relationship with a long-time friend because you go shopping and gossip together. Instead, I suggest simply exploring other areas in your life and see where they lead.

Positive Relationships

It was the end of our wedding reception, and Sarah and I were worrying about several last-minute details. Yet, as he had been all that week, my best man, John, was right there. He just looked at me and said the same thing he'd said many times already that week. "Don't worry, I'll take care of it." Sarah and I left, and John stayed behind, once again taking care of the little details and giving us the freedom to enjoy this day with as little worry as possible. As Sarah and I walked away, I looked over my shoulder and saw him taking down some decorations, and I realized that the more friends like John I had in my life, the better my life would be.

June 2003

On the flip side of that negative relationship coin is positive relationships—ones that reinforce your positive traits. Positive relationships are based on exchanging value with one another and encouraging each other's best attributes.

Catherine Krikorian, a mortgage underwriter from Bellevue, WA, is adamant that personal relationships laid the foundation for her career and saved her through economic downturns. "I can't think of any job that I have had over the past 20 years that I landed just because my resume was the best fit. I always knew someone that got me an 'in.' Mind you, there were many people interviewing for the positions, and I was eventually hired on my own merits because I interview well and I am good at what I do, but would I have even had the chance to interview without that contact? I can guarantee you with the last two jobs, especially with the recent real estate implosion and the many underwriters out of work, the answer would have been 'no.'"[4]

In my own life, I've found this to be true. The John I mention in the previous anecdote has been my closest friend (besides my wife) over the last fifteen years of my life. No matter what I happen to be doing in life, he takes the time to listen to what I'm saying and offer genuine and useful advice and help. He rarely speaks negatively of anyone and usually finds the positive in any situation. He's also very content to engage in activities that don't require money to be spent—in fact, John can often be found at our dining room table playing a board game with us.

The difference between John and the circle of friends I described earlier is that John cares about *me*, whereas the others care more about *gratification*. In the other circle, I am easily replaceable because I don't truly matter. If I'm unavailable, they'll just call someone else to go out on the town with them. If I'm unavailable, John will immediately ask what he can help with. In the other circle, negative expressions toward others is rewarded and, over time, leads to a more negative sense of the world. With John, positive expressions toward others is rewarded and, over time, builds into a more positive sense of the world.

Most of us have a mix of negative and positive people in our lives. The easiest way to maximize the value of the positive people and minimize the impact of the

4   Personal interview.

negative is to simply make the choice to spend our free time with the positive ones. Instead of heading out to go shopping with the gossip girls, have a movie night with some of your other friends. Instead of heading out to the golf course for another afternoon of drinking and betting and insults, go play ultimate frisbee at the park with some of your other friends. You'll find that, over time, your outlook on life and attitudes toward money will change in a positive direction.

Another vital aspect of bringing positive relationships forward in your life is that positive relationships constantly contribute opportunities and value to your life. A positive friend, upon seeing an opportunity you may be interested in, will immediately strive to inform you of that opportunity—and, similarly, as your attitude becomes more positive, you'll do the same. If you need help, a positive friend will come forward to help you instead of turning away at when you need it most.

From a Negative to a Positive: Cultivating Opportunities

I left a meeting with my academic advisor, who had informed me that the job market was incredibly poor for people graduating this spring and that only a small handful of people in my major had found any sort of work—mostly with pretty low salaries. I had sent out dozens of applications and resumes and letters, but had so far only received one bite—and it required moving to a new part of the country by myself, leaving behind my family and the woman that I loved and would eventually marry.

I trudged back to work in the research lab, wondering what was going to happen. When I arrived, my boss was waiting for me with a big smile on his face. "Your work here has been excellent over the past several years. Would you like to work on a new project for me after you graduate? I think it's something you'll be interested in." A wonderful job, delivered at my feet thanks to my effort in building a positive relationship.

March 2002

Most of the time, our relationships are formed by circumstance. We're related to these people. We work with these people. We live near these people. Our children are friends with their children. We went to college together. We go to the same church. We're in the same book club.

I call these groups **cohorts**. Within each cohort, there's usually a wide mix of people, both negative and positive. Quite often, though, our friends within a given cohort happen to be the first people we "clicked" with in some way. We found a common interest with the guy two doors down at the neighborhood barbecue. We started hanging out with the "after-dinner drink" group because someone invited you on your second day of work.

The best way to slowly transition your relationships from negative ones to positive ones is to explore each of your cohorts. Get to know a wide variety of people at your church, not just the group that you first befriended. Have dinner with the parents of each of your child's friends, just to get to know them. Plan another neighborhood barbecue and make it your goal to meet as many of the people who attend as possible.

As you meet more and more people, you'll find more and more people that you click with on some level. As you begin to connect, ask yourself: *Will this new person I'm connecting with improve me as a person?* Is that person positive, complimenting and helping people, or is that person negative, spreading gossip behind their back? Does that person offer helpful advice to you, or do they look down their nose at you? Does that person enjoy spending time with people no matter what the activity or are they always chasing the latest thing?

As you discover more positive people around you, make an effort to deepen your connection with them. Invite them over. Help them with projects. Ask for their advice and ideas, and offer your own to them freely. From such a seed, a powerful positive relationship will bloom. By osmosis, that positive relationship will affect your life in countless positive ways.

Even more compelling, having positive relationships in many different cohorts can radically benefit your life. People from different cohorts will be exposed to different information and different opportunities and, by the nature of a positive relationship, they'll want to share that information and those opportunities with you.

Five Ways to Maximize Your Positive Relationships

The relationships that fill your life have a profound impact on your personal and financial success. Positive relationships open opportunities; negative relationships close them. Thus, one major step that any person can take to improve his or her personal and financial position is to open the door to as many positive relationships as possible. Here are five ways to begin doing just that:

1. **Explore your cohorts.** Make an effort to get to know as many people as possible that you already have something in common with. Have conversations with people you don't know very well in the workplace, at church, at group meetings, and in the neighborhood. Unless you open yourself up to finding new relationships, you'll have a very difficult time establishing more positive relationships.

2. **Evaluate the people you meet and build relationships with the positive ones.** Are these people positive or negative people? Do they speak well of others? Do they offer genuinely useful and helpful information? Are they enjoyable to be around? One good way to delve into this is to ask for their opinions on various subjects and listen to whether they offer positive, helpful information or negative, useless information. Focus on building relationships with the interesting, positive people you discover by inviting them over for events and engaging them in regular conversation and interaction.

3. **Focus on being more positive.** If you have information you know will be useful to people in your life, share it. If someone asks for help, give it to the best of your ability. Reduce (or even eliminate) the amount of negative information

you share about others. Most importantly, *don't worry about what you will get in return for it.* What you'll get, over time, is a positive reputation and a set of positive relationships that will help you when you need it. In the end, positive people tend to attract other positive people.

4. **Mix positive people in different cohorts.** Introducing the positive people you know from different cohorts to each other often produces a multiplying effect. Positive people are often able to make each other better, and not only have you been able to easily improve two people you're connected to, you also happen to be one of the things they have in common. You're the one that connected them, and they'll remember you for that. One effective way to do this is to have a dinner party at your home in which you invite positive friends from different cohorts who may not all know each other, giving you the opportunity to make introductions and perhaps helping the people you care about to build new, valuable relationships.

5. **Don't lament negative relationships that end.** Quite often, negative relationships are replaceable. Rather than missing you, a negative person will simply find a replacement in their social circle without any real damage to their self-esteem. Quite often, the manner in which a relationship ends—with silence or with a flurry of negativity—gives a great indication that the relationship wasn't about valuing you at all, which is a relationship you're better off without.

Chapter 10

The New Career Rules

I wasn't supposed to be the one speaking, yet there I was, presenting and flipping through the slides. The responsibility had fallen to me. I was scared to death. Every single person in that room had more knowledge of this stuff than me. I could have said no. As I looked at the two people sitting in the back of the room, I realized why I had said yes. One was my former boss, the one who had opened the door to this job for me. The other one was a loyal coworker, the one person who had come through time and time again and made this project work, even through some desperate crises and adversity. I looked at the two of them, took a deep breath, and kept on delivering my first presentation.

October 2002

My father worked for thirty-five years for the same company. He was loyal to them through restructurings, layoff periods, downsizings, drastic changes to their retirement plans, constant management shufflings, aborted technology shifts, and countless other obstacles. Today, he sits at home retired, watching the news and hoping the company doesn't go under, dragging his pension down with it.

My father's loyalty to the company was bought with a long series of promises. Today, though, we see countless examples of how such loyalty to an organization often falls through in the long run.

Where is my father's loyalty now? It still lives on in an altered form: his friends. Many of the long-term friendships he built in the workplace are still thriving. These workplace friends visit him often, and he's often engaged in any number of activities with them.

In the end, his loyalty wasn't to some monolithic organization that was supposed to take care of him. His loyalty is to the people around him, the ones who actually came through on that promise.

Where Is Your Loyalty?

Today, we all face a similar question. As we can clearly see, loyalty to a business that's likely to downsize us at the first sign of economic trouble isn't an entity that can earn our trust. Yet being loyal to no one but ourselves is an empty bargain as well—when the chips are down, the man or woman who is only beholden to himself or herself has no one to help him or her.

The solution stares us in the face every single day: our coworkers and peers.

Organizations are transient. Once you leave, an organization no longer supports you or cares for you, nor do you support or care for it. What you do still care for, however, are the people that remain—the peers still in your field, the former boss who might write you a great recommendation down the road, the people who will still give you advice and perhaps toss some work your way in the future.

The same phenomenon holds true even within an organization. In the end, your true loyalty is best served if it's directed toward your peers, particularly as we move more and more toward an information- and collaboration-based economy. It is your coworkers and your peers who have the power to make you successful—or ensure that you don't succeed, either through negligence or through sabotage.

Quite often, loyalty toward your coworkers overlaps very nicely with efforts that help the company. If you work hard to support your coworkers in completing a great project, that project benefits the company. If you help your coworkers with the problems that they have, the solution to that problem benefits the organization.

Similarly, if you request help from peers in your field—or offer them help in the same way—it benefits the organization. You need to only look at the open source software movement, where companies employ people to write, share, and support software freely usable by everyone, for evidence of this phenomenon.

A Community of Peers

In this peer-based loyalty, you see the phenomenon of the community, discussed in Chapter 5, "Running to

Stand Still," come back into clear focus. Your co-workers and professional peers are the community in which you conduct your professional business, and you're best served by putting forth effort to improve that community.

What does that mean? Share your knowledge freely. Be helpful. Don't gossip, and don't spread negative information. Strive to build lots of value-based relationships with people in your workplace, as well as others in your field who work elsewhere. Participate in community forums, where people share information and resources that everyone can access. Pass along information and opportunities to appropriate peers.

If you don't know where to find such resources, start your own. Initiate a new group on Facebook or LinkedIn where people can share comments, ideas, and resources as well as simply get to know each other.

As a personal finance and personal growth writer, I participate in a number of different forums where people engaged in the same area can share ideas and opportunities. I strive to help them when I can, offering advice and information and assistance whenever possible. I'll advise new writers on ways to market their writing, provide guest articles to publishers who need them, and encourage group participation in writing and brainstorming projects.

At some point, I'll need help as well and, thanks to my participation in this community, I'll have all the professional help I need.

Such communities of peers don't require an organization or a single common focus. They just require people with overlapping interests who are genuinely interested in helping each other. Over time, such a group develops into a true community, supporting the people involved in a myriad of ways.

That's where the new loyalties lie.

The Power Shift

In the past, the value you can provide to others needed to be bullet points that could be neatly summarized on a resume.

As the world becomes more connected, however, the evaluation of new employees, contractors, or free-lancers often goes far beyond a cover letter and a hand-ful of slick bullet points. In the modern era, it's often easy for a Human Relations person to get a good idea of the value of the person the company is hiring from a few timely Google searches. Does the person have a large network of connections on LinkedIn? Is the person an active and positive participant in Internet communities based around their profession? Is the person's reputation positive enough that others link to what he or she says?

Along those same lines, when individuals look to form new startups or new divisions in a particular field, the first place they'll go to look for strong candidates is within that very community.

To put it simply, the Internet has contributed greatly to the power of the community in terms of opening doors for people. It facilitates the growth of communities of professional peers—and makes them more powerful and more deserving of loyalty—at the same time corporate destabilization is reducing the loyalty workers once felt for their organizations.

Another advantage of the growth of peer-based communities is that the gatekeeper for entry into such communities isn't knowing someone powerful or having a particular degree from a particular university. Instead, entry into and respect within such communities comes much more from what you can offer to the community to make everyone better. Instead of being differentiated by who you know or what university you attended, peers are often differentiated by your contributions to the community.

So what can you contribute?

Learning, Growing, and Synthesizing

In an era where overwhelming amounts of information are available at everyone's fingertips, there is substantial value in being able to sift through that information, extract what's valuable, and synthesize it into something meaningful and new. Such synthesis is something that everyone finds valuable—it's the reason that certain blogs and message boards can become incredibly popular and influential. It often doesn't require expertise, just enough ability to synthesize an abundance of information into something compelling.

Thus, the first thing you can do to contribute to a community is to never stop learning and growing. Strive to constantly take on new challenges, absorb new information, try new things, and learn from your failures and your successes. It is only through this filter of real-world learning and experience that you can begin to provide valuable answers and help to others.

Obviously, such growth is not only valuable to your peers, it's also valuable to your potential clients and employers. When you share your knowledge and skills within your community, your reputation as someone who provides genuine value grows along with the positive social connections you've made. That's the backbone of the new career.

Passion

Of course, the desire must be there to actually dig in and learn more about the field in which you're involved. That's where passion comes in.

Georg Wilhelm Friedrich Hegel once said, "Nothing great in the world has ever been accomplished without passion."[1] Passion is something that can't be taught or earned or bought. It's something that comes from within. It's the activity or enterprise that fills us with an endless desire to learn more, to try more, to experience more.

As information becomes more and more accessible and peer communities become more and more powerful, passion becomes a central part in who excels and who does not. It is the passionate person who will write up a detailed helpful response to someone at two in the morning. It is the passionate person who is constantly trying new things and looking for ways to improve

---

1   GWF Hegel. The Philosophy of History.

what's already know. It is the passionate person who contributes to the resources of the community. Find what you're passionate about. Get involved with the community around that passion. See where it takes you.

Deliberate Practice

The third vital factor in determining who will contribute most powerfully to a community and rise to the top of a given field comes in the form of how they practice their skills.

In an article for *Fortune*, Geoffrey Colvin investigated the practice regimens of people who excel in specific fields and found that in almost every circumstance, deliberate practice was behind their success. Deliberate practice refers to practice with lots of repetition and very specific goals that strives to improve your ability in a very specific way. "For example: Simply hitting a bucket of balls is not deliberate practice, which is why most golfers don't get better. Hitting an eight-iron 300 times with a goal of leaving the ball within 20 feet of the pin 80 percent of the time, continually observing results and making appropriate adjustments, and doing that for hours every day—that's deliberate practice."

This phenomenon holds true in almost every field. "In a study of 20-year-old violinists by Ericsson and colleagues, the best group (judged by conservatory teachers) averaged 10,000 hours of deliberate practice over their lives; the next-best averaged 7,500 hours; and the next, 5,000. It's the same story in surgery, insurance sales, and virtually every sport. More deliberate practice equals better performance. Tons of it equals great performance."[2]

Malcolm Gladwell, in his book *Outliers*, makes a similar case, arguing that individuals who practice obsessively within their field of interest are often the ones that rise to the top. Gladwell cites a study by K. Ander Ericsson in which students at Berlin's Academy of Music are grouped according to their skill and then asked how much they practiced. In each distinct discipline, there was a direct correlation between practice time and ability level, with the most gifted students not excelling because of raw talent, but because of thousands of hours of practice beyond what their lower-skilled peers had applied. Gladwell points out a similar phenomena in other fields, including computer programming.[3]

The point is not that you need to devote years of your life to mastering your specific craft, but that deliberate practice plays a huge role in setting you apart from the rest of your field. Setting aside time to practice the fundamental skills required in the area you're passionate about makes it easier to excel in that area—and to share your excellence with others.

Transferable Skills

The fourth area of valuable contribution to a professional community—and to a career—is in the

2   Geoffrey Colvin. "What it takes to be great." *Fortune Magazine.* Volume 154, Number 9, October 30, 2006. http://money.cnn.com/magazines/fortune/fortune_archive/2006/10/30/8391794/index.htm . (Retrieved September 12, 2009.)

3   Malcolm Gladwell, *Outliers*, pp. 38–47. ISBN: 9780316017923.

development of transferable skills, mentioned earlier in Chapter 3, "A Visit from the Black Swan," as tools to help individuals succeed in an ever more random world. Transferable skills, such as communication skills, information organization, time management, and creativity, are skills that apply effectively to almost any professional field of interest, leading not only to success among one's peers but to countless professional opportunities. More importantly, these skills are often developed outside of a classroom environment; thus, mere possession of transferable skills often indicates an individual of value. Here are six specific transferable skills you may want to polish for professional success:

1. *Leadership* refers to the ability to inspire and motivate a group of people to work together toward some greater purpose. The best way to learn leadership skills is to learn them in the laboratory of life, and organizations provide the perfect opportunity. Join a community or student organization and take charge of a large project. Later, run for a leadership position within that group.

2. *Administrative skills* refers to the ability to prioritize tasks and to appropriately assign tasks to people. Administrative skills are often best learned by taking charge of the planning of a large project, either at work or through an organization that you might be a part of.

3. *Information management* refers to the ability to handle a large volume of information in a cohesive fashion. Aside from simply maintaining a detailed address book and calendar and keeping

ahead of one's emails, one great way to do this is to volunteer to create a presentation on a specific topic, as it will require you to research that topic (dredging up an abundance of information) and then distill that information down to a manageable size. You can also improve your information management skills by becoming the secretary or treasurer of a large group. Both positions require the careful management of lots of discrete pieces of information.

4. **Creativity** refers to your ability to generate solutions without specific guidelines. It's easy to exercise your creative muscles—get involved in brainstorming sessions and play games that reward open-ended thinking.

5. *Interpersonal communications* refers to the ability to easily start or join in a conversation, as well as the ability to present ideas to others. You can practice interpersonal communication skills by actively participating in conversations and meetings (reminding yourself that, if you have an idea in mind but are hesitant to share it, half of the people in the room likely have a similar idea but don't have the courage to speak up), volunteering for public-speaking opportunities, and taking on documentation projects.

6. **Personal development** refers to one's ability to learn from one's mistakes, to deal with stress, and to handle challenges. The best way to grow in this area is to simply step up to challenges before you. Relish major projects and tasks instead of

fearing them. At the same time, keep a journal and reflect honestly in it about how you feel about the situations you're in, the people around you, and what you can genuinely learn from them.

Finding (and Being) a Mentor

A final ingredient for professional success both personally and within a peer community is mentorship. A *mentor* is simply any person with significant experience within that field who is willing to provide advice and basic assistance to individuals who lack that experience.

Early on, finding a mentor can be an invaluable step toward getting a foothold within a particular area of interest. A mentor often knows the hurdles that a beginner will face along the way and can help a new person overcome these hurdles before they turn into genuine obstacles.

Finding a mentor isn't that difficult. Simply seek out an experienced person in your field who you respect and with whom you won't be in direct competition in the reasonable future. Instead of asking that person to be a mentor, keep in mind the giving nature of a successful community and also keep in mind the fact that a good mentor is likely already loaded with demands. Instead, offer whatever you can to your potential mentor, in the form of special connections to others you may have, information you may have, or perhaps even as simple as a helping hand in a tight position.

Later on, you may have the opportunity to mentor new members of your professional community. As a mentor, it's important to recognize that, for the moment, you have substantially more value to offer them than they have to offer you. Keep the long view in mind—if you provide valuable mentorship to someone who blossoms into a success in your field, then your value to the community (and to that person) will be substantially increased.

Five Steps on a Journey of a Thousand Miles

This chapter outlines a path to career success that's quite different than you'll find in many career books. Rather than focusing on how to get a job and how to get ahead in a specific company, the new career rules point to a different community-based path, where passionate peers help each other find the opportunities that best fit them and support each other throughout their career growth. Here are five key steps in this journey:

1. **Discover what you're passionate about.** Ideally, you're already involved in a career that you're passionate about. If you're not, all hope is not lost. Spend some time engaging in a diversity of activities and learning experiences until you begin to find the things that awaken your senses and interests and make you want to stay up all night learning more and trying new things.

2. **Get involved in communities that facilitate your passion in a positive way.** When you've found a passion, get involved in a community of like-minded people, particularly those who have followed that passion to professional success. If you have difficulty finding such a community, seek out individuals who have already found success in your area, find a way to help them, and ask them to be your mentor.

3. **Find ways to join your passion with the transferable skills you already have.** People who combine their passion with a skill set that makes it easy to share that passion and work well with others often find many routes to success. Perhaps you have a strong set of communication skills, making it easy for you to evangelize for what you're passionate about. It may be that you're good at organizing projects, in which case you might be a perfect person to corral a project revolving around your area of passion.

4. **Dig deep into your passion through learning, synthesis, and deliberate practice.** If you're engaged in a particular area, you'll naturally want to learn more about it through experience and other modes of learning. Excellence, however, often comes from incorporating deliberate practice into your area of expertise. Use passion as your fuel to drive you through the challenge of deliberate practice.

5. **Find ways to translate your passion and developed skills into your current career—or find a new one.** As your new passion develops into a surprising new set of skills, seek ways to incorporate these skills into your current career. You may send your current career trajectory into overdrive—or you may find yourself relaunching in a new area. In either case, you're on board with a skill set that differentiates you from the rest, and you have a strong community supporting and backing you. That is the ticket to career success in the twenty-first century.

Chapter 11

Life Design—Building Something New

"Are you sure this is actually something you want to do?" my supervisor asked me. She sat across the desk from me with a look of utter surprise on her face. I was walking away from a great job that paid me almost $50,000 a year with strong benefits. I was choosing instead to work as a freelance writer for an unclear income. I was also choosing to make this move with two children under three years of age at home and less than a year after taking out a six-figure mortgage for a home. "Absolutely," I told her with a sense of elation and freedom, something I hadn't felt in a long time.

February 2008

Why would I jump off such a big financial cliff right after spending two years getting us completely out of credit card debt, paying off student loans and car loans, and finally building up a good emergency fund? At first glance, one would think that this is a position to accumulate wealth and secure a strong financial future—

after all, that's the perspective constantly preached by other personal finance gurus.

My reason for turning my financial life around, though, was to live the life I wanted to live, free from the shackles of debt. I wanted a writing career that I could control. I wanted the flexibility to be able to spend many days with my children while they were young. I wanted a job that didn't have to follow me with a load of stress everywhere I went. I wanted a job that would allow me to just get up and walk away from it for a while and follow whatever windmill I saw in the horizon.

In short, I wanted a very different life than the one I was leading.

In the film *American Beauty*, the central character, Lester Burnham, tells his wife something that has stuck in my mind for years: "This isn't life, it's just stuff. And it's become more important to you than living." The typical American lifestyle—buying an expensive home that pushes what you can afford, constantly striving to keep up with the affluence of others, working a job that you can't even consider leaving because the pay is just too good—adds up to a broken American dream, one in which the joys of life are often pushed aside in a never-ending chase for something we cannot quite attain. Once we get the thing we want, we always find that there is something else to want.

I realized that the thing that was missing in my life wasn't a material thing—it was a way of life. It was spending time with my family without the pressure of work hanging over my head. It was writing—perhaps creating that elusive Great American Novel, perhaps not, but always enjoying the chase of the written word. It was the ability to wake up in the morning and realize that I *wanted* to do all of the things on my checklist for the day.

My family's financial efforts in the two years between hitting financial bottom and walking away from my job were intense and, at times, extreme. We lived very cheaply, learning new skills and new interests along the way. I launched a side business—TheSimpleDollar.com— that earned a small measure of income and also allowed me to dig into my passion for writing as well as my passion for self-improvement. We threw every extra penny into eliminating debt, which meant that we went without many material things that might have provided us with a burst of short-term enjoyment.

My reward for that effort was an opportunity to wipe the slate clean and create the kind of life I'd always dreamed of. You can do it, too.

Building a Solid Foundation

Consider the human hierarchy of needs as described by Abraham Maslow. To put it simply, once one's basic needs are met—clothing, food, shelter, companion-ship—humans then tend to have higher aspirations, such as self-actualization and professional fulfillment.

This hierarchy is subverted in many ways—advertising, peer pressure, our own psychology—and it leaves us taking actions that undermine our basic needs while making futile attempts at grabbing at our higher needs.

Add into this mix the increasing unpredictability of modern life, and you've got a painful situation. It's no wonder that many people see such radical life choices as effectively being "impossible."

They're not.

The first step to achieving the life you dream of is assembling a solid foundation that not only ensures your basic needs, but protects them over the long haul. Here are six essential pieces of that foundation:

1. **Self-understanding.** Why do you make the choices you do? Why do you choose to make impulse buys? What criteria do you use before making a purchase? Why do you choose to go into debt? Why do you choose to associate with certain people? The answers to such questions are a key part of understanding yourself and why you make the choices you do. The greater your understanding of your internal decision-making, the more likely you are to change how you make choices—usually for the better. Self-understanding leads directly to self-control, which is the key to personal and financial success.

   Begin by spending time contemplating every poor choice you make in a given day, from drinking one soda too many or hanging out with someone who is demeaning to you to spending extra money or choosing not to exercise. Keeping a daily journal is a good way to push this journey along.

2. **Freedom from debt.** Debt is a prison, as we so thoroughly discussed in Chapter 6, "With or Without You." It foists unnecessary monthly payments on you, which in turn require you to have a high income just to maintain the status quo. Eliminating those debt payments eliminates the need for that income, vastly widening the scope of possible life and career choices you can make. Implementing a debt repayment plan, committing significant effort to it, and following through with it to the end will free you from the shackles of debt.

3. **Frugal sensibilities.** As discussed in Chapter 7, "Minding the Gap," this doesn't mean subsisting on ramen noodles and avoiding anything fun. Instead, it means cutting back hard on the things that matter less in your life so that you have the resources to reach your dreams in the areas you do care about.

4. **A substantial emergency fund.** As discussed in Chapter 2, "What's Missing?," and Chapter 3, "A Visit from the Black Swan," life is incredibly chaotic. A large cash emergency fund greatly reduces the effect that this chaos can have on your day-to-day life, making it much easier for you to ride through the bad events and take advantage of the opportunities.

5. **Retirement planning.** Note that I did not necessarily say retirement saving. What's important is that you think ahead to what your needs will be in your later years and take whatever measures

are necessary to ensure that future. It never hurts
to save more now so that you can put away less
later on.

6. **Insurance.** Insurance is a final protection against
uncertainty. Term life insurance (because you just
want the insurance, not any sort of investment
product), health insurance independent of
employer, and long-term disability insurance are
all strongly worth considering if you have
dependents who rely on your livelihood. I won't
go into the specifics of each type of insurance, as
insurers are constantly changing policy standards
and numerous products are currently in the market. Use the Internet to research your options in
each area and choose the plan that fits your
needs.

The Rules of Your Life

"So you're quitting that great job just so you can sit
at home all day and do nothing? What will you do
for money?" My old friend looked at me incredu-
lously, as though he suspected I was feeding him a
story.

"For one, I don't really need all that much money.
And for another, I'm not just going to sit at home all
day. I'm going to be a more involved parent, and I
have a writing career that seems to be starting to
take off."

"But what about insurance? And all of the people who rely on you? I think you're making a big mistake."

I looked at him and scooped up another bite of pad thai. I was breaking the rules, and he didn't like it.

March 2008

One of the biggest challenges that many people have when they begin to think outside the box in terms of their overall life choices is the sense that things simply aren't done this way. It's not how everyone else does it, so there must be something inherently wrong with it.

This impression is a reasonable one. As we discussed in Chapters 2 and 3, our minds deal with all the random events in our life by creating the impression that our lives are incredibly orderly. We remember the general pattern we've established, but we forget the countless unexpected good and bad events that disrupt that pattern all the time.

In short, all of us have a set of "rules" for how we expect our lives to go—and how we expect the lives of our friends and associates to go. Most of us go to work. Most of us earn a paycheck. Most of us do similar things on weekdays and on weekends. When we actually think of our lives significantly changing from that pattern, it can seem really uncomfortable because it involves breaking that pattern that we've established in our minds.

Here's a perfect example. Every single morning, like clockwork, I wake up, spend an hour or two uninterrupted with my children, and eat breakfast with them.

Whenever that pattern of quality time in the morning with my children is interrupted, I get uncomfortable. I don't like it. It breaks a rule—and it happens to be a rule that I cherish.

Household chores follow much the same logic. I usually spend about an hour each day on household chores—doing dishes, doing laundry, cleaning the carpet, and so on. If I *don't* do it, there are negative consequences. Dishes pile up, Sarah gets upset, and I don't have adequate clean clothes. I don't like it. It breaks a rule for how I live my life.

Our days are all filled with tons of these little patterns and rules. We treat others with courtesy. We mow the yard. We go to work following a certain route. We stop at the coffee shop and say hello to the barista. We give our mother a call on the way home from work. We plan a dinner party and invite our usual group of friends over. We get our hair cut at the salon. We can't possibly miss NBC's Thursday night lineup. We pick up our kids from daycare. We surf the Web for an hour or so every evening. It often feels unnatural to choose to disrupt these simple patterns, even though the chaotic nature of our lives often does disrupt them.

Rules Are Made to Be Broken

Yet, if we allow ourselves to be governed solely by these rules, we find ourselves missing out on countless opportunities for a better life.

I puzzled over the decision to leave my career behind for more than a year. I felt like I was breaking countless rules—leaving a high-paying job with children in the home, leaving a job where my skill set was valued, and not working a nine-to-five job like everyone else in my family and my immediate circle of friends. I'd also be throwing away my entire daily routine—the morning chat with my coworkers, the inside jokes, the lunch routines, the relative peace of the daily commute, and the regular stops at the library and my other regular haunts after work. All of those rules and safety nets and routines would be going out the door—and the thought of it held me back from making the leap.

Yet, the moment I finally walked out the door—breaking countless "rules" in the process—I felt nothing but relief and joy. It was the single best decision I made in my adult life. It reaffirmed my relationship with my kids. It gave me the time and space to engage in work I am deeply passionate about. It left me with a renewed energy and zest for life.

Yes, I faced the scorn and misunderstanding of many of the most important people in my life. I was breaking their rules as well. I confounded expectations and challenged their definitions of what it means to be an adult and a parent. That, too, is a cloud with an enormous silver lining, because they also began to see that the rules in their lives are made to be broken.

Your rules are made to be broken, too.

Shoot the Moon

"I am going to write a book. By the end of next year, I'm going to be doing book signings. I'm going to be able to walk into a Barnes and Noble anywhere in the country and find my book for sale."

Sarah grinned. "Yeah, and while you're at it, how about a big house in the country with a small forest in the back? If we're talking big...." She knew as well as I did that my goal was pretty audacious. I knew no one in the publishing industry. I had never had a single article printed in a major publication. I was not at all what one might call an "expert" in any field. Yet I was promising to have a book bought by a major publishing house and distributed widely enough that I could walk into any bookstore in the country and find my work. I wanted it, though. I wanted to be a published author my entire life. And I was willing to do whatever it took to make it happen.

October 2007

Fourteen months after setting that ridiculously audacious goal, I walked into a Barnes and Noble and saw a stack of copies of my first book, *365 Ways to Live Cheap*, sitting on the featured table. In fourteen months, I raised my profile high enough to get the attention of a book publisher, signed a deal, wrote the entire manuscript, ushered it through the editing process, and watched as my finished work went to press and appeared on bookstore shelves all across the country.

What I found was that by setting an enormous, life-changing goal—and, yes, getting that book published was a life-changer, as it's much more impressive to be introduced as "best-selling author Trent Hamm"—my enthusiasm for the project was substantially higher. I was much more likely to take big steps to make it happen, like contacting well-known people out of the blue and asking for help or editing my manuscript while cooking supper and rocking my infant daughter with my foot.

A truly audacious goal offers many advantages over an ordinary one.

Enhanced enthusiasm. Engagement in something wild and exciting gets our adrenaline flowing as we push our boundaries and personal expectations. Choosing something far beyond what's expected offers the thrill of adventure and naturally piques our enthusiasm.

In my own experience, I found that setting an enormous, life-changing goal—and, yes, getting that book published was a life-changer, as it's much more impressive to be introduced as "best-selling author Trent Hamm"—my enthusiasm for the project was substantially higher. I was much more likely to take big steps to make it happen, like contacting well-known people out of the blue and asking for help or editing my manuscript while cooking supper and rocking my infant daughter with my foot.

Support from others. A daring goal is much more likely to attract the positive attention—and support—of people outside your inner circle, the very people who are likely to be able to help you make that goal into a reality. People are always inspired by a story of an individual bucking the odds and seeking to make their dream a reality, and it is the most incredible of goals that get their attention.

By wearing my large goals on my sleeve publicly at TheSimpleDollar.com (and, at the same time, committing to helping others in my peer community, as described in Chapter 9, "Cultivating People and Opportunities"), I was able to solicit help from many, many people in reaching my goals. If my goals were ordinary—just simply to make a few dollars—people would not have become engaged in what I was doing. Instead, my goal was to remake my life, share my successes and failures openly along the way, and become a published author in the process—and that sort of gumption attracted a great deal of support from many, many wonderful readers and supporters.

Unexpected rewards. If you shoot for something truly audacious, you're going to have to pass through some unexplored territory along the way, and there is often hidden treasure to be found here. New skills, new relationships, and new opportunities abound when you go beyond where your limits are and explore uncharted space.

When I sat at home poring over personal finance books at the lowest point of our financial meltdown, I would have never expected that I would wind up meeting, engaging with, and in some cases, building a friendship with most of the authors of those books. I would have never expected that producers would contact me soliciting my help on pilots and proposals for television series. I would have never believed that I would have the phone numbers of CEOs, chairmen, and other leaders within the financial industry. These rewards all came in the wake of setting enormous goals and moving toward them with passion and earnestness.

Tim Ferriss, author of *The Four Hour Work Week*, has been intimately involved in life design for more than a decade. He also advocates for enormous, audacious goals. "Small goals are paradoxically harder to achieve than big goals. If the potential payoff is small, your enthusiasm won't be sufficient to get through the inevitable obstacles. Aim for the home run when everyone else is aiming for base hits. It improves your odds."[1]

If you're going to even bother stepping up to the plate to chase a dream, you might as well swing for the fences. Win or lose, it will bring out the best in you. Dreams don't come true if you settle for something less, and even in failure, you can still succeed beyond your wildest imagination. After all, Flynn and Blake may have been the ones to actually get on base, but the poem is called "Casey at the Bat."

Think big. Envision that secret dream you've always wanted. Write it down, make it real, and throw all of your energy toward achieving it.

Five Steps to Designing a New Life

For many people—myself included, not too long ago—thinking of such massive life-changing goals seems overwhelming and out of reach. In truth, those big goals are often much more reachable than the smaller goals we often set for ourselves. It's much easier to get our own dream job than to get someone else's dream job, after all.

---

1   Personal interview.

Here are five simple steps to get you started on your journey:

1. **Get your foundation in order.** Understand why you make the decisions you make—and get control over those decisions. Live with a more frugal mindset. Eliminate your debt and build up a healthy emergency fund. Even if you never accomplish your big goal, getting this kind of foundation in place will make any life you choose to lead substantially easier and more fulfilling.

2. **Know what *you* want.** It is you—and you alone—who is always there when you close your eyes at night and when you open them in the morning. It is you who will be the driving force behind achieving your dreams. Chase the dreams that *you* have. The positive people around you will be on board with you and support you. As for the negative people, they're doing nothing more than holding you back.

3. **Envision the worst-case scenario.** Often, the worst-case scenario for a truly transformative goal is much less painful than the worst-case scenario for a much lesser goal. Case in point: Making a film out of your own script, even if it's a failure, is still a far more impressive result than never bothering at all, as it's likely to build you connections and resources that you would have never otherwise had.

4. **Look at the personal rules you use to govern your life—there are many of them.** How many of them can be broken to your net benefit, without harming your reputation or harming those around you? There are countless seemingly "unbreakable" rules in our lives that are, in fact, just tired habits. Picking through these, evaluating them, and eliminating the ones that don't actually benefit us can not only refresh our lives, but strongly weaken the barriers to an audacious goal.

5. **Associate with people who are attempting audacious goals in their own life.** You can use them for inspiration, foster a new relationship by helping them toward their goal, and perhaps find a foothold for you to make your own leap of faith.

Chapter 12

Managing the Gap

"What do we do now?" Sarah asked me as she watched me lick the envelope on our final credit card payment.

After a year of frenzied debt repayment, we had finally reached a plateau. Our debts were paid off, yet our income remained steady. The gap between our income and our required monthly payments had never been higher—we were spending substantially less than we were earning, and we were thriving.

I ran my tongue across the envelope and watched my son roll around on the floor, chasing our two cats. He giggled, enraptured with the innocent play with the felines, not realizing that his parents had transformed their financial situation and started securing a wonderful future for him.

I turned to her and looked deep into her eyes. "Now we keep rolling, honey."

March 2007

You're debt free. You've got a healthy emergency fund. You're living the life you want to live, engaged in a career that fulfills you and surrounded by people who support you.

What's next?

Financial stability is trickier than you might think. It's tempting to backslide into bad spending habits now that you're "safe." It's also tempting to simply inflate your lifestyle a bit and enjoy the material spoils of your hard work.

On the other hand, you can find incredible rewards by simply staying the course and maintaining the enjoyable lifestyle you already have. True financial independence—the ability to live your life without earning an income through work—is an attainable goal for everyone, as is the achievement of financial goals you once thought to be impossible.

Avoiding Lifestyle Inflation

Lifestyle inflation occurs when you make the choice to adopt a higher standard of material living, often as a result of an increase in income or a decrease in monthly bills (due to debt repayment). You're convinced by advertising and by a desire to keep up with the neighbors that you need to "upgrade" the perfectly enjoyable and functional items you already have. The Toyota in the driveway becomes a BMW. The cell phone you mostly use to chat with your family and friends becomes an iPhone (with its requisite expensive service).

A romantic candlelight dinner at home becomes a romantic candlelight dinner at the most expensive restaurant in town. That elegant, simple ring on your finger that you've worn happily for the last decade simply must become a diamond-encrusted extravaganza.

Before you know it, you're right back where you were before—an empty life, except surrounded by a few nicer things. Your big dreams in life take a backseat to a higher class of stuff.

In our modern world, lifestyle inflation is incredibly hard to avoid. A person must be incredibly well-disciplined to overcome such material upgrade desires. In my experience, I've found only two techniques that truly help avoid lifestyle inflation, as follows:

- **Create an artificial sense of scarcity through automation.** At the end of each pay period, a significant portion of our family's income is immediately and automatically locked away in investments and savings accounts for specific goals, such as our emergency fund, our automobile savings, our Christmas savings, and our savings for our dream home in the country. We simply do not allow a large checking account balance to build up. If one of us ever notices a large balance in our checking account and starts to use that as motivation for the idea that we now *deserve* some wholly unnecessary material item, we know it's probably time to alter our savings strategy, likely by increasing our automatic savings a bit.

- **Keep your savings in a hard-to-reach place.** At the same time, simply having a savings account at your local bank with an enormous balance is also incredibly tempting. Such savings is easy to access quickly by ATM, and it often takes little more than a phone call to have that savings balance transferred right over to checking for easy access to fulfill lifestyle inflation desires. Our solution for this is incredibly simple: We keep our checking account and a small savings account for emergency purposes at one bank—the local one in our town so that we have teller access—and the rest of our money is stored either in certificates of deposit (CDs) that financially penalize us for early use or at an online bank that cannot be as easily accessed. These barriers are just enough to force us to think about and talk about large lifestyle-inflating purchase and gives us the time we need for our more rational minds to take over.

As we shopped for our next car, we test drove many different models in many different price ranges. Some of them offered exquisite experiences—leather seats, perfect leg room, full surround sound, a DVD player, an in-dash GPS, clever storage, exquisite handling, and so on.

After trying them all, Sarah and I walked back to one of the least-expensive models that we drove, a Toyota Prius with almost no bells and whistles on it. It did what we wanted—it provided fuel efficiency for her lengthy commute and a high level of reliability and safety for the dollar.

We could have afforded the Lexus with the leather seats or the BMW with the superb engineering. In the end, though, that expensive car would have just served the same function as the Toyota would—getting my wife back and forth on her daily commute.

We smiled at each other as we drove away in the Prius, knowing that the tens of thousands of dollars we saved in not keeping up with the Joneses and simply buying what we needed left us that much closer to our dreams.

March 2009

The Crossover Point

The crossover point, as popularized in the book *Your Money or Your Life* by Joe Dominguez, Vicki Robin, and Monique Tilford, refers to the point at which the income from your savings and investments exceeds your living expenses, making it unnecessary for you to work for an income.

It's easy to understand this with an example. Let's say Leo lives happily on $30,000 a year. His local bank has long-term certificates of deposit that earn a 4% return. If Leo is able to buy $1,200,000 worth of these CDs, the CDs will return the stable $30,000 a year that Leo needs to live on. Obviously, this is simplified—I'm excluding tax implications—but the basic principle is clear.

For many people, the sum required to reach the crossover point seems tremendous—an insurmountable goal. They give up before they even begin. However, consider these four points.

A partial crossover point allows you to leap into your dreams. Let's say Leo wants to be spending his free time as a gardener at the local greenery, earning minimum wage doing what he loves doing: putting plants in the ground. This job earns Leo about $25,000 a year. So, for Leo to be able to take this job, he just has to come up with that extra $5,000 a year. In order to earn that amount, Leo merely needs $125,000 worth of CDs to make that life-changing leap.

Your investments as you approach the crossover point help push you over the top. As you save toward the crossover point, the income from the investments you already have can be rolled over into the investment. In Leo's case, let's suppose that he's buying a $500 CD each month that returns the steady 4% we discussed previously. In the first year, he only buys the first twelve CDs for a total of $6,000. The second year, he buys twelve more, giving him a total of $12,000 in CDs. However, the first year's worth of CDs each return 4% on that investment, giving him an extra $240, which he uses to buy another CD. In the third year, he buys twelve more CDs, giving him a total of $18,240 in CDs. However, the first $12,240 is returning 4% to him, giving him another $489.60 to invest in additional CDs. Each year, his initial investments help push him toward his big goal.

As you push toward your crossover point, you can be more aggressive with your investments. Once you reach the crossover point, you'll want your money to be in a very safe investment where the return is steady and there is minimal risk of losing your initial layout. Before then, though, you're supported by the income from your work, which means you can afford more risk in how you invest the money. Stocks, for example, are a good place to invest this money. In a given year, stocks might go up 16% or they might go down 16%, but over

the long haul of history, a broadly-based stock investment will go up an average of 7% per year.

Taking that into account, let's look at Leo's progress
with an investment in a stock index fund instead of
CDs. Each month, he's putting aside $500 for stock
investing and, at the end of the year, he rolls that $6,000
into his stock index fund. In the first year, he only buys
$6,000 worth of stocks. The second year, he buys an
additional $6,000 worth of stocks. However, the first
year's worth of stocks returns 7%, giving him an extra
$420 that he can roll into his investment. In the third
year, he buys $6,000 worth of additional stocks.
However, the first $12,420 is returning 7% to him, giv-
ing him another $869.40 in his investment. Over the
course of the investment, the acceleration given by his
early aggressive investments will cause him to reach his
goal more than a year earlier.

Snowflaking is an incredibly powerful strategy.
Back in Chapter 6, "With or Without You," we discussed snowflaking as a useful strategy for reducing
debt. Simply put, snowflaking means making small
choices to save money and turning the money saved
from those choices toward your financial goals.
Receiving a windfall, cooking at home instead of going
out, finding a $50 bill in the parking lot—these are all
sources for snowflaking. Each little step seems small
and insignificant, but it's the combination of a lot of little actions that makes a profound difference.

If Leo did nothing more than give up a $5 breakfast
once a week and replaced it with a piece of toast before
leaving the house, he'd contribute $260 more toward
his goal each year and move his partial crossover point

almost two months earlier. Even one single, simple action can have a surprising impact on your life. A collection of simple choices can bring about truly profound change.

Protecting What You Have

As you begin to accumulate significant wealth, you'll want to put some safeguards in place to preserve this wealth in the event of a personal crisis. After all, this wealth is the result of a lifetime of careful planning and work, and in a world that grows ever more filled with randomness, you don't want an extreme negative random event to undo all of your hard work.

Here are some options to carefully consider if you have hard-earned financial resources that you want to protect against the unknown.

A will and/or a living trust are vital tools for ensuring that your property is handled in the way you desire after your passing. A will is simpler and less expensive, but it requires that your property goes through probate, which is the legal administration of your will in court. In cases where your will is unclear, a judge will likely be the person making the decision as to the final destination of your property. On the other hand, a living trust allows you to identify trustees for your property, allowing these people that you trust to make any such decisions about your property that you didn't specify. However, living trusts can often be quite expensive to set up and to maintain. The choice often comes down to more precise control with higher costs or less precise control with much lower fees. If you have substantial assets, you should consult an estate attorney to go over your options in your jurisdiction.

A *living will or advance health care directive* sets in stone the actions you want to have taken on your behalf in a medical emergency. Getting this document in place ensures that, if it is against your wishes, you never become a medical burden to your family, sapping away your life's work just to maintain you in an incomplete state. Take this difficult choice out of the hands of your loved ones—protect them from having to decide and protect yourself from a life that you may not want.

Umbrella insurance covers you in the case of additional liability beyond the limits of your already existing insurance policies, like life insurance, homeowner insurance, and automobile insurance. If you have wealth that extends beyond the limits of the protection such insurance offers, your personal wealth may be in danger if you're at fault in an incident. If you have it, in such high-liability instances, umbrella insurance steps in and protects your hard-earned money against legal attacks.

Long term care insurance provides coverage for the cost of long-term care if you're struck with a medical condition that causes you to have long-term health care expenses, such as a nurse or expensive equipment that goes beyond the coverage provided by typical health insurance or Medicare coverage. Long-term care insurance merely makes sure that, if you find yourself in such a situation, your lifelong earnings aren't drained in the cost of your care.

Five Methods for Maintaining the Gap

You've mastered the art of the gap, and the gap has helped you achieve things you never thought possible. What can you do to keep the momentum going?

1. **Don't stop saving just because you reached your first goal.** Achieving debt freedom or buying the house you've always wanted is cause for celebration—it means you've climbed a great mountain. But as you stand on the summit and look out in the distance, you'll see greater mountains to climb that will bring you to a rarefied air that few people around you will ever experience. You've lived quite well without the money you've been investing toward your goal—now, channel that money toward your next one.

2. **Don't judge your own experience by the rules of others.** You are not a failure because your neighbor has a nicer car than you. They've simply chosen to place a high value on their automobile, a value much higher than you place on your automobile. Your values are elsewhere, represented in other areas of your life, ones that don't sit in the driveway while you live your life. Make your own rules and judge your own life by those rules.

3. **Protect what you have.** Plan a will *now*, even if you're young and it seems unnecessary. Create a living will and file it appropriately. If you have significant assets, look into umbrella insurance and long-term care insurance.

4. **Automate yourself into a sense of scarcity.** If you find that you're convincing yourself to make unnecessary spending choices simply because you have an abundance of cash available in your checking account, increase your automatic savings policies so that this is no longer a temptation. Not only will this help prevent you from making poor financial choices in the short run, but it will also help you move closer to your big financial goals in the long run.

5. **Create a barrier that removes easy access to your savings.** If accessing your long-term savings is as easy as swiping a card into an ATM machine, it will become much easier to tap that money for an impulsive purchase. Instead, put that money into another financial institution entirely and don't give yourself tools for such easy access to the money.

Chapter 13

The Personal-Financial Boundary

We looked out the windows of the airplane as it rested on the tarmac, waiting to take off. Our fingers were entwined. Just twenty-four hours earlier, we had walked out of the church, husband and wife. Now we were beginning our new life together with a honeymoon in the United Kingdom.

I squeezed Sarah's hand and she looked back at me, her hazel eyes shining. "It's just me and you now, honey," I said, and she gave me one of her patented crooked smiles. As the plane took off, I leaned back to relax. After all, we had a lifetime ahead of us. This was no time to think of money. The rest would take care of itself, or so I thought.

June 2003

We are all emotionally invested in our money and in our spending decisions.

The money we have is the result of our hard work, our hours and our energy given over to someone else so that we can have the things we need and a few of the things we want. Our spending decisions are often a window into our imperfections, full of impulsiveness and materialism. The investment of our time and the revelations provided by our buying choices are areas that we often protect.

There's a big reason why money is often something that's avoided in polite conversation.

But in the real world, we have deep, intimate relationships with other people and our choices, when it comes to money, can affect them greatly.

This is where our conflicting interests can run into trouble. On the one hand, we value our privacy and our hard work, as well as a sense that we make good spending decisions. On the other hand, we need positive intimate relationships with other people; often, we need to provide care and resources for them.

Balancing this equation is simple once you recognize that the people with whom you share a deep relationship love you for who you are and are invested in your success. Their criticisms come from a desire to see you both succeed and their defensiveness comes from the difficulty in opening yourself fully to another person. If either of these statements fails to hold true, then the relationship itself is in danger.

The challenges of dealing with money and interpersonal relationships balance on the utilization of three key ingredients: communication, honesty, and time.

Communication

We were angry, shouting accusations at each other. It was late at night. We had sat down together to get a grip on how bad our financial situation was. In the process, we found mistakes that we both had made. The mistakes were kindling—our fear and worry about our situation was the spark. After an hour's worth of the worst argument our marriage had ever had, Sarah and I sat next to each other on the couch, holding hands. She turned to me and said one simple but incredibly wise thing. "We need to actually talk about this stuff before it blows up into this kind of mess again."

April 2006

For the longest time, my biggest obstacle to financial success was simply discussing matters with Sarah. Money was the most uncomfortable subject between the two of us—every time we discussed it, even with the best intentions, one of us wound up very upset. So, for years, it was a complete taboo topic outside of the functional "Did you pay the electric bill?" type question.

When we finally sat down and had a real financial heart-to-heart, it was revelatory. We realized that we were on the same page on a lot of things, and that in our own separate ways, we were making many of the same mistakes.

Time and time again, I've found that communication problems in a relationship are often like water backed up behind a dam. If nothing is relieved, pressure builds up and results in an explosion—painful for everyone involved. However, if communication of one's feelings and ideas in a safe environment without retribution becomes a normal thing, the pressure is relieved and life flows forward like never before.

Here are six key points to consider when talking about money with your partner:

1. **Check your emotions at the door.** When you talk about money honestly with your partner, it's going to hurt sometimes. Getting overly emotional or angry solves nothing—it simply creates new problems. If you find yourself getting angry or upset, stop the conversation. Call a time-out and come back to the conversation later.

2. **Focus on goals.** Ask your spouse when he/she wants to retire and what he/she wants to do after retirement. Ask what his/her dreams are—where would he/she like to be in five years, or ten years. The point is to think positively about money by asking where it can get you.

3. **Look the other person right in the eye, and hold his/her hand.** No matter how egregious the mistakes of your partner are, avoid giving any sign that you are anything other than compassionate and loving. If your partner is admitting a major mistake, it likely means that he/she is summoning a great deal of courage to do this—and by reacting with anger, you're encouraging him/her to not trust you with future issues.

   If/when your spouse admits to overspending, don't blow up at him/her. We live in a consumerist society that is designed to push our buttons and trick us into spending. Even worse, it's a pattern that's very difficult to break—it's a very socially acceptable addiction.

4. **Look at numbers.** Don't talk about your *impression* of your money situation. Get out the papers, go through them, and create a real picture of your financial situation.

5. **Create goals that you both agree on and develop a written plan to reach those goals.** Often, the difficulty that people have in terms of working toward goals in a relationship isn't the absence of goals. Quite often, both partners have individual goals that they're working toward; however, these goals often are incompatible with the goals of their partner.

Each of you should make a list of the goals you'd like to reach, both in the short term and in the long term. Then, find the ones that mesh together and agree to work toward them. For example, my wife and I are both interested in eventually moving to a home in the country with access to basic farming and woodlands, so we've made that one of our primary goals, and we now think of our spending in terms of this goal.

Once you've identified some common goals, spend some time figuring out how you can get there. Do you need to cut down on the Starbucks visits? Does your spouse need to spend less cash on authentic baseball jerseys? Each of you needs to be willing to make some sort of sacrifice to reach the goal, and if you're initiating this, you should be the first one to offer up something.

From there, write down the goal on paper, along with the steps that you're both willing to take to achieve it, and have both people keep a copy of this document. Writing down a goal and a plan to achieve it makes it tangible and real, separating it from merely talking about it.

6. **Talk about money regularly.** I am a big fan of a monthly family meeting about money issues. Doing this is a great way of ensuring that both partners are taking action toward achieving the goals they share (as well as their individual goals) and that individual problems are dealt with quickly and efficiently.

Of course, communication about money (or anything else) isn't useful if it's underlined with the second key ingredient of a successful relationship.

Honesty

Do I tell her or not? I sat out in the truck, watching the rain pour down on the windshield. I had just stopped by the bookstore on my way home from work, convinced that I was just looking for a single title. But I was weak. By the time I walked out of the store, I had purchased six new books and thrown another $100 on our credit card. An amount we didn't need at all.

Even worse, on the way out to the car, I had dropped the bag in the parking lot, soaking the edges of the books. They were unreturnable, even if I wanted to do so, though they would still be readable after drying out. I sat there, feeling ashamed to admit my mistake to her, but I knew that she was invested in this, too. I made my decision. I opened up the door, picked up my bag of books, and headed inside.

March 2006

No one is proud of mistakes, yet they're a basic part of human existence. We all make mistakes. We all fall flat on our faces. We all make choices that fly right in the face of our goals. We do things that undermine the relationship we have with the people we cherish the most.

Because of this shame, it's human nature to want to hide our mistakes from everyone, even the ones we love the most. Yet, quite often, our mistakes negatively affect the ones we love. We made some bad spending choices and now we're taking money away from the dreams we share. We jumped on a great investment opportunity that fell flat on its face. We signed up for a credit card secretly to buy Christmas gifts and managed to charge $18,000 on it.

These mistakes affect the people we care most about, and yet often we continue to hide them, hoping that we can somehow fix the problem before anyone else has to know about it. Quite often, though, it's far harder to solve the problem on our own and, eventually, our partner finds out. Our deception is revealed, and the problem is substantially worse than before, threatening the very fabric of our relationship.

Honesty is the solution to all of these problems. Simply confessing your mistakes to the people who are affected by them and asking for their help in fixing the mistake not only retains and reaffirms the trust in the relationship, but also finds you with a helping hand toward fixing the problem.

Being honest about your mistakes also creates a standard of honesty for your relationship. By being honest and straightforward, you encourage those around you to match that standard.

Time

In Chapter 4, "The Power of Goals in a Random World," I pointed to statistics from the Department of Labor that indicated that the average worker in the United States spends just over fifty-six hours per week at work. Add in time spent for sleep, commuting, and personal activities, and it turns out that the people with whom we spend the most time in a given week is our coworkers.

To put it simply, the demands of our daily lives often takes away most of the time we have to devote to the relationships in our lives that matter the most. It is those relationships, built up over time, that provide much of the value in our lives.

Time is the one resource that can never be bought back. Once the moment has passed, it can never be reclaimed. Your son's first step. An evening on the porch with your wife and a bottle of wine. Your daughter's piano recital that she's practiced for months. A slow dance beneath the moonlight. These are the experiences that we work so hard to preserve—and yet in that hard work, they often slip through our fingers. We leave town on a business trip and miss our son's first word. We simply can't make it to the recital because a client is in town. We're too tired to dance with our husband and hold him close.

What are we sacrificing to earn a little more money?

After all, not getting that promotion might mean that you have to wait a little longer to upgrade your stuff, but no amount of money in the world will get your daughter's first loose tooth back. Establishing a firm financial foundation ensures that your job is not your master and that you're free to decide for yourself what's most important to you.

Friends, Family, and Lending Money

Ask yourself this: Do you like your mortgage company? Do you have a close, personal relationship with your credit card company? Do you love the loan officer down at the bank?

Most of us would be quite happy to not have to deal with these financial entities. These financial arrangements cost us thousands of dollars in interest and deliver a nice healthy bill to our doorstep to be paid each month. There's little love lost between most borrowers and most lenders.

Look at it from their perspective. If you pay your bills on time, you're nothing more than a useful number in a database. If you don't pay your bills on time, they have to start harassing you in various ways to get the money that is theirs.

Does this sound like the type of relationship you want to have with your family and friends? In its simplest terms, this is the exact arrangement you agree to whenever you make the choice to loan money (or to borrow money) from someone you have an established relationship with. Your relationship goes from a familial bond or a friendship into a lender-borrower relationship, with all of the negativity that goes with it.

If you lend someone money and they fail to pay it back, you begin to feel some serious strain in the relationship. Should you confront them or should you just let it slide? The pressure builds up over time and the acid corrodes the previously-existing good relationship. The same thing happens for the borrower—they begin to feel guilty about the money left unpaid and begin to avoid the lender.

There are three simple solutions to this conundrum, as follows:

1. **If someone you care about owes you money, forgive that debt.** Do it right now, before it has the chance to damage your relationship even more. If you're still left with hard feelings, chalk it up to a negative experience and move forward with life.

2. **If you have a desire to lend money to someone you care about, make it a one-time gift.** Yes, we all want to help our friends in need, but lending them money often results in damage to that relationship—one that's obviously valuable enough that you're willing to lend money. Find ways to help them that do not result in a lender-borrower relationship, because that type of relationship ends in heartache.

3. **Don't borrow money from family or friends.** If you're in a financially difficult spot, it's fine to ask your friends for advice, temporary living space, or a helping hand. Just don't ask them to lend you money because, merely by asking, you put them in a difficult and unfair spot. Instead, seek their advice and help in other ways.

Five Steps to Getting Your Relationships on Track

There is no better day than today to get the important relationships in your life in better shape. These relationships are central to who you are as a person and form a big part of the foundation for your personal success. Here are five steps to get started on right away:

1. **Set aside some time to talk to your partner about money—and about life.** Set aside an hour one evening to talk about the goals you share, then go through your entire financial state and determine where you are and what you need to do to accomplish those goals. Don't be surprised if such discussions bleed far outside this hour—and relish those discussions, as they'll become the foundation of your financial future together.

2. **Recognize that your partner is human and makes mistakes, just as you do.** We're all human. We all make mistakes. Getting enraged at your partner's missteps does nothing at all to solve the problem— it just makes it worse. Put yourself in your partner's shoes—if you had made a financial mistake, would

you want to admit it if you knew your partner would go into a snarling rage? Instead of reacting with pure emotion, react with compassion and look for solutions to those problems.

3. **Confess your mistakes to your partner and work with your partner to fix them.** Just as your partner is willing to admit mistakes and seek solutions, you should be willing to do the same. Admit your mistakes, bear the emotional response to them, and work with your partner to come up with a solution to these mistakes. Only by working together can you come up with a truly effective solution.

4. **Forgive the debts and misdeeds (financial and otherwise) of those who we care about and attempt to re-establish a connection with them.** A past mistake (often on both of your parts) is not worth destroying a valued personal relationship over. Step back and ask yourself what's really valuable here.

5. **Set aside focused time to build (and rebuild) the relationships most important to us.** Call your parents. Spend an afternoon with your kids with the cell phone off. Take a few days to go visit your sibling and his/her family. Call up an old friend and ask them to lunch. These core relationships are a big part of what we work so hard to maintain and protect—don't allow them to wither on the vine. Distinguish between what's "important but not urgent" and what's "urgent but not important"—and choose wisely between the two.

Chapter 14

Recasting Retirement

"Where do you think we'll be when we're his age?" Sarah asked me, with a nod in the direction of her grandfather, who was kneeling on the porch and scratching the ears of his faithful dog Ole. Sarah and I were lying in the grass in his yard, side by side. We were engaged to be married and saw a long life spread out in front of us. "I don't know," I told her. "But I do know one thing. I want to keep going until I can't go any more." "Me, too," she said.

May 2009

As you considered in Chapter 10, "The New Career Rules," the traditional path of working for the same company for a number of years, and then gliding off into a golden sunset paved with pension money, has vanished. Today's worker is loyal to his or her community of peers and shuffles from job opportunity to job opportunity, saving money in individual retirement plans along the way.

In fact, the very nature of the traditional retirement at age 65 is outdated. Today, the average American has a life expectancy of 77.7 years,[1] with an annual increase in life expectancy of 0.2 years *every year* over the past decade.[2] To put it simply, people are living longer than ever and the trends point toward even longer lives in the future.

With a longer life comes a longer period of vitality. People now commonly work into their seventies and eighties; many people *begin a new career* in their sixties.

Retirement no longer means kicking back in the Barcalounger watching *The Price is Right* and waiting for the grandkids to come and visit. It means an exciting new stage in life, complete with new challenges.

Retirement Rarely Equates to Idleness

My father stood there in his hip waders, holding on to the back of the truck, panting. He and his assistant had just brought in an enormous catch of fish, and the exertion of unloading hundreds of pounds of catfish from his boat had winded him. He caught his breath and looked up at his catch with a sly grin on his face. In that moment, I didn't see my retirement-age father. For just a moment, I saw him exactly as he was when I was a little kid, running constantly on a boundless supply of energy and joy. He stood up,

1   National Vital Statistics Reports, p. 1, Vol. 57, No. 16. "Deaths: Final Deaths for 2006." http://www.cdc.gov/nchs/data/nvsr/nvsr57/nvsr57_14.pdf. Retrieved July 16, 2009.

2   Child Trends Data Bank. "Life Expectancy." http://www.childtrendsdatabank. org/indicators/78LifeExpectancy.cfm. Retrieved July 16, 2009.

grabbed a bucket of fish, and headed off the bench to dress them for his customers. So much for his retiring to the living room.

July 2009

Remember my story about my father from Chapter 10? His retirement didn't exactly turn out as planned. He's often worried about the company's long-term stability and the future of that very pension that he had been promised for so long.

His solution, like many other retirees, was to do something about it. In his sixties, he transformed his lifelong hobby of fishing into a lucrative side business, earning a solid supporting income for himself and my mother. To further supplement his income, he also launched a tomato-growing business with another member of his family, selling his wares directly to supermarkets and local restaurants.

This is not what most people think of when they hear the word "retirement," but it's becoming the trend for retirees who find themselves at the age where they can start cashing in on their pensions and their 401(k)s but discover they have a lot of vitality left in them.

With the longer lifespans and greater vitality that we all have in store, retirement no longer equates to idleness.

What's Your Next Act?

In his book *Free Agent Nation*, Daniel Pink looks at burgeoning movement of retirees who are doing exactly what my father did: reinventing themselves at a traditional retirement age. "Legions of [...] sixty-plus Americans are becoming freelancers, micropreneurs, self-employed knowledge workers, temps, home-based businesspeople, and independent professionals. They're working as part-time, some time, and anytime free agents—using the Internet as a platform for finding and executing work."[3]

As discussed in Chapter 10, the new frontier of building professional opportunities for yourself comes from connecting with communities of your peers who are also engaged in your career. These communities often develop online, sharing resources and making themselves ever more open to opportunities of all stripes. Rather than focusing on who you are, these communities place value on what you can provide to the community, and Americans near retirement age, with an enormous wealth of knowledge and experience built up over a long career, have a lot to offer.

What's your next act? What excites you? What do you want to do with the rest of your years? Your lifetime of work has given you the tools and resources you need to succeed, and the Internet provides the access you need to a community of supportive peers. There's no better time than now to dive in and find out where this new path will lead you.

Recasting Retirement Savings

From this perspective, saving for retirement no longer has the same goal that it once had. Previously, retirement

3   Daniel Pink, Free Agent Nation. p. 234. ISBN: 9780446678797.

savings was intended to allow people whose vitality was slipping to live out their final years in financial peace. Today, however, retirement age arrives, and people still have vitality. They still have the desire and the ability to work on projects that challenge and excite them.

What does that do to the traditional role of retirement savings?

To put it simply, it turns retirement savings into a tool to support challenging professional and personal choices. Instead of fully supporting you in a reduced lifestyle, retirement savings can maintain you in the lifestyle you're accustomed to while you take on personally fulfilling challenges that might not be financially lucrative. Doing things like becoming the secretary of your church, becoming a freelance artist, or taking a job at a nonprofit are no longer financial suicide if you have retirement savings to supplement such a position. Instead, they become deeply fulfilling personal opportunities.

For many, retirement savings has a depressing feel. People don't want to visualize their life during the period that many of us think of as retirement. However, the nature of those retirement years is changing fast. Instead of being a slow ride into the sunset, retirement is an opportunity to claim a lifelong dream, and retirement savings makes that possible.

Instead of saving for retirement, you're saving (in part) to support your next act in life.

Retirement Savings Versus College Savings

"The last thing I want to do is become a burden to you when I reach the end of my years," my mother told me on the phone. She had spent the last two months slowly digging through her mother's estate, going through giant boxes of unsorted paperwork, trying to make sense out of the mess of my grandmother's final year of life, which involved a slow slide into dementia. My thoughts drifted to my own children. How would I be able to ensure that they would not be burdened by me in their adult years? I would have no problem taking care of my own mother, and I'd like to believe that my children would be willing to take care of me. I looked at the picture of my two children that serves as my desktop wallpaper and asked myself what I really wanted out of my golden years.

May 2009

Parents often have a challenging choice to make once their children are born. At a time in their lives when their money is tied up on many fronts—saving for a down payment on a home, struggling with the relatively low income level one earns early in a career—they're hit with the double whammy of needing to save for retirement and also needing to save to support their child's education.

It seems like a difficult choice, but it really isn't. Save for retirement and let the cards fall where they may when it comes to college savings. There are several reasons for this.

First, *a college education can be earned without college savings, while retirement cannot.* Many students earn a college education with minimal financial support from their parents—myself included. Not having such support requires students to seek out more scholarships and take more responsibility for the value of their education instead of having it handed to them on a silver platter. It also provides a better case for financial aid. At the same time, the early years of retirement savings—the ones that provide the longest timeframe for aggressive investing and the most years for compound interest to work in your favor—are absolutely vital and should be maximized.

Second, *eschewing retirement savings in favor of college savings puts your children at risk later in life.* Many parents choose to forego retirement savings and save for their children's education under the belief that the best assistance they can give their child in adulthood is to not saddle them with student loan burdens. However, by doing that, you put them at a much higher risk of having to support you financially in your old age due to inadequate retirement savings.

Third, *college savings may not even be necessary for the path your child chooses.* Your child might choose an entrepreneurial path. Your child might choose a lucrative trade school, choosing to become an electrician, a plumber, or a carpenter. Your child also could earn enough in scholarship money to make college savings redundant. In any case, following a typical savings plan for college may be redundant.

Often, caring parents—such as myself—are unconvinced of this argument. Yet, there's a simple solution for balancing both of these conflicting desires: *Save for retirement in a Roth IRA.*

A Roth IRA is an individual retirement account that you set up on your own, independent of your job. You put money into this account *after taxes*, which means that it doesn't go straight out of your paycheck like 401(k) savings does. However, a Roth IRA has a huge advantage: You can withdraw your Roth IRA contributions for any reason without penalty. If you are saving for retirement but then decide to make a withdrawal to help with educational expense, you can do so with minimal consequence—the only drawback is that you cannot replace the contributions once you withdraw them.

A final point: *Involve your adult children in your estate planning.* This goes far beyond merely involving them in the preparation of a will. Prepare a document with them that explains every significant step that needs to be taken to cash in all of your insurance policies, cancel your accounts, and settle your affairs. Keep this document updated. It's a simple step that you can take to make the burden of your eventual passing much easier on your next of kin.

Revisiting the Crossover Point

In Chapter 12, "Managing the Gap," we discussed the idea of the *crossover point*—the point at which the income from your savings and investments exceeds your living expenses. We also referred to the *partial crossover point*, the point at which the income from your savings and investments plus the reduced income from a job that deeply fulfills you (but perhaps doesn't earn as well) exceeds your living expenses.

This "partial crossover point" is *exactly* what you want to shoot for in this brave new age of retirement. As you transition into a second act, you'll likely find new avenues for income—but these income sources may be a significant drop from what you're currently earning. Transitioning from middle management to a job at a charity can equate to a huge drop in income, as can switching from a career in nursing to a career as a church organist. Even switching to a potentially lucrative freelancing career can have challenges, as income is wildly uneven for people in such careers. Your retirement savings becomes the bridge between paydays.

The most amazing part? The tax advantages and matching funds for retirement savings make all of this look easy.

Five New Steps Toward "Retirement"

Here are five steps you can take as you approach this new kind of retirement:

1. Spend some time thinking about what you would do with your time if you had a small supplementary income to help you live the life you wanted to lead as long as you stayed productive. What dreams would you chase? What opportunities would you grab hold of?
2. Plan ahead for your second act. Look for opportunities in the career path you have now to build the skills you will need when you reinvent

yourself. In particular, always work on your transferable skills—communication skills, leadership, information management, and so on.

3. **Take advantage of all matching funds in your 401(k)/403(b).** Matching funds are essentially free money given to you by your employer to accelerate your retirement savings. Take advantage of them.

4. **Open a Roth IRA for additional retirement savings.** Because you're able to withdraw contributions from a Roth IRA without penalty, their flexibility for retirement savings and for other major goals make them valuable.

5. **Make a master information document.** A master information document simply lists every significant piece of information about your life and your financial state that someone might possibly need to know in the event of your passing. Include descriptions, contact names, business names, addresses, phone numbers, account numbers, and other such necessary information. Keep it all in one place, somewhere safe, and let the most important people in your life know where it is.

Chapter 15

The New Path to Adulthood

"I don't know much about college. But I know you'll figure it out." My father wasn't much for giving verbal advice. Instead, he often stood back and let me try new things, watching as I sometimes failed and sometimes succeeded, and only encouraging me to pick myself up and try again. In that moment, though, just as he was about to leave me on that college campus for the first time, he did the last thing I expected him to do. He gave me a bear hug, slapped me on the back a few times, and said, "Go get 'em, boy." Even at the peak of my rebellious years, I knew that someday I wanted to be half the father he was.

August 1996

The path from childhood to professional success has been repeated and nearly etched in stone for the last thirty years. You've got to get excellent grades in high school and load up on Advanced Placement courses and perhaps a few extracurriculars that look good on a college application. Then, you need to score a nice number on the SAT and/or the ACT to get your foot in the door at a good school. There, you need to work your tail off earning a strong GPA so that you can earn a degree that will get your foot in the door with a great job.

This pathway was incredibly powerful in the past, when universities and workplaces had difficulty evaluating the true breadth of a student. Today, however, new skills are needed. Success in the global economy requires young people who stand out beyond the test scores and the old checklist of extracurricular activities. The world demands a more well-rounded skill set, one that goes far beyond classroom learning and branches into how they approach the world.

If you want your child to succeed in this new world, you might need to sacrifice a few sacred cows in the process.

Setting Your Child Apart—Money Lessons

In her book *Raising Financially Fit Kids*, Joline Godfrey identifies ten basic money skills that every child should have:

1. How to save.
2. How to keep track of money.
3. How to get paid what you are worth.
4. How to spend wisely.
5. How to talk about money.
6. How to live on a budget.
7. How to invest.

8. How to exercise the entrepreneurial spirit.

9. How to handle credit.

10. How to use money to change the world.

Godfrey suggests giving your child a taste of experience in each of these categories beginning as early as age four.[1]

What's the best way to approach these goals? Give your child as many independent choices as you can when it comes to money decisions.

Give your child a small allowance independent of chores. The amount of the allowance should be small enough that it will take many weeks worth of saving for your child to save up enough money to purchase a much-desired item.

Offer your child the opportunity to earn more. Tie a financial reward to household work that goes far beyond the normal household chores the child should be expected to do—and encourage him or her to negotiate a fair price with you. Encourage your child to try out entrepreneurial endeavors, such as collecting aluminum cans, selling lemonade, or doing basic lawn care for others.

Talk about goals with your child and help him develop plans to reach those goals. If your child wants a specific item, help your child come up with a savings plan to save for that item. It's often useful to have a "savings jar" or a piggy bank in a place where he can visualize the savings, particularly when he's young. As

1   Joline Godfrey, *Raising Financially Fit Kids*, p. 5. ISBN: 9781580085366.

the child grows older, introduce him to other concepts—investing for the future and giving your money to a greater cause.

Give your child the tools for adult finance before he even leaves the nest. Get your child a checking account, a checkbook, an ATM card, and, yes, even a credit card (with a low limit) at least a year before he leaves for college. Encourage him to use these items and understand how they work and how they affect daily life. Encourage your child to get a part-time job with limited hours to provide grist for this financial mill.

Don't stop there, though. Such basic financial lessons are only the first element of a much larger toolset that you need to give your child to ensure his or her personal, financial, and professional success in life.

Setting Your Child Apart— A Growth Mindset

Joe stood there tentatively, unsure if he had the courage inside of him to reach for the gymnastics rings yet again. He had fallen twice in his attempts to grab onto the rings, and each time he had fallen to the ground as the rings slipped through his fingers. "Are you pushing him a little hard? He's only three." My mother looked at me inquisitively as we watched the boy from afar. My eyes never left my son as I watched him build up the fortitude to reach for the rings again. He stretched out his arms, took a brave leap, and suddenly found himself hanging in the air, a ring in each hand.

"Look, Daddy, I did it!" he shouted.

"You certainly did! Good job picking yourself up and trying again until you got it!" I shouted back at him.

June 2009

In her book *Mindset*, Dr. Carol Dweck argues that there are two basic mindsets that define how people approach the world. "Believing that your qualities are carved in stone—the *fixed mindset*—creates an urgency to prove yourself over and over. If you have only a certain amount of intelligence, a certain personality, and a certain moral character—well, then you'd better prove that you have a healthy dose of them. It simply wouldn't do to look or feel deficient in these most basic characteristics."

On the flip side of the coin is the growth mindset. "This *growth mindset* is based on the belief that your basic qualities are things that you can cultivate through your efforts. Although people may differ in every which way—in their initial talents and aptitudes, interests, or temperaments—everyone can change and grow through application and experience."[2]

The fixed mindset is one of inadequacy, of a sense that you can never really stack up to your competition. Instead of actually attempting to grow, people with a fixed mindset simply "fake it." Sometimes it works, sometimes it fails miserably, but in any case, individuals with a fixed mindset either get in way over their heads without the tools to dig out or are left behind.

2   Dr. Carol Dweck, *Mindset*, p. 6–7. ISBN: 9780345472328.

A growth mindset is much different, as a person with a growth mindset believes that he or she *can* improve and measure up to any situation. People with growth mindsets constantly work not to create an appearance of having a certain set of skills, but to actually attain those skills, no matter what the situation.

The most valuable gift you can give your children is a growth mindset, as it will put them in a position to handle whatever challenges life throws at them. This leads directly to personal and financial independence, which is what we want most for our children—and for ourselves in our later years.

Here are three basic tactics a parent can utilize to encourage a growth mindset in their child:

- **Don't praise talent, praise effort.** "Parents think they can hand children permanent confidence— like a gift—by praising their brains and talent. It doesn't work, and in fact has the opposite effect. It makes children doubt themselves as soon as something is hard or anything goes wrong."[3] Instead of praising a child's talent and skill, praise his or her effort toward completing something. Instead of praising the result, praise the process he or she went through to get there. It's more challenging, but it teaches that the real key to success isn't in the end result, but in the journey to get there.

- **Don't attack attributes.** Your child will make mistakes and not meet your expectations quite often as he grows up. Your response should not be to criticize the child. If a child gets a poor grade,

---

3   Dr. Carol Dweck, *Mindset*, p. 176. ISBN: 9780345472328.

don't demean the child's intelligence by calling him "stupid." Instead, figure out what went wrong in the learning process. Go over the child's work with him and find out where exactly the struggle is coming from. Similarly, if your child doesn't succeed at sports, don't call him "weak" or "uncoordinated" or "a loser" (such terms seem harsh until you witness the behavior of parents on the sidelines at a youth sporting event). Instead, encourage him to work on the fundamentals of his game. Don't define your child—leave that up to your child.

- **Never conditionalize love.** You should be the one source of unconditional love in your child's life— your child *needs* that. You should provide comfort when they fail, but you need to allow them to fail, too. Your love is there to convince him or her to get up and take another crack at that challenge. By withdrawing that love, children will fold in on themselves and truly believe that they are unworthy of the love of the one person who should love them.

Setting Your Child Apart—Self-Reliance

My father was never one for giving specific directions. When there were chores to be done, he would often describe them in the minimum amount of words and then wander off to do something else.

As a child, I found this incredibly frustrating. Sometimes, I would have only the vaguest idea of what needed to be done. Clean the garage? I had only the scarcest idea of where most of the stuff belonged. Prep some fishing lines? I didn't know where the bait was or the line boxes were. Water the garden? The garden was at a twenty-degree slope, there was no hose within reach of the garden, and the different plants had different watering needs.

Later on, I found that my mischievous old man *was often vague on purpose*. "How else would you figure out how to figure out things?" he asked, channeling the spirit of Yogi Berra.

As adults, we have an enormous amount of personal latitude in our day-to-day choices. We are constantly presented with situations and problems without any sort of specific direction on how to handle them. The more opportunities we give our children to experience problems and situations without specific directions, the more training we give them on how to deal with day-to-day life.

As early as possible, start giving your child unspecific tasks to work on. Give him a blank piece of paper and tell him to draw you a picture. Ask him to put everything away in the living room. Tell him to write a story. Give him $10 when you enter the grocery store and tell him to plan tonight's dinner (seriously).

Yes, they'll mess things up. When that happens, compliment their effort in doing so and then walk through two or three things they might have done to accomplish it. Along the way, they'll learn that there's a great virtue in solving problems themselves—and this goes hand in hand with the money lessons that you'll be teaching them.

Setting Your Child Apart—Self-Learning

Many people buy into the notion that the classroom is the primary source of education in a child's life and that education ends when a degree is received. In the real world, however, people are often responsible for teaching themselves a wide variety of things, often very quickly, and the people who are best able to do this are the ones who succeed in life.

In short, your children need to master the ability to teach *themselves* things without simply asking you for answers.

Start simple. Have days where you identify items of a specific color when you're out and about, or find items that come in sets of a specific number. Encourage your child to find these things on his own and identify aloud what they are.

As they grow, start a family reading time where everyone reads a book of their own choosing. Most books, particularly ones written for children, offer some sort of learning, but you can guide your children to better choices by talking positively about books that make you think. Fostering a love of reading encourages lifelong learning.

Go on explorative journeys. Go to a park with a tree identification guide and see how many trees you can identify—or use a rock identification guide, or a plant identification guide, or a bird identification guide. Have your child investigate the things he is interested in and encourage him to report back to you about it.

The more a person uses their faculties for learning new things, the easier learning new things becomes.

Independent learning is a lifelong skill that pays dividends over and over again throughout your personal, professional, and financial life.

Setting Your Child Apart— Unique Experiences

Like it or not, the global economy is here to stay. Assuming that your child achieves even a small degree of professional success, he or she will be interacting with people from different cultures and assimilating cultural experiences as a fundamental part of their day-to-day lives.

Corporations, as well as universities, are waking up to this reality and actively seeking students with the tools to navigate this brave new world. To put it simply, exceptional experiences as a child grows toward adulthood are more important now than ever before.

Here are three ways you can give your children exceptional experiences that will help them grow as people while also providing them with outstanding career fodder:

- **Student exchanges.** A year-long international student exchange is a powerful way to give your child experience with other cultures in a way that will not only help him grow as a person, but provide him with a resume bolster that's hard to beat. It provides an independent experience for your child (demonstrating that he is able to function without mom and dad's guidance), while also immersing them deeply in another culture and in the nuances of another household.

- **Large self-directed projects.** Many children join service organizations as a resume booster, but such groups are often filled with disinterested kids looking to sew up their college applications. Rather than follow that route, encourage your child to figure out an area that he or she is passionate about and then construct his or her own large-scale project to lead to completion in that area. Such a project teaches leadership, self-direction, and communication skills while also helping your child dig deep into his or her potential interests.
- **A family sabbatical.** In her book *The New Global Student*, Maya Frost offers up this exceptional idea for immersing your child in another culture without disrupting their familial structure: a sabbatical in another country. "[T]he biggest reason [our family lived abroad for a time] was to experience life abroad with our kids and give them a chance to gain some global skills. If you don't want to wait until your kids are high school or college age and you want to spend time abroad *with* them, a sabbatical can be a fantastic experience for the whole family."[4] This often works extremely well if one or both parents are self-employed or are teachers (as it's often easy for teachers to find work abroad).

---

4   Maya Frost, *The New Global Student*, p. 233. ISBN: 9780307450623.

Setting Your Child Apart—
Educational Priorities

With globalization and the radical growth of the information economy, one might expect that the forefront of modern careers would be found in high-tech industries and commercial enterprises, the kinds of places where a college degree is require to compete.

Here's the truth: The U.S. Bureau of Labor Statistics forecasts that the career paths that offer the most outstanding income and work opportunities over the next ten years includes plumbers, pipefitters, pipelayers, steamfitters,[5] electricians,[6] trained carpenters,[7] and installation, maintenance, and repair technicians.[8] None of which, by the way, require a college degree.

In such a thoroughly modern, high-tech world, how can this be? It's simple. Never has it been more important for the physical infrastructure of the world to be secure, strong, and reliable. As more and more commerce is conducted electronically, there's never been more of a need to build the high-quality physical elements to support this commerce.

5   U.S. Bureau of Labor Statistics. Occupational Outlook Handbook, 2008-09 Edition. "Pipelayers, Plumbers, Pipefitters, and Steamfitters." http://www.bls.gov/oco/ocos211.htm. (Retrieved October 2, 2009.)

6   U.S. Bureau of Labor Statistics. Occupational Outlook Handbook, 2008-09 Edition. "Electricians." http://www.bls.gov/oco/ocos206.htm. (Retrieved October 2, 2009.)

7   U.S. Bureau of Labor Statistics. Occupational Outlook Handbook, 2008-09 Edition. "Carpenters." http://www.bls.gov/oco/ocos202.htm. (Retrieved October 2, 2009.)

8   U.S. Bureau of Labor Statistics. Occupational Outlook Handbook, 2008-09 Edition. "Installation, maintenance, and repair occupations." http://www.bls.gov/oco/oco1008.htm. (Retrieved October 2, 2009.)

Remember this: There are many, many routes that your child may follow to financial, personal, and professional success. Avoid the temptation to project what you want. Instead, give him the tools to achieve whatever it is that he chooses to do in life.

Five Little Steps

We all want to encourage our children to be on the right track for a successful and independent personal, professional, and financial life. Here are five things you can immediately help your child with at any age to cultivate that kind of success:

1. **Introduce money lessons to your child early, repeat them frequently, and grow them to maturity.** The ten basic money lessons identified earlier in this chapter provide a good foundation to start, but keep all ten in mind, as it is very easy for even the most diligent parent to put aside some of the more challenging lessons. Start young and, more importantly, give your children strong tastes of real-world money lessons as early as possible, while you still have a chance.

2. **Immerse your child in new experiences.** New experiences are incredibly powerful for everyone. They force us to interact with the world in a new way, adapting our own behavior to overcome obstacles that we've previously not faced. The more new experiences you give to your child, the more adaptable he or she will become to ever-changing conditions.

3. **Allow your child to independently manage as much as he can.** Give him self-directed tasks. Give him responsibilities. Allow him to discover that he can solve problems on his own without your help. Such self-reliance is the backbone of successful people.

4. **Recognize when you're substituting your own fears for your child's.** Quite often, we avoid allowing our children to face difficult challenges because we're afraid that they'll fail. Quite often, we don't allow our children to follow the road less traveled because we fear what that road might contain. Never forget that this is your child's journey, not your own. Give him the tools to succeed at whatever challenge he faces or whatever path he chooses.

5. **Give your child opportunities that truly set him or her apart from the crowd.** The people who are able to claim great rewards in life are often the ones who have done something exceptional to set themselves apart from the crowd. Give your child these opportunities, even if it means conquering your own fears in the process. Look into study-abroad opportunities, exceptional adventures, and projects that can blossom into something far outside the experiences of his peers.

Chapter 16

The Power of Giving

It was late on a Saturday afternoon, and I was walking near the edge of a rough part of Des Moines, Iowa. I saw a young boy, about six years old, climbing out of a dumpster behind an apartment building. He was dressed in a dirty tank top and shorts and was barefooted. In his hand he held a wadded-up fast food bag. When the boy's feet hit the ground, he ran around to the far side of the dumpster, opened up the bag, and pulled out a handful of fries, which he stuffed in his mouth as though he were starving. I have never in my life felt so compelled to help someone out, but I didn't know what to do. I looked around and spied a McDonald's about a block away, and so I walked over near the child and said hello to him. He looked scared and started to run away.

I told him loudly that I wanted to buy him some food. He stopped and looked back at me for a minute. I told him that I was going to go down to the McDonald's down the street and buy him some food and that I would come back and leave it by the dumpster. He could come and get it if he wanted. I decided to do it this way because I figured the kid wouldn't follow me there, and I also didn't want to create the appearance that I was abducting him. He seemed to understand the arrangement, so I walked down to an ATM, withdrew $20, went to McDonald's, bought about $15 worth of food (thinking he could perhaps share some with his mother or any siblings or friends he might have), and put the change from my twenty dollar bill in the bag—four ones and some coins.

I came back to the dumpster and the boy was gone—which I kind of expected. I put the bag on the ground by the dumpster, looked around, and walked away. I watched for a little while, but I never saw the boy come back. I ended up just leaving the food there in hopes that the boy would eventually come back and find it, but to this day I don't know if he did or not. I like to think that he came back, found the bag, took it to his mother and his little sister, and they were able to at least get some calories in their system to sustain them for a little while. I walked away with this simple vision in my head, and that thought lifted my mood for the rest of the day—and for days afterward.

Did this gift help the world? I can't tell, but I can certainly say that it helped me.

June 1999

One central thread throughout this book has been the power of community. By participating in a community, we are doubly rewarded. First, we live out the ideal of utilitarianism, in which our actions bring about a positive change in the lives of many others. Second, our lives are improved by the utilitarian actions of the other participants in that community—their giving benefits us.

Leo Babauta, author of *The Power of Less*, sums up this idea nicely: "Every successful person knows that you become successful because of how much value you give to others. [...] *By helping others, they are more inclined to help you in return.*"

He goes on. "I think it's interesting how we intuitively know these things, but somehow our ego gets in the way. Our *self-importance* makes us think that we need to receive to justify giving. This is the same part of you that seeks to be *right* instead of *happy*. Is it worth it? [...] [I]t's a much more empowering position to be the one that gives first. Otherwise, who knows how long it will take the other person to initiate, if it even happens at all. To wait for others to give is like waiting for someone to give you what you want. [...] When you can give without expecting anything in return, you have mastered the art of living."[1]

The golden rule is at work here, but it goes far, far beyond that.

---

1   Leo Babauta, *How Giving Changes Everything.* http://zenhabits.net/2009/07/how-giving-changes-everything/. Retrieved September 24, 2009.

Giving Is Part of Participating in a Community

The power of communities in the modern world is growing. Thus, by corollary, the power of giving is growing as well.

In our lives, we participate in a plethora of communities—the community we live in, the workplace, the professional community of our peers, our church, the organizations we belong to, our circle of friends, our city, our state, our nation, the world itself. Within each of those communities, the power of giving is in force.

Simply by giving of yourself first without expecting a thing in return, we implicitly build the communities that we're participating in. Those communities become more powerful, as each person in those communities has more resources upon which to draw. Those resources open the doors to more opportunities for that community, some of which may be of value to you.

Our giving not only strengthens those who we give to, it strengthens us as well. Giving is an essential part of community participation.

When we give to the food bank in our town, we expect nothing in return for that gift. Yet, subtly, that gift strengthens the very community we live in. The food winds up on the table of a family that needs it, giving them strength in their moment of need and enabling them to contribute more in the workplace and in the classroom. They contribute more to the community through this renewed energy, and that contribution, in countless unforeseeable ways, finds its way back to you.

When we contribute documentation and information to our professional community, we expect nothing in return for that gift. Yet, again, the community is strengthened. Others read and offer helpful edits to that documentation. Others read that documentation and utilize it to solve their own problems. Yet others are inspired to contribute their own materials and opportunities to the community. The community thrives in countless indirect ways, growing in unforeseen directions because of your initial contribution.

When we help a friend, we bring them up from their low point. We give them solace and hope for the future. They're more able to contribute to the network of people in their own life, many of whom you know and who are better off simply because the friend you helped is now in a better place.

When we contribute to a political or social cause, we give that cause more leverage. Their resources are able to spread their message and their assistance a little bit wider, reaching a few more people and perhaps changing their way of thinking or even their way of living. As we learned in 2000, it only takes a handful of votes to swing an election and, by extension, the entire direction of a nation. Giving to a cause we believe in increases the chances of such a swing.

All of this, and it feels good, too.

Doing It Different

Quite often, the idea of giving is directly attached to money. Groups and individuals constantly ask for financial support. Our friends and family ask us for loans.

Our church passes around a collection plate. Giving often feels like it saps away from the resources we need to achieve our own goals.

Financial giving is vital, don't give me wrong. Without financial giving, many organizations would not be able to survive and many of the most powerful forms of giving would go undone. Financial giving is a powerful part of human and spiritual life.

At the same time, most people overlook the many, many ways we all have to give to others every single day. These gifts foster community, building a stronger network that not only helps countless others around us, but also supports us in our time of need.

Here are four exceptional gifts you can give every day.

Give Your Attitude

Having a positive attitude simply warms the room. It lifts the attitude of those around you. It encourages people to step outside of their normal routines. It makes people sit up and want to participate.

You can start by simply encouraging others. Give positive feedback when people contribute to the community. Speak up when a positive voice is really needed. Act energetic and enthusiastic about the things you care about.

Your positive attitude can spur others on to actions beyond what you could ever provide to the community, and that is a truly powerful gift, indeed.

Give Your Talents and Knowledge

I flipped the power switch and the computer hummed to life. The problem had been simple after all—a faulty power supply.

"The computer's all fixed!" I shouted into the next room.

I heard shuffling, then the elderly man came into the room just as the Windows logo flashed on the monitor. "Thank you!" he said. "What do I owe you for that?"

"Nothing. I'm just glad to help," I said as I put on my jacket to leave. I shook his hand and left.

A few days later, the old man stopped by our house to visit my dad. In his hand, he had a small package for me. "You collect baseball cards, don't you? I have a few of these lying around in the attic, and I thought you might enjoy them."

Inside the box was a number of vintage baseball cards—manna from heaven for a baseball-loving young man.

"One good turn deserves another," he said after seeing the obvious look of delight on my face. I've held those words close to me ever since.

June 1994

Every single one of us is a warehouse of information and skills, both useful and otherwise. Although we are

sometimes tempted to preserve these things for ourselves, it is only when we share these attributes that they
have value.

Contribute documentation online that relates to
your area of expertise and thus to the professional or
interest-based community you belong to. Help people
by answering the questions that you can provide a useful answer for. Share your musical talents with a church.
Teach others how to participate in an activity that
you're skilled at.

You have an abundance of talent and knowledge
within you. Find ways to share that talent with those
who need it and you'll bolster a community that you're
a part of.

Give Your Time

Quite often, skill isn't required so much as time is.
There are many incredibly simple tasks that can greatly
help a community to thrive—administrating message
boards, filing paperwork, stuffing envelopes, manning
the food bank, answering the phone, and so on.

Many such tasks can easily be multitasked. For
example, it often just takes a moment or two several
times a day to effectively administer an Internet message
board, but that time helps keep a message board clean
and usable for the other members of the community.
You can stuff envelopes for a cause while kicked back
on the couch watching a movie. Errands for an organization can often be intermingled with your own
errands.

Such simple tasks are often just what's needed to help a community to grow and thrive.

Give Your Connections

With the wide array of communities each one of us finds ourselves with a toehold in, each of us likely knows a substantial number of people who are doing interesting things in the world. You might have a sister-in-law who's involved with writing grants for the National Science Foundation and a childhood friend who's a successful architect, for example.

Those connections you have are themselves a valuable resource to be shared with others. Simply doing something as simple as calling in a favor to an old friend can often be transformative in the life of someone else. This gift, simply done on your part, can create a tremendous sea change not only in an individual life, but in an entire community. After all, a rising tide lifts all boats.

Five Ways to Get Started

Excited to observe the power of giving in your own life? Here are five simple ways to get started.

1. **Take a look at the needs of the communities you're involved in.** You're a part of a wide array of communities, from familial communities and professional communities to geographical communities and political communities. What's needed in these communities? What can you easily give to these communities that fulfills a need?

2. **Make giving a habit.** Commit yourself to a regular diet of giving something of value to someone or to a community as a whole. Make it a daily thing. It can be as simple as serving as a moderator for a low-traffic email list or it can be as big as collecting cans every day for the local food pantry. Do something every day.

3. **Alternate between the communities you support.** By diversifying your giving, you increase the likelihood that you'll make personal connections in different communities, which themselves can be the source of powerful giving—as well as powerful opportunities for yourself.

4. **Give in a way that stretches you.** Giving can often be a powerful way to improve yourself and discover where your own personal limits are. Offer to write a document describing something in detail that will require you to do research. Give your time and energy to a building project that will physically push you and teach you construction skills.

5. **Enjoy it.** Giving of yourself in a way that makes others thrive feels *good*.

Chapter 17

Holding You Back

I pulled into the bookstore parking lot, got out of the truck, and began walking into the store before I realized what I was doing. The whole experience—stopping at the bookstore, strolling inside, buying a book or two, and going home to read them—had become so routine that I didn't even think about it. Even after hitting our financial breaking point a few weeks ago, I still found myself going through the motions of my old life. I was about to make the same mistake again simply because this was the routine of my life. It fit like an old glove—spending in such a frivolous manner was second nature to me. I realized that this was going to be harder than I thought.

May 2006

Earlier we discussed how we use routines to help keep our lives in some semblance of order. Without these routines—or at least the perception of them—our lives would be too filled with randomness for us to comprehend. It would be impossible to plan ahead and set goals.

Yet, at the same time, this very routine-oriented nature of ours works against us when we're attempting to establish real change in our lives. We have great, powerful intentions when it comes to making the changes in our life that we need to make, but when the rubber meets the road, many of us falter.

Resolutions fail not because they're not something we truly want, but because they require us to break through a lot of routines in our life—and those routines are very powerful things to break, indeed.

This chapter focuses on some of the most powerful tactics you can use to break through these routines and bring about the personal, professional, and financial changes that we want in our lives.

What We Say Versus What We Do

It's easy to commit to a change verbally. We can easily tell ourselves that we're going to lose weight or tell our partner that we're really committed to trimming our spending.

Our actions, though, often fly directly in the face of our words and our best intentions. We fill our plate at dinner and devour the whole thing without thinking about it. We go out with our friends and drop $40 almost reflexively. It's no wonder that such promises often leave us feeling far worse than we did before those words came out of our mouth.

All of the words and the great intentions in the world add up to very little if they're not coupled with the actions to back them up.

Instead of focusing on words, focus on actions. Instead of pledging to lose weight, forget the pledge and concentrate on eating smaller portions at meal time. Instead of promising to alter our spending habits, focus your energy on avoiding situations where you're tempted to spend.

Setting a goal can be a powerful thing, indeed, but a goal, in the end, is just a framework for a set of actions you have to take. Instead of making grand promises to yourself and to others about the goal itself, use your energy to simply ensure that you make the next step on the long road to your goal.

Words don't matter. Your next action is all that matters.

Passive Barriers

Ramit Sethi, author of, *I Will Teach You To Be Rich*, argues that one incredibly effective way to force yourself to establish a new routine in your life is to introduce a *passive barrier* that ensures better behavior. In his words: "Passive barriers are subtle factors that prevent you from changing your behavior. Unlike 'active' barriers, passive barriers describe the *lack* of something, making them more challenging to identify. But once you do, you can immediately take action to change your behavior."[1]

---

1   Ramit Sethi, "The Psychology of Passive Barriers: Why Your Friends Don't Save Money, Eat Healthier, or Clean Their Garages." http://www.getrich-slowly.org/blog/2009/03/17/the-psychology-of-passive-barriers-why-your-friends-dont-save-money-eat-healthier-or-clean-their-garages/. Retrieved October 19, 2009.

Here are five examples of passive barriers that can be used to achieve greater financial success:

1. **Leave your credit cards outside of your wallet.** Instead of carrying credit with you wherever you go, just leave your cards on your desk at home. Then, whenever you feel the urge to pull out the plastic to make a purchase, you'll find that the credit card isn't with you. It's at home, safe and sound, where you can't rack up a balance on it. Some people go further and actually freeze their credit card in a block of ice (this is actually quite easy—fill a pan half full of water, freeze the pan, put your credit cards on top, add more water to fill the pan, then freeze it again), creating an even stronger passive barrier against unplanned credit card use.

2. **Set up an automatic savings plan.** Saving money regularly seems like a good idea until you meet the reality of actually having to conduct a bank transaction every time you want to do it. Instead, set up an automatic transaction that transfers money from your checking account to your savings account each time. Your savings account, held in a distinct place from your checking account, is itself a passive barrier to easy access for your money. This same philosophy works for any automated savings, whether in your retirement account at work or in an investment account.

3. **Unplug the Internet cable.** One of my friends loves to spend her evenings checking eBay auctions. She seems to constantly have dozens of

bids going on things that are "bargains," but she'll sheepishly admit that most of the stuff she buys isn't really a bargain. It's just a pattern for her. One effective way to curb such a spending addiction is to add a passive barrier to the mix. Just unplug the Internet cable from the computer. This way, if she sits down to check her eBay auctions, there's suddenly a passive barrier—she has to climb under the desk, figure out which wire goes where, and hook it back up.

4. **Find a different route home from work.** When I worked in an office environment, my traditional route home from work took me directly by a bookstore and an electronics store. These two places were painful on my pocketbook as it was incredibly easy for me to just stop in for a quick peek. I put a passive barrier in place against these stores by coming up with a better route home from work. This new route was actually a bit shorter and kept me from going near those temptations, erecting a passive barrier against wanton book buying.

5. **Play the "why" game.** This is a general solution for uncovering passive barriers in your life. When you notice something in your life that you'd like to change, ask yourself why you do this. Then ask yourself why you do that. Keep asking yourself "why" until you hit upon something that can easily be changed with a passive barrier.

Here's an example. Let's say you want to find more time to read, but you always seem to be exhausted before bedtime:

Why are you exhausted?

Because you go to sleep too late.

Why do you go to sleep too late?

Because I watch the late local news on television.

Why do you watch the late local news?

Because it's after whatever show I'm watching that evening.

Why do you watch "whatever show" each evening?

Because I'm in the family room and it's so easy to switch on the television.

Your solution is self-evident—make it harder to watch television by doing something like getting rid of the remote (or storing it in the opposite end of the house), and you'll bump against a passive barrier, freeing you to spend your time on other activities. You can still actively choose to turn on the television, but it now requires much more action than before, which is often more than enough to direct you down a different path.

Clutter

Clutter is actually a specific kind of passive barrier, one that often keeps us from accomplishing important things in our lives. Clutter is the result of having more material items that we can deal with in our lives.

Clutter, by its very nature, represents financial and personal loss. By having more things than we have time to deal with, we've invested our money into material items that don't add up to the value we invested in them. At the same time, clutter often functions as a barrier against doing the things we want to do—finding a particular item to solve a need we have (sometimes even resulting in unnecessary and redundant purchases), inviting people over to visit and building your social circles and communities, finding time to adequately enjoy each item we already have, and so on.

Erin Doland, author of, *Unclutter Your Life in One Week*, recommends using the "three piles" system to declutter an area: " The first thing you do is that you pick an area you want to declutter. Don't try to do too much at once; focus on what's causing you the most stress. (Let's say it's your closet, but it could be your files, or your kitchen, or anything else.) Schedule ample time to dedicate to the task and go through every item in your cluttered space. Place each item into one of three piles: the 'love and use' pile, the 'recycle' pile, and the 'ambivalence' pile."[2]

The real trick of using the "three piles" method is to recognize that the vast majority of the stuff you put into the "ambivalence" pile (the things you're unsure about) should actually be in the "recycle" pile (things you don't need to have).

A simple decluttering can accomplish several things at once. The "recycle" pile can become a source of financial revenue (think eBay and the "snowflaking" strategy discussed earlier). The items you do choose to keep can now be found much easier, eliminating passive

2   Erin Doland, "Getting Started with Getting Organized." Unclutterer.com. http://unclutterer.com/2007/01/08/getting-started-with-getting-organized/. Retrieved on October 21, 2009.

barriers to enjoying some of your property and keeping you from spending money unnecessarily on entertainment. Plus, it freshens up your home and makes it much more accessible to guests.

Focus

One of the biggest challenges in establishing a new habit is repeating it often enough that it begins to seem like the norm in our lives. If we do something every day for an extended period of time, it eventually becomes a normal part of our day and we naturally *want* to include it in our routine.

Software developer Jerry Isaac shared a brilliant tactic (that he attributes to the comedian Jerry Seinfeld) for maintaining the focus on establishing a new habit on LifeHacker.com. "[G]et a big wall calendar that has a whole year on one page and hang it on a prominent wall. The next step was to get a big red magic marker. [...] [F]or each day that I do my task of writing, I get to put a big red X over that day. After a few days, you'll have a chain. Just keep at it and the chain will grow longer every day. You'll like seeing that chain, especially when you get a few weeks under your belt. Your only job next is to not break the chain."[3]

This tactic actually creates a simple psychological barrier *against* your tendency to revert to your old habits. The idea of breaking a "chain" of successes can seem incredibly negative and something to avoid, but by

3   Brad Isaac, "Jerry Seinfeld's Productivity Secret." Lifehacker.com. http://lifehacker.com/281626/jerry-seinfelds-productivity-secret. Retrieved on October 21, 2009.

continuing that chain, you're pushing yourself into the establishment of a new personal habit.

Choosing to Be Happy

For most of us, happiness—and, conversely, unhappiness—is a habit, part of the routine that we follow in life. Quite often, the routine has been in place for so long that anything else seems impossible. Yet, just as often, unhappiness with aspects of one's life can fuel poor financial moves, as we attempt to "cure" the sense of unhappiness by spending recklessly. Marketers prey on this sense of unhappiness, often convincing us that the peace we want can be found in this product—but that promise of happiness is a mirage.

Happiness is a choice. We can choose to see the glass half full and be aware of all the opportunities and joys life has for us. Conversely, we can choose to see the glass half empty and dwell on all of the things missing in our life. A happier life, a more contented life, makes it much easier to control our spending and keep our finances in a healthy place.

Kim Bentz, an administrator in Colorado Springs, Colorado, reflects on making a similar choice. "Up until the time I was about 26, I thought that you were as happy as the personality you were born with or that circumstances allowed you to be. Some people had won the lottery in both of those, having naturally sunny dispositions and having very little trouble in their lives, and some of us were naturally morose, and circumstances and tragedies conspired to keep us that way.

"Naturally I resented happy people, thinking that they had simply won life's lottery and, but for a twist of fate, that could have been me. Once I was told it was a choice, I began to study happy people. What I found was truly eye-opening. Happy people have no fewer problems than I or anyone else, but they were making a conscious choice to be happy anyway. If they could choose, so could I. The *habit* of unhappiness was deeply ingrained, so it took years for me to really learn how to make that choice. "[4]

Five Ways to Overcome Your Barriers

All of us have barriers in our lives that keep us from accomplishing the things we want and keep us from making profound changes in our lives. Overcoming those barriers is often the real challenge in the process of turning our financial, personal, and professional state around. Here are five steps you can take toward identifying the barriers in your own life and devising solutions for them:

1. **Use the "whys" game for every aspect of your life that makes you unhappy.** Ignore the things you cannot control. Instead, keep asking "why" until you come up with something that you do have some control over—a personal choice or an ongoing state in your life.
2. **Use simple passive barriers to your advantage.** If you want to break the television habit, hide the remote. If you want to break the smoking habit,

4   Personal interview.

throw away all the cigarettes. Make it as difficult as possible for you to access the tools you need to continue to engage in the behavior you want to break.

3. **Dwell on the positive aspects of your life, not the negative ones.** The negative aspects of your life—the sense that you're not pretty enough, not smart enough, and not happy enough—are the areas that marketers like to feed on to convince you to buy products you don't need. Instead, look at the many things you *do* have in your life—the friendships, the hobbies, the fulfilling career, the family.

4. **Stop making promises and focus on actions.** Instead of making grand pronouncements about where you're headed, focus on today's behaviors. What can you do *today* to establish a better routine for yourself? Once you have that new behavior in place, use the chain technique to put together strings of consecutive days utilizing that new behavior. Eventually, the behavior will become the norm, and you'll have achieved the goal without the bluster and hubris.

5. **Declutter.** Evaluate the possessions you have and determine which ones contribute real value to your life and which ones do not. Sell the items that don't have value (netting you a minor windfall, perfect for pushing you into a better financial place) and focus on enjoying the things that do have value while decreasing your maintenance time and also making your home more inviting to others.

Chapter 18

Original of the Species

"So, what exactly do you do all day?" My oldest brother Alan leaned across the table. I had just told him about my decision to quit my full-time job and take up a drastically different lifestyle. Aside from family farmers, I was the first self-employed person in my family. As I described how I now filled my days with a new mix of personal life and professional work, I could see his face change from a look of incredulity to a look of curiosity and interest. "That sounds awesome!" he said. "I wonder if I could do that?"

April 2008

Most of this book has revolved around making changes in a life that you're unhappy with. In fact, I assume that you picked up and read this book because you are in fact unhappy with your financial or professional position in life, and you're seeking answers for a better life.

Most of us, however, *are* happy with much of what goes on in our lives. We have friends and family that we love and care for and who love and care for us. We have a career that we enjoy. We have hobbies and activities that fill our remaining hours in interesting ways.

Yet something still made you pick up this book. Something is still not quite right in your life. Here are a few potential answers for your conundrum.

Experiences Trump Things

When I think back to the summer of 2004, I don't remember the DVDs I bought or the video games I collected or the new furniture we picked up. Instead, the first thought that comes to mind is sitting on a low bridge with my sister-in-law Rachel. It was a hot summer day, and we had both pulled off our shoes to dangle them in the water—and the water was freezing cold.

When I reflect on the high points in my life, I don't remember *things*. I remember experiences—the people I was with, the activity I was engaged in, and the place where I was doing it.

When I have conversations with my friends, we rarely talk about the things we have. Instead, we talk about our experiences—the things we're doing in our lives. We don't brag about the fact that we use the expensive laundry detergent; instead, we talk about the hike we went on last weekend or the ultimate Frisbee game earlier in the week.

Experiences always trump things. Experiences do not require maintenance. They do not take up space in your home. They stay with you in your heart.

Fill your life with experiences. Chase the things you've always dreamed of doing, and leave the things on the store shelves where they belong.

Insanity: Doing the Same Thing and Expecting Different Results

"Someday, things will change for me and my ship will come in," Helen said.

Helen and I had each just gone through a trial by fire at our respective new jobs. Since we were old friends from our college days, we agreed to eat lunch together and effectively allow each other to vent about the difficult and sometimes seemingly unfair challenges we faced.

When I heard Helen talk about her ship coming in, though, I had a strange feeling inside of me. If she keeps sitting there by the dock waiting, her ship will never come in. If she's genuinely unhappy with things to the point that she's pinning her hopes on an unforeseen windfall, she's doing nothing more than ensure the continuation of her own misery.

In Helen's comment, I saw myself. It scared me, and it made me want to start something new.

July 2004

The title of this section is a truism often attributed to Albert Einstein. It speaks to a fundamental truth about the world: **If you want something different out of life, you need to try something different** and change the rules a bit.

If I had not committed to trying something different in my life, you would not be holding this book in your hands today. Instead, my wife and I would likely be buried up to our necks in debt, I'd still be working in a career that stressed me out while dreaming about another career, and our children wouldn't be getting the attention that they so richly deserve.

If you want to make change, you have to try something different. If you've made it this far in the book, you've likely had dozens of ideas for how to make change in your life. As you read through these final pages, ask yourself this: *Do I expect change to happen in my life if I don't actually do some of these things?* Then close the book and get started.

Success Is About Differentiation

People often tend to resist making changes in their life because they're afraid of sticking their neck out. Such fears are based on the idea that we're essentially helpless, like chickens in a henhouse hoping that the fox doesn't catch us.

In the real world, success is often earned by the person who does make the change in their life to stand out from the pack. If you strive to hide in the crowd, you'll simply be passed over time and time again until, of course, you become one of the nameless faces included in the latest downsizing. On the other hand, if you choose change, you stick your neck out—and you're likely to be the first face seen when opportunity comes knocking.

If you simply keep repeating the behaviors of your friends who spend more than they earn, you'll continue to slip slowly downward in a spiral of debt. On the other hand, if you choose change, you escape that downward spiral and likely retain all of the powerful positive relationships you had before while only eliminating the negative ones that were pulling you down.

Success comes from being different, not from simply repeating the moves of everyone else.

Stop Caring What Other People Think

A thirteen-year-old truck sits in our driveway. I've driven it for the better part of a decade, and the wear of a dozen Iowa winters is beginning to show on it. There are a few rust spots around the edges and the paint simply doesn't glisten any more, even after a good washing and waxing. It doesn't run all that well, either—it desperately needs a new flywheel and, sometime after that, a new transmission.

Throughout our neighborhood, I can see shiny new vehicles parked in front of people's homes. In fact, I'd say that my truck is perhaps the oldest vehicle on the block.

At one point in my life, this state of affairs would have bothered me. I would feel jealousy toward the beautiful cars owned by our neighbors and wonder if they thought less of me because of my truck.

After having clawed my way back from the brink of financial destruction, though, I see things a bit differently. Each month, the bills for those beautiful cars arrive in their mailboxes. Each month, those families have to make some hard decisions about what they can afford to do. They have to worry about toeing the line at work and jumping at every suggestion from their manager. They have to tell their children that they won't be going on a memorable family vacation this year—or else they'll put the whole thing on plastic and have yet another giant bill to fret about.

Yet, when I stroll through my neighborhood and chat with my neighbors, we see that we're all equals. We're all struggling through the challenges of everyday life. We all make mistakes, and we all have triumphs.

It doesn't really matter, in the big scheme of things, what my neighbors think of my car. It does the job that I want it to do—taking me to the library and helping me run other local errands.

Does it cause my neighbors to treat me differently? It makes a real difference only to a few of them, and those individuals, by virtue of caring so deeply about what car someone else is driving, are inherently negative people anyway, looking for criteria with which to bring someone else down. As we discussed in Chapter 9, "Cultivating People and Opportunities," one of the best financial moves you can make in your own life is to minimize your negative relationships and stop caring what negative people think.

I buy things that have value to *me*, not because I anticipate the look of jealousy on someone else's face. Such anticipation is pure negativity, because you are attempting to feel better about yourself due to bringing someone else down.

The less you worry about what others think of what you do, the easier it becomes to blaze your own path in the world without the shackles of debt holding you in place.

"Live Like No One Else So You Can Live Like No One Else"

The preceding quote was popularized by television and radio personality Dave Ramsey, who often uses it to extol the virtues of getting oneself out of debt.[1]

In a much broader sense, however, it represents a key truth about any sort of change we undergo in our lives. Almost always, change feels negative at first. We're breaking rules. We're upsetting the expectations others have for us—and the expectations we have for ourselves.

To put it simply, change means choosing to live in a way that's somehow different than the people around us. We have to make the choice to separate ourselves from what they expect—and what we expect from ourselves—in order to have a chance to touch the dreams we have.

Take me, for example. In my entire circle of friends and family, I knew *no one* that had ever attempted a writing career, let alone a self-employed career of any kind. It was an incredibly difficult choice to make—it took me more than a year to finally make it—and I faced a lot of doubt and resistance from many people in my life.

1   Dave Ramsey, "FPU Church Home." DaveRamsey.com. http://www.daveramsey.com/fpu/church/. Retrieved October 27, 2009.

Looking back, the last two years of my life have been the happiest two years of my life. I made the change for myself, and my life couldn't be better for it.

Five Steps for Going Your Own Way

Committing to genuine change in one's life is always an incredibly challenging thing. You have to shatter not only your own ideas, fears, and psychological barriers, but you often have to work through the fears and barriers of others in your life. Here are five final pieces of advice for finding the courage to go your own way:

1. **Imagine the worst-case scenario.** Quite often, the worst-case scenario of attempting change is a simple return to the state you're at now. If you decide to commit to a new financial life and find later that it doesn't work, what's the worst-case scenario? You simply return to the financial state you're in right now. If you decide to take on new challenges at work, what's the worst-case scenario? You discover it's beyond your reach, and you revert back to your old tasks.

2. **Imagine the best-case scenario.** What happens if your decision to make a change in your life works well? You'll wind up in a better life position than the one you find yourself in now. When you pair that best-case scenario with the "worst case"— the way your life is right now—there's no reason *not* to make a sincere attempt at changing your behavior.

Trying change is much like asking a beautiful, intelligent, and interesting woman out on a date—she might say "no," but how is that any different than where you are before you asked her? But if she says "yes," all of your dreams might come true.

3. **Take change one day at a time.** It's easy to jump in over your head, making a number of changes all at once in your life. The problem with that approach is that it compounds the difficulty of each individual change because of the number of routines, rules, and expectations you're attempting to break all at once. Instead, focus at first on just a change or two, and work on those changes one day at a time. Ask yourself each day what you can do toward achieving your new goal and strive to make those actions a reality.

4. **Minimize the impact of unexpected events.** One of the very first changes everyone should make is securing their lives against the impact of an unexpected event. Commit to building up a month or two of living expenses in the bank and set up an automatic transfer each week to begin building toward that goal. Once you have that in place, an unexpected negative turn of events is no longer disastrous in your life, which means that you're even more open to the positive possibilities of further changes in your life.

5. **Don't give up due to a bump in the road.** We don't just wake up one morning, decide that we're going to change a major part of our lives, and then just cruise to victory. There will be mis-steps and minor failures along the way. Accept that. Don't give up and undo the good you've done over a long period just because of a single mistake or setback.

Chapter 19

11 O'Clock Tick Tock

It's eleven o'clock at night. The children are asleep, as is my wife. I'm still awake, alone in this quiet house. I'm sitting in a quiet, well-lit room with a notebook in front of me. Pen in hand, I begin to fill the paper, not with more personal finance and life management writings, but with the beginnings of the novel I've wanted to write since I was a young boy. A new journey is about to begin.

November 2009

If there's a single overriding point of this entire book, it's this: Money is nothing more than a tool with which you can create the life you truly want. The true challenge is knowing what you truly want, taking control of your situation, and putting yourself in a position to take advantage of the opportunities that come your way while protecting yourself from the obstacles life throws at all of us.

If you're ready to embark on that journey, here are ten essential tools to take along with you.

The Single Most Important Part of Personal Finance Is Truly Knowing Yourself.

Why do you buy the things that you do? Why are you worried about this situation? Why do you feel this way about this product? Why do you respond to guilt in this way?

The answer to all of these questions lies with introspection. The answer to all of these questions is also a *tremendous* boost when it comes to personal finance. If you understand fully the internal reasons why you desire something, you can work through those reasons, validate them or throw them aside, and then make a clear, enlightened, and rational decision about whether to acquire it.

The more introspection you do, the more naturally the true answers to those questions become and the easier it becomes to recognize your more dangerous and frivolous impulses for what they are. This leads not only to tremendous financial success, but great personal success as well.

The Second Most Important Part of Personal Finance Is Setting Clear, Concrete Goals.

This covers everything from daily to-do lists to a lifetime plan—and everything in between.

You can't go anywhere if you don't know where you are headed. The more specific and clear your goal, the easier it is to head in that direction. The more concrete your goal—in other words, a goal that has clear and realistic steps to get there and has a clear definition of achievement—the easier it is to achieve it.

I spend some time *every week* defining and re-defining my own goals. Doing this helps me keep in mind where I want to go and what I need to be doing today to get to that point. Over the last few years, this process has served me very well.

The World Is More Random Than You Think It Is.

We're psychologically tuned to minimize all of the random events in our life—both negative and positive—and maximize the idea that our lives run smoothly. Without this trick, it would be difficult for us to navigate through our daily lives.

The truth, however, is that our lives are full of unexpected events, and the more we can do to prepare ourselves to survive the negative events and take advantage of the positive ones, the better our life will be over the long haul.

The Most Valuable Resource in the World Isn't Money, It's Time.

Money is an infinite resource—you can always acquire more money. Time is a finite resource—you can never acquire more time.

We earn money through how we use our time. The more money we can earn in a given amount of time, the better off we are. Of course, the contrary is true—we spend our money making the remaining time we have more pleasurable.

The question that often entangles people is defining what exactly pleasurable time is. The definition is different for everyone, but I can say for certain that one thing is true: There are many people and marketers out there attempting to muddy the water for you. Advertising tries to make it seem as though using their product will make the time you have more pleasurable, even when it often won't.

Again, it comes back to knowing yourself. What is your idea of pleasurable time? For me, my time isn't made more enjoyable by having a name-brand household product. My time is made more enjoyable by having a product that gets the job done well at the lowest possible cost, freeing up my money to create more pleasure in other areas that matter to me.

Money is just a mechanism to improve the quality of our time. The question is whether or not we understand ourselves well enough to do that.

The More Supportive People You Have in Your Life, the Better Off You Are.

Supportive people in your life make countless good things possible. They provide connections. They open doors. They provide advice. They provide help for your challenges. They support you in whatever you choose to do. They help build your self-esteem. They're not necessarily just yes-men, though—a good supportive person can provide fierce criticism when it's warranted.

The more you migrate toward supportive people in your life, the better you'll feel about yourself and the more capable you will be to handle the challenges that life throws at you.

The Fewer Unsupportive People You Have in Your Life, the Better Off You Are.

On the flip side of that coin, removing unsupportive people from your life also improves the quality of your life.

Unsupportive people criticize you and damage your self-esteem. They take from you without replenishing. They aren't there for you when you need them, but they expect you to be there for them when they need you.

These relationships devour the energy and passion and resources from your life without providing anything of value in return. Ending such relationships—and, ideally, replacing them with more positive ones—is a net positive in your life.

Blaming Others for Your Problems Is a Dead-End Road.

It's incredibly easy to blame others when something goes wrong. It's someone else's fault that you lost your job. It's the fault of the marketers that you're in debt.

It's the fault of the lender that you can't make your mortgage payment.

In each case, though, the blame often falls much closer to home. The willingness to accept that you're often at fault when things go wrong is a major step toward being in control of your finances and your life. Analyzing those faults and figuring out what you can do differently so you're not susceptible to such problems is vital.

Yes, sometimes it really isn't your fault. Yet you did put yourself in the position so that you could be damaged by the ineptitude of others. Was there not actions you could have taken to prevent such things from happening? What can you learn from that the next time you try?

The More Time You Spend Improving and Educating Yourself, the Better Your Personal and Financial Life Will Be.

Virtually every successful person I know has a hobby that improves them in some way. They're either passionate about reading and learning or some other area of specific interest. Quite often, they have a variety of interests, each of which leads to some degree of personal improvement.

What do you do in your spare time that also improves you? Are you exercising your body? Are you exercising your mind? Are you exercising your soul? Are you exercising your skills and talents?

Time spent engaged in activities that don't push us to grow leads to one thing: atrophy. Falling behind.

Karma Always Comes Around.

People who act in negative ways have negative things happen to them. People who act in positive ways have positive things happen to them.

It happens over and over again. Why? I think it's because humans are better at reading each other than many people think. On a very basic level, people can sense what kind of person you are. Are you the kind of person who is constructive and seeks to help and support others? Or are you destructive—one who seeks to attack and bring down others? Which side of the coin do you enjoy—the success story or the failure story?

Your actions define you, even the ones that you think are hidden from everyone around you. Those choices affect your personality—they alter who you are. Choose good acts, and you become a better person, one others are more likely to help. Choose negative acts, and you become a worse person, one that drives others away. It's up to you, with every little action you take.

There Are Very Few Aspects of Your Life That Cannot Be Changed.

Most aspects of who you are—your financial situation, your skill set, your appearance, your social circle, even your personality—can change and improve with focused work in those areas. Don't accept the things about yourself that you don't like—work to change them.

Yes, some aspects cannot be changed. Some people have medical conditions that are difficult to overcome. Others may struggle with psychological issues. However, these are often burdens to fight through that can make you stronger as you overcome them, like ankle weights on a figure skater.

You don't have to be content with your lot in life. Recognize that the place you're at can merely be a stepping stone, and strive to step above it.

The clock is ticking. The next step toward having the life that you want is up to you.

Index

L

Lastovica, John, 84
leadership, 132
leftovers, 99
lending money to family/friends, 6, 175-177
libraries, 106
life
  barriers
    clutter, 218-220
    focus, 220
    overcoming, 222
    passive, 215, 218
    unhappiness, 221
  changes
    actions versus words, 214
    committing, 232-234
    experiences trump things, 226
    living like no one else, 231
    success from differentiation, 228
    trying something different, 227
    worrying about what others think, 229-231
  designing new
    audacious goals, setting, 148-151
    five steps, 151-153
    foundation, creating, 142-144
    rule breaking, 145-147
  future self reliability, 55
  hobbies, 240
  negative experiences, 16
  power of today, 55
  running in place, 49
  unexpected events
    emergency funds, 26-28
    examples, 23
    luck, maximizing, 32
    minimizing, 237
    personal risk sources, 29-31

    positive, 26
    preparation, 26-29, 34
    random, 25
    reliability, 33-34
    unwinding with mindless tasks, 58
lifestyle inflation, avoiding, 156, 159
Lifestyle of the Tight and Frugal: Theory and Measurement (Lastovica), 84
living trusts, 162
living wills, 163
local communities, 62
long term care insurance, 163
long-term financial security, 4
long-term goals
  achieving with short-term goals, 42
  benefits, 41
  self-reliance, 42-44
  setting, 40-42
  success framework, 46
loyalties
  coworkers/peers, 124-125
  organizations, 124
luck, maximizing, 32

M

maintaining financial stability, 164-165
making life changes
  actions versus words, 214
  committing, 232-234
  experiences trump things, 226
  living like no one else, 231
  success from differentiation, 228
  trying something different, 227
  worrying about what others think, 229-231
Maslow, Abraham, 141
Matthews, Dr. Gail, 38

FT Press

FINANCIAL TIMES

In an increasingly competitive world, it is quality
of thinking that gives an edge—an idea that opens new
doors, a technique that solves a problem, or an insight
that simply helps make sense of it all.

We work with leading authors in the various arenas
of business and finance to bring cutting-edge thinking
and best-learning practices to a global market.

It is our goal to create world-class print publications
and electronic products that give readers
knowledge and understanding that can then be
applied, whether studying or at work.

To find out more about our business
products, you can visit us at www.ftpress.com.

Ramona Quimby, age 8

Ramona bent over her paper and wrote slowly and carefully in cursive, Ramona Quimby, age 8. She admired the look of what she had written, and she was happy. She liked feeling tall in her new school. She liked— or was pretty sure she liked—her nonfussy teacher. Yard Ape— Well, he was a problem, but so far she had *not let* him get the best of her for keeps. Besides, although she might never admit it to anyone, now that she had her eraser back she liked him—sort of. Maybe she enjoyed a challenge.

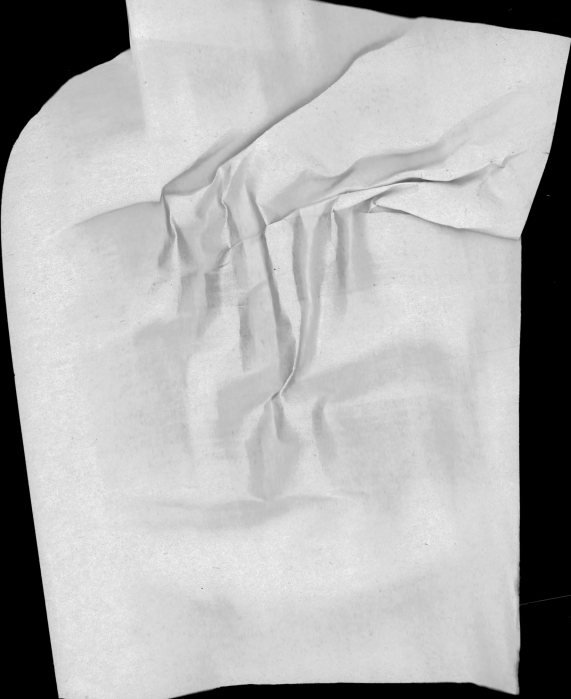

Enjoy all of Beverly Cleary's books

FEATURING RAMONA QUIMBY:

Beezus and Ramona

Ramona the Pest

Ramona the Brave

Ramona and Her Father

Ramona and Her Mother

Ramona Quimby, Age 8

Ramona Forever

Ramona's World

FEATURING HENRY HUGGINS:

Henry Huggins

Henry and Beezus

Henry and Ribsy

Henry and the Paper Route

Henry and the Clubhouse

Ribsy

FEATURING RALPH MOUSE:

The Mouse and the Motorcycle

Runaway Ralph

Ralph S. Mouse

MORE GREAT FICTION BY BEVERLY CLEARY:

Ellen Tebbits

Otis Spofford

Fifteen

The Luckiest Girl

Jean and Johnny

Emily's Runaway Imagination

Sister of the Bride

Mitch and Amy

Socks

Dear Mr. Henshaw

Muggie Maggie

Strider

Two Times the Fun

AND DON'T MISS BEVERLY CLEARY'S AUTOBIOGRAPHIES:

A Girl from Yamhill

My Own Two Feet

Beverly Cleary

Ramona Quimby, Age 8

ILLUSTRATED BY
Tracy Dockray

HarperTrophy®
An Imprint of HarperCollins*Publishers*

Harper Trophy® is a registered trademark of
HarperCollins Publishers.

Ramona Quimby, Age 8
Copyright © 1981 by Beverly Cleary
Library of Congress Catalog Card Number: 2005938682
ISBN-10: 0-380-70956-2 — ISBN-13: 978-0-380-70956-4
Typography by Amy Ryan

❖

Reillustrated Harper Trophy edition, 2006
Visit us on the World Wide Web!
www.harpercollinschildrens.com
11 12 13 LP/BR 90 89 87 86 85 84 83

Contents

1

The First Day of School

Ramona Quimby hoped her parents would forget to give her a little talking-to. She did not want anything to spoil this exciting day.

"Ha-ha, I get to ride the bus to school all by myself," Ramona bragged to her big sister, Beatrice, at breakfast. Her stomach felt quivery with excitement at the day ahead, a day that would begin with a bus ride just the

1

right length to make her feel a long way from home but not long enough—she hoped— to make her feel carsick. Ramona was going to ride the bus, because changes had been made in the schools in the Quimbys' part of the city during the summer. Glenwood, the girls' old school, had become an intermediate school, which meant Ramona had to go to Cedarhurst Primary School.

"Ha-ha yourself." Beezus was too excited to be annoyed with her little sister. "Today I start high school."

"*Junior* high school," corrected Ramona, who was not going to let her sister get away with acting older than she really was. "Rosemont Junior High School is not the same as high school, and besides you have to walk."

Ramona had reached the age of demanding accuracy from everyone, even herself. All summer, whenever a grown-up asked what grade she was in, she felt as if she were fibbing when she answered, "third," because she had not actually started the third grade. Still, she could not say she was in the second grade since she had finished that grade last June. Grown-ups did not understand that summers were free from grades.

"Ha-ha to both of you," said Mr. Quimby, as he carried his breakfast dishes into the kitchen. "You're not the only ones going to school today." Yesterday had been his last day working at the checkout counter of the ShopRite Market. Today he was returning to college to become what he called "a real, live school teacher." He was also going to work one day a week in the frozen-food warehouse of the chain of ShopRite Markets to help the family "squeak by," as the grown-ups put it, until he finished his schooling.

"Ha-ha to all of you if you don't hurry up," said Mrs. Quimby, as she swished suds in

the dishpan. She stood back from the sink so she would not spatter the white uniform she wore in the doctor's office where she worked as a receptionist.

"Daddy, will you have to do homework?" Ramona wiped off her milk moustache and gathered up her dishes.

"That's right." Mr. Quimby flicked a dish towel at Ramona as she passed him. She

giggled and dodged, happy because he was happy. Never again would he stand all day at a cash register, ringing up groceries for a long line of people who were always in a hurry.

Ramona slid her plate into the dishwater. "And will Mother have to sign your progress reports?"

Mrs. Quimby laughed. "I hope so."

Beezus was last to bring her dishes into the kitchen. "Daddy, what do you have to study to learn to be a teacher?" she asked.

Ramona had been wondering the same thing. Her father knew how to read and do arithmetic. He also knew about Oregon pioneers and about two pints making one quart.

Mr. Quimby wiped a plate and stacked it in the cupboard. "I'm taking an art course, because I want to teach art. And I'll study child development—"

Ramona interrupted. "What's child development?"

"How kids grow," answered her father.

Why does anyone have to go to school to study a thing like that? wondered Ramona. All her life she had been told that the way to grow was to eat good food, usually food she did not like, and get plenty of sleep, usually when she had more interesting things to do than go to bed.

Mrs. Quimby hung up the dishcloth, scooped up Picky-picky, the Quimbys' old yellow cat, and dropped him at the top of the basement steps. "Scat, all of you," she said, "or you'll be late for school."

After the family's rush to brush teeth, Mr. Quimby said to his daughters, "Hold out your hands," and into each waiting pair he dropped a new pink eraser. "Just for luck," he said, "not because I expect you to make mistakes."

"Thank you," said the girls. Even a small present was appreciated, because presents of any kind had been scarce while the family

tried to save money so Mr. Quimby could return to school. Ramona, who liked to draw as much as her father, especially treasured the new eraser, smooth, pearly pink, smelling softly of rubber, and just right for erasing pencil lines.

Mrs. Quimby handed each member of her family a lunch, two in paper bags and one in a lunch box for Ramona. "Now, Ramona—" she began.

Ramona sighed. Here it was, that little

talking-to she always dreaded.

"Please remember," said her mother, "you really must be nice to Willa Jean."

Ramona made a face. "I try, but it's awfully hard."

Being nice to Willa Jean was the part of Ramona's life that was not changing, the part she wished would change. Every day after school she had to go to her friend Howie Kemp's house, where her parents paid Howie's grandmother to look after her until one of them could come for her. Both of Howie's parents, too, went off to work each day. She liked Howie, but after spending most of the summer, except for swimming lessons in the park, at the Kemps' house, she was tired of having to play with four-year-old Willa Jean. She was also tired of apple juice and graham crackers for a snack every single day.

"No matter what Willa Jean does," complained Ramona, "her grandmother thinks it's my fault because I'm bigger. Like the time

Willa Jean wore her flippers when she ran under the sprinkler, pretending she was the mermaid on the tuna-fish can, and then left big wet footprints on the kitchen floor. Mrs. Kemp said I should have stopped her because Willa Jean didn't know any better!"

Mrs. Quimby gave Ramona a quick hug. "I know it isn't easy, but keep trying."

When Ramona sighed, her father hugged her and said, "Remember, kid, we're counting on you." Then he began to sing, "We've got high hopes, try hopes, buy cherry pie-in-July hopes—"

Ramona enjoyed her father's making up new words for the song about the little old ant moving the rubber tree plant, and she liked being big enough to be counted on, but sometimes when she went to the Kemps' she felt as if everything depended on her. If Howie's grandmother did not look after her, her mother could not work full time. If her mother did not work full time, her father could not go to school. If her father did not go to school, he might have to go back to being a checker, the work that made him tired and cross.

Still, Ramona had too many interesting things to think about to let her responsibility worry her as she walked through the autumn sunshine toward her school bus stop, her new eraser in hand, new sandals on her feet, that quivery feeling of excitement in her stomach, and the song about high hopes running through her head.

She thought about her father's new part-time job zipping around in a warehouse on a fork-lift truck, filling orders for orange juice, peas, fish sticks, and all the other frozen items the markets carried. He called himself Santa's Little Helper, because the temperature of the warehouse was way below zero, and he would have to wear heavy padded clothing to keep from freezing. The job sounded like fun to Ramona. She wondered how she was going to feel about her father's teaching art to other people's children and decided not to think about that for a while.

Instead, Ramona thought about Beezus going off to another school, where she would get to take a cooking class and where she could not come to the rescue if her little sister got into trouble. As Ramona approached her bus stop, she thought about one of the best parts of her new school: none of her teachers in her new school would know she was Beatrice's little sister. Teachers always like Beezus; she was so prompt and neat. When both girls had gone to Glenwood School, Ramona often felt as if teachers were thinking, I wonder why Ramona Quimby isn't more like her big sister.

When Ramona reached the bus stop, she found Howie Kemp already waiting with his grandmother and Willa Jean, who had come to wave good-by.

Howie looked up from his lunch box, which he had opened to see what he was going to have for lunch, and said to Ramona, "Those new sandals make your feet look awfully big."

"Why, Howie," said his grandmother,

"that's not a nice thing to say."

Ramona studied her feet. Howie was right, but why shouldn't her new sandals make her feet look big? Her feet had grown since her last pair. She was not offended.

"Today I'm going to *kidnergarten*," boasted Willa Jean, who was wearing new coveralls and T-shirt and a pair of her mother's old earrings. Willa Jean was convinced she was beautiful, because her grandmother said so. Ramona's mother said Mrs. Kemp was right. Willa Jean was beautiful when she was clean, because she was a healthy child. Willa Jean did not feel she was beautiful like a healthy child. She felt she was beautiful like a grown-up lady on TV.

Ramona tried to act kindly toward little Willa Jean. After all, her family was depending on her. "Not *kidnergarten*, Willa Jean," she said. "You mean nursery school."

Willa Jean gave Ramona a cross, stubborn

look that Ramona knew too well. "I am too going to *kid*nergarten," she said. "*Kid*nergarten is where the kids are."

"Bless her little heart," said her grandmother, admiring as always.

The bus, the little yellow school bus Ramona had waited all summer to ride, pulled up at the curb. Ramona and Howie climbed aboard as if they were used to getting on buses by themselves. I did it just like a grown-up, thought Ramona.

"Good morning. I am Mrs. Hanna, your bus aide," said a woman sitting behind the driver. "Take the first empty seats toward the back." Ramona and Howie took window seats on opposite sides of the bus, which had a reassuring new smell. Ramona always dreaded the people-and-fumes smell of the big city buses.

"By-byee," called Mrs. Kemp and Willa Jean, waving as if Ramona and Howie were going on a long, long journey. "By-byee." Howie pretended not to know them.

As soon as the bus pulled away from the curb, Ramona felt someone kick the back of her seat. She turned and faced a sturdy boy wearing a baseball cap with the visor turned up and a white T-shirt with a long word printed across the front. She studied the word to see if she could find short words in it, as she had learned to do in second grade. *Earth. Quakes. Earthquakes.* Some kind of team. Yes, he looked like the sort of boy whose father would take him to ball games. He did not have a lunch box, which meant he was going to buy his lunch in the cafeteria.

A grown-up would not call him a purple cootie. Ramona faced front without speaking. This boy was not going to spoil her first day in the third grade.

Thump, thump, thump against the back of Ramona's seat. The bus stopped for other children, some excited and some anxious. Still the kicking continued. Ramona ignored it as the bus passed her former school. Good old Glenwood, thought Ramona, as if she had gone there a long, long time ago.

"All right, Danny," said the bus aide to the kicking boy. "As long as I'm riding shotgun on this bus, we won't have anyone kicking the seats. Understand?"

Ramona smiled to herself as she heard Danny mutter an answer. How funny—the bus aide saying she was riding shotgun as if she were guarding a shipment of gold on a stagecoach instead of making children behave on a little yellow school bus.

Ramona pretended she was riding a stagecoach pursued by robbers until she discovered her eraser, her beautiful pink eraser, was missing. "Did you see my eraser?" she asked a second-grade girl, who had taken the seat beside her. The two searched the seat and the floor. No eraser.

Ramona felt a tap on her shoulder and turned. "Was it a pink eraser?" asked the boy in the baseball cap.

"Yes." Ramona was ready to forgive him for kicking her seat. "Have you seen it?"

"Nope." The boy grinned as he jerked down the visor of his baseball cap.

That grin was too much for Ramona. "Liar!" she said with her most ferocious glare, and faced front once more, angry at the loss of her new eraser, angry with herself for dropping it so the boy could find it. Purple cootie, she thought, and hoped the cafeteria would serve him fish portions and those canned green beans with the strings left on. And apple wedges, the soft mushy kind with tough skins, for dessert.

The bus stopped at Cedarhurst, Ramona's new school, a two-story red-brick building very much like her old school. As the children hopped out of the bus, Ramona felt a little thrill of triumph. She had not been carsick. She now discovered she felt as if she had grown even more than her feet. Third graders were the biggest people—except teachers, of course—at this school. All the little first and second graders running around the playground, looking so young, made Ramona feel tall, grown up, and sort of . . . well, wise in the ways of the world.

Danny shoved ahead of her. "Catch!" he yelled to another boy. Something small and pink flew through the air and into the second boy's cupped hands. The boy wound up as if he were pitching a baseball, and the eraser flew back to Danny.

"You gimme back my eraser!" Encumbered by her lunch box, Ramona chased Danny, who ran, ducking and dodging, among the first and second graders. When she was about to catch him, he tossed her eraser to the other boy. If her lunch box had not banged against her knees, Ramona might have been able to grab him. Unfortunately, the bell rang first.

"Yard apes!" yelled Ramona, her name for the sort of boys who always got the best balls, who were always first on the playground, and who chased their soccer balls through other people's hopscotch games. She saw her

pink eraser fly back into Danny's hands. "Yard apes!" she yelled again, tears of anger in her eyes. "Yucky yard apes!" The boys, of course, paid no attention.

Still fuming, Ramona entered her new school and climbed the stairs to find her assigned classroom, which she discovered looked out over roofs and treetops to Mount Hood in the distance. I wish it would erupt,

she thought, because she felt like exploding with anger.

Ramona's new room was filled with excitement and confusion. She saw some people she had known at her old school. Others were strangers. Everyone was talking at once, shouting greetings to old friends or looking over those who would soon become new friends, rivals, or enemies. Ramona missed Howie, who had been assigned to another room, but wouldn't you know? That yard ape, Danny, was sitting at a desk, still wearing his baseball cap and tossing Ramona's new eraser from one hand to another. Ramona was too frustrated to speak. She wanted to hit him. How dare he spoil her day?

"All right, you guys, quiet down," said the teacher.

Ramona was startled to hear her class called "you guys." Most teachers she had known would say something like, "I feel I am talking very loud. Is it because the room is noisy?" She chose a chair at a table at the front of the room and studied her new teacher, a strong-looking woman with short hair and a deep tan. Like my swimming teacher, thought Ramona.

"My name is Mrs. Whaley," said the teacher, as she printed her name on the blackboard. "*W-h-a-l-e-y*. I'm a whale with a *y* for a tail." She laughed and so did her class. Then the whale with a *y* for a tail handed Ramona some slips of paper. "Please pass these out," she directed. "We need some name tags until I get to know you."

Ramona did as she was told, and as she walked among the desks she discovered her new sandals squeaked. *Squeak, creak, squeak.* Ramona giggled, and so did the rest of the class. *Squeak, creak, squeak.* Ramona went up one aisle and down the other. The last person she gave a slip to was the boy from the bus, who was still wearing his baseball cap. "You give me back my eraser, you yard ape!" she whispered.

"Try and get it, Bigfoot," he whispered back with a grin.

Ramona stared at her feet. Bigfoot? Bigfoot was a hairy creature ten feet tall, who was supposed to leave huge footprints in the mountain snows of southern Oregon. Some people thought they had seen Bigfoot slipping through the forests, but no one had ever been able to prove he really existed.

Bigfoot indeed! Ramona's feet had grown, but they were not huge. She was not going to let him get away with this insult. "Superfoot to you, Yard Ape," she said right out loud, realizing too late that she had given herself a new nickname.

To her astonishment, Yard Ape pulled her eraser out of his pocket and handed it to her with a grin. Well! With her nose in the air, Ramona squeaked back to her seat. She felt so triumphant that she returned the longest way around and bent her feet as much as she could to make the loudest possible squeaks. She had done the right thing! She had not let Yard Ape upset her by calling her Bigfoot, and now she had her eraser in her hand. He would probably call her Superfoot forever, but she did not care. Superfoot was a name she had given herself. That made all the difference. She had won.

Ramona became aware that she was squeaking in the midst of an unusual silence. She stopped midsqueak when she saw her new teacher watching her with a little smile. The class was watching the teacher.

"We all know you have musical shoes," said Mrs. Whaley. Of course the class laughed.

By walking with stiff legs and not bending her feet, Ramona reached her seat without squeaking at all. She did not know what to think. At first she thought Mrs. Whaley's remark was a reprimand, but then maybe her teacher was just trying to be funny. She couldn't tell about grown-ups sometimes. Ramona finally decided that any teacher who would let Yard Ape wear his baseball cap in the classroom wasn't really fussy about squeaking shoes.

Ramona bent over her paper and wrote slowly and carefully in cursive, Ramona Quimby, age 8. She admired the look of what she had written, and she was happy. She liked feeling tall in her new school. She liked—or was pretty sure she liked—her nonfussy teacher. Yard Ape— Well, he was a problem, but so far she had not let him get the best of her for keeps. Besides, although she might never admit it to anyone, now that she had her eraser back she liked him— sort of. Maybe she enjoyed a challenge.

Ramona began to draw a fancy border, all scallops and curliques, around her name. She was happy, too, because her family had been happy that morning and because she was big enough for her family to depend on.

If only she could do something about Willa Jean. . . .

2
AT Howie's House

"Now be nice to Willa Jean," said Mrs. Quimby, as she handed Ramona her lunch box. Grown-ups often forgot that no child likes to be ordered to be nice to another child.

Ramona made a face. "Mother, do you have to say that every single morning?" she asked in exasperation. Deep down inside, where she hid her darkest secrets, Ramona sometimes longed to be horrid to Willa Jean.

"OK, OK, I'll try to remember," said Mrs. Quimby with a little laugh. "I know it isn't easy." She kissed Ramona and said, "Cheer up and run along or you'll miss your bus."

Being a member of the Quimby family in the third grade was harder than Ramona had expected. Her father was often tired, in a hurry, or studying on the dining-room table, which meant no one could disturb him by watching television. At school she was still not sure how she felt about Mrs. Whaley. Liking a teacher was important, Ramona had discovered when she was in the first grade. And even though her family understood, Ramona still dreaded that part of the day spent at Howie's house in the company of Mrs. Kemp and Willa Jean.

Those were the bad parts of the third grade. There were good parts, too. Ramona enjoyed riding the bus to school, and she enjoyed keeping Yard Ape from getting the best of her. Then another good part of the third grade began the second week of school.

Just before her class was to make its weekly visit to the school library, Mrs. Whaley announced, "Today and from now on we are going to have Sustained Silent Reading every day."

Ramona liked the sound of Sustained Silent Reading, even though she was not sure what it meant, because it sounded important.

Mrs. Whaley continued. "This means that every day after lunch we are going to sit at our desks and read silently to ourselves any book we choose in the library."

"Even mysteries?" someone asked.

"Even mysteries," said Mrs. Whaley.

"Do we have to give book reports on what we read?" asked one suspicious member of the class.

"No book reports on your Sustained Silent Reading books," Mrs. Whaley promised the class. Then she went on, "I don't think Sustained Silent Reading sounds very interesting, so I think we will call it something else." Here she printed four big letters on the blackboard, and as she pointed she read out, "D. E. A. R. Can anyone guess what these letters stand for?"

The class thought and thought.

"Do Everything All Right," suggested someone. A good thought, but not the right answer.

"Don't Eat A Reader," suggested Yard Ape. Mrs. Whaley laughed and told him to try again.

As Ramona thought, she stared out the window at the blue sky, the treetops, and, in the distance, the snow-capped peak of Mount Hood looking like a giant licked ice-cream cone. *R* could stand for *Run* and *A* for *And*.

"Drop Everything And Run," Ramona burst out. Mrs. Whaley, who was not the sort of teacher who expected everyone to raise a hand before speaking, laughed and said, "Almost right, Ramona, but have you forgotten we are talking about reading?"

"Drop Everything And Read!" chorused the rest of the class. Ramona felt silly. She should have thought of that herself.

Ramona decided that she preferred Sustained Silent Reading to DEAR because it sounded more grown-up. When time came for everyone to Drop Everything And Read, she sat quietly doing her Sustained Silent Reading.

How peaceful it was to be left alone in school. She could read without trying to hide her book under her desk or behind a bigger book. She was not expected to write lists of words she did not know, so she could figure them out by skipping and guessing.

Mrs. Whaley did not expect the class to write summaries of what they read either, so she did not have to choose easy books to make sure she would get her summary right. Now if Mrs. Whaley would leave her alone to draw, too, school would be almost perfect.

Yes, Sustained Silent Reading was the best part of the day. Howie and Ramona talked it over after school and agreed as they walked from the bus to his house. There they found two of the new friends he had made at Cedarhurst School waiting with their bicycles.

Ramona sat on the Kemps' front steps, her arms clasped around her knees, her Sustained Silent Reading book of fairy tales beside her, and looked with longing at the boys' two bicycles while Howie wheeled his bicycle out of the garage.

Because Howie was kind and because Ramona was his friend, he asked, "Ramona,

would you like to ride my bicycle to the corner and back?"

Would she! Ramona jumped up, eager to take a turn.

"Just once," said Howie.

Ramona mounted the bicycle and, while the three boys silently watched, teetered and wobbled to the corner without falling off.

Having to dismount to turn the bicycle around was embarrassing, but riding back was easier—at least she didn't wobble quite so much—and she managed to dismount as if she were used to doing so. All I need is a little practice, thought Ramona, as Howie seized his bicycle and rode off with his friends, leaving her with nothing to do but pick up her book and join Willa Jean in the house.

Now that Willa Jean was going to nursery school, she was full of ideas. Dressing up was one of them. She met Ramona at the door with an old curtain wrapped around her shoulders. "Hurry up and have your snack," she ordered, while her grandmother sat watching television and crocheting.

The snack turned out to be pineapple juice and Rye Crisp, a pleasant change for Ramona, even though Willa Jean stood impatiently beside her, watching every swallow until she had finished.

"Now I'll be the lady and you be the dog," directed Willa Jean.

"But I don't want to be a dog," said Ramona.

Willa Jean's grandmother looked up from her crocheting, reminding Ramona with a glance that Ramona's job in the Quimby family was to get along at the Kemps'. Did she have to be a dog if Willa Jean wanted her to then?

"You have to be the dog," said Willa Jean.

"Why?" Ramona kept an eye on Mrs. Kemp as she wondered how far she dared go in resisting Willa Jean's orders.

"Because I'm a beautiful rich lady and I say so," Willa Jean informed her.

"I'm a bigger, beautifuler, richer lady," said Ramona, who felt neither beautiful nor rich, but certainly did not want to crawl around on her hands and knees barking.

"We can't both be the lady," said Willa Jean, "and I said it first."

36

Ramona could not argue the justice of this point. "What kind of dog am I supposed to be?" she asked to stall for time. She glanced wistfully at her book lying on the chair, the book she was supposed to read at school, but which she was enjoying so much she brought it home.

While Willa Jean was thinking, Mrs. Kemp said, "Sweetheart, don't forget Bruce is coming over to play in a few minutes."

"Bruce who?" asked Ramona, hoping Willa Jean and Bruce would play together and leave her alone to read.

"Bruce who doesn't wee-wee in the sand-box," was Willa Jean's prompt answer.

"Willa Jean!" Mrs. Kemp was shocked. "What a thing to say about your little friend."

Ramona was not shocked. She understood that there must be a second Bruce at Willa Jean's nursery school, a Bruce who did wee-wee in the sandbox.

As things turned out, Ramona was saved

from being a dog by the arrival of a small boy whose mother let him out of the car and watched him reach the front door before she drove off.

Willa Jean ran to let him in and introduced him as Ramona expected, "This is Bruce who doesn't wee-wee in the sandbox." Bruce looked pleased with himself.

Mrs. Kemp felt a need to apologize for her granddaughter. "Willa Jean doesn't mean what she says."

"But I don't wee-wee in the sandbox," said Bruce. "I wee-wee in the—"

"Never mind, Bruce," said Mrs. Kemp. "Now what are you three going to play?"

Ramona was trapped.

"Dress up," was Willa Jean's prompt answer. She dragged from the corner a carton piled with old clothes. Willa Jean shoved one of her father's old jackets at Bruce and handed him an old hat and her blue flippers. She unwound the curtain from her shoulders, draped it over her head, and tied it under her chin. Then she hung a piece of old sheet from her shoulders. Satisfied with herself, she handed a torn shirt to Ramona, who put it on only because Mrs. Kemp was watching.

"There," said Willa Jean, satisfied. "I'll be Miss Mousie, the beautiful bride, and Bruce is the frog and Ramona is Uncle Rat, and now we are going to have a wedding party."

Ramona did not want to be Uncle Rat.

"Mr. Frog would a-wooing go," sang Willa Jean. Bruce joined in, "*Hm-m, hm-m.*" Apparently this song was popular in nursery school. Ramona *hm-m*ed too.

"Say it," Willa Jean ordered Bruce.

"Willa Jean, will you marry me?" sang Bruce.

Willa Jean stamped her foot. "*Not* Willa Jean! Miss Mousie."

Bruce started over. "Miss Mousie, will

you marry me?" he sang.

"Yes, if Uncle Rat will agree," sang Willa Jean.

"*Hm-m, hm-m.*"

"*Hm-m, hm-m,*" hummed all three.

The two nursery-school children looked to Ramona for the next line. Since she did not remember the words used by Uncle Rat to give Mr. Frog permission to marry Miss Mousie, she said, "Sure. Go ahead."

"OK," said Willa Jean. "Now we will have the wedding party." She seized Bruce and Ramona by the hand. "Take Bruce's other hand," she ordered Ramona.

Ramona found Bruce's hand inside the long sleeve of the old coat. His hand was sticky.

"Now we'll dance in a circle," directed Willa Jean.

Ramona skipped, Willa Jean pranced, and Bruce flapped. They danced in a circle, tripping on Miss Mousie's train and wedding veil and stumbling over Mr. Frog's flippers until Willa Jean gave the next order. "Now we all fall down."

Ramona merely dropped to her knees while Willa Jean and Bruce collapsed in a heap, laughing. Above their laughter and the sound of the television, Ramona heard the shouts of the boys outside as they rode their bicycles up and down the street. She wondered how much longer she would have to wait until her mother came to rescue her. She hoped she would arrive before Howie's parents came home from work.

Willa Jean scrambled to her feet. "Let's play it again," she said, beaming, convinced of her beauty in her wedding veil. Over and over the three sang, danced, and fell down. As the game went on and on, Ramona grew bored and varied the words she used to give Mr. Frog permission to marry Miss Mousie. Sometimes she said, "See if I care," and sometimes she said, "Yes, but you'll be sorry." Willa Jean did not notice, she was so eager to get to the party part of the game where they all fell down in a heap.

Still the game went on, over and over, with no sign of Bruce and Willa Jean's tiring. Then Beezus came in with an armload of books.

"Hi, Beezus," said Willa Jean, flushed with laughter. "You can play too. You can be the old tomcat in the song."

"I'm sorry, Willa Jean," said Beezus. "I don't have time to be the old tomcat. I have homework I have to do." She settled herself at the dining-room table and opened a book.

Ramona looked at Mrs. Kemp, who smiled and continued crocheting. Why did Ramona have to play with Willa Jean when Beezus did not? Because she was younger. That was why. Ramona was overwhelmed by the unfairness of it all. Because she was younger, she always had to do things she did not want to do—go to bed earlier, wear Beezus's outgrown clothes that her mother saved for her,

run and fetch because her legs were younger
and because Beezus was always doing homework. Now she had to get along with Willa
Jean—her whole family was depending on
her—and Beezus did not.

Once more Ramona looked at her book
of fairy tales waiting on the chair beside the
front door, and as she looked at its worn
cover she had an inspiration. Maybe her idea
would work, and maybe it wouldn't. It was
worth a try.

"Willa Jean, you and Bruce will have to

excuse me now," Ramona said in her politest voice. "I have to do my Sustained Silent Reading." Out of the corner of her eye she watched Mrs. Kemp.

"OK." Willa Jean was not only impressed by a phrase she did not understand, she had Bruce to boss around. Mrs. Kemp, who was counting stitches, merely nodded.

Ramona picked up her book and settled herself in the corner of the couch. Beezus caught her eye, and the two sisters exchanged conspiratorial smiles while Willa Jean and Bruce, now minus Uncle Rat, raced happily around in a circle screaming with joy and singing, "She'll be coming 'round the mountain when she comes!"

Ramona blissfully read herself off into the land of princesses, kings, and clever youngest sons, satisfied that the Quimbys had a clever younger daughter who was doing her part.

3

The Hard-boiled Egg Fad

With all four members of the family leaving at different times in different directions, mornings were flurried in the Quimby household. On the days when Mr. Quimby had an eight o'clock class, he left early in the car. Beezus left next because she walked to school and because she wanted to stop for Mary Jane on the way.

Ramona was third to leave. She enjoyed

these last few minutes alone with her mother now that Mrs. Quimby no longer reminded her she must be nice to Willa Jean.

"Did you remember to give me a hard-boiled egg in my lunch like I asked?" Ramona inquired one morning. This week hard-boiled eggs were popular with third graders, a fad started by Yard Ape, who sometimes brought his lunch. Last week the fad had been individual bags of corn chips. Ramona had been left out of that fad because her mother objected to spending money on junk food. Surely her mother would not object to a nutritious hard-boiled egg.

"Yes, I remembered the hard-boiled egg, you little rabbit," said Mrs. Quimby. "I'm glad you have finally learned to like them."

Ramona did not feel it necessary to explain to her mother that she still did not like hard-boiled eggs, not even when they had been dyed for Easter. Neither did she like soft-boiled eggs, because she did not like slippery, slithery food. Ramona liked deviled eggs, but deviled eggs were not the fad, at least not this week.

On the bus Ramona and Susan compared lunches. Each was happy to discover that the other had a hard-boiled egg, and both were eager for lunchtime to come.

While Ramona waited for lunch period, school turned out to be unusually interesting. After the class had filled out their arithmetic workbooks, Mrs. Whaley handed each child a glass jar containing about two inches of a wet blue substance—she explained that it was oatmeal dyed blue. Ramona was first to say "Yuck." Most people made faces, and Yard Ape made a gagging noise.

"OK, kids, quiet down," said Mrs. Whaley. When the room was quiet, she explained that for science they were going to study fruit flies. The blue oatmeal contained fruit-fly larvae.

."And why do you think the oatmeal is blue?" she asked.

Several people thought the blue dye was some sort of food for the larvae, vitamins maybe. Marsha suggested the oatmeal was dyed blue so the children wouldn't think it was good to eat. Everybody laughed at this guess. Who would ever think cold oatmeal was good to eat? Yard Ape came up with the right answer: the oatmeal was dyed blue so the larvae could be seen. And so they could— little white specks.

As the class bent over their desks making labels for their jars, Ramona wrote her name on her slip of paper and added, "Age 8," which she always wrote after her signature. Then she drew tiny fruit flies around it before she pasted the label on her very own jar of blue oatmeal and fruit-fly larvae. Now she had a jar of pets.

"That's a really neat label, Ramona," said

Mrs. Whaley. Ramona understood that her
teacher did not mean tidy when she said
"neat," but extra good. Ramona decided she
liked Mrs. Whaley after all.

The morning was so satisfactory that it
passed quickly. When lunchtime came,
Ramona collected her lunch box and went
off to the cafeteria where, after waiting in
line for her milk, she sat at a table with Sara,

Janet, Marsha, and other third-grade girls. She opened her lunch box, and there, tucked in a paper napkin, snug between her sandwich and an orange, was her hard-boiled egg, smooth and perfect, the right size to fit her hand. Because Ramona wanted to save the best for the last, she ate the center of her sandwich—tuna fish—and poked a hole in her orange so she could suck out the juice. Third graders did not peel their oranges. At last it was time for the egg.

There were a number of ways of cracking eggs. The most popular, and the real reason for bringing an egg to school, was knocking the egg against one's head. There were two ways of doing so, by a lot of timid little raps or by one big whack.

Sara was a rapper. Ramona, like Yard Ape, was a whacker. She took a firm hold on her egg, waited until everyone at her table was watching, and *whack*—she found herself

with a handful of crumbled shell and something cool and slimy running down her face.

Everyone at Ramona's table gasped. Ramona needed a moment to realize what had happened. Her egg was raw. Her mother had not boiled her egg at all. She tried to brush the yellow yolk and slithery white out of her hair and away from her face, but she only succeeded in making her hands eggy. Her eyes filled with tears of anger, which she tried to brush away with her wrists. The gasps at her table turned into giggles. From another table, Ramona caught a glimpse of Yard Ape grinning at her.

Marsha, a tall girl who always tried to be motherly, said, "It's all right, Ramona. I'll take you to the bathroom and help you wash off the egg."

Ramona was not one bit grateful. "You go away," she said, ashamed of being so rude. She did not want this third-grade girl treating her like a baby.

The teacher who was supervising lunch period came over to see what the commotion was about. Marsha gathered up all the paper napkins from the lunch boxes at the table and handed them to the teacher, who tried to sop up the egg. Unfortunately, the napkins did not absorb egg very well. Instead, they smeared yolk and white around in Ramona's hair. Her face felt stiff as egg white began to dry.

"Take her to the office," the teacher said to Marsha. "Mrs. Larson will help her."

"Come on, Ramona," said Marsha, as if Ramona were in kindergarten. She put her hand on Ramona's shoulder because Ramona's hands were too eggy to touch.

Ramona jerked away. "I can go by myself." With that reply, she ran out of the cafeteria. She was so angry she was able to ignore the giggles and the few sympathetic looks of the other children. Ramona was mad at herself for following a fad. She was furious with Yard Ape for grinning at her. Most of all she was angry with her mother for not boiling the egg in the first place. By the time she reached the office, Ramona's face felt as stiff as a mask.

Ramona almost ran into Mr. Wittman, the principal, which would have upset her even more. He was someone Ramona always tried to avoid ever since Beezus had told her that the way to remember how to spell the kind of principal who was the principal of a school was to remember the word ended in *p-a-l*, not *p-l-e*, because the principal was her pal. Ramona did not want the principal to be her pal. She wanted him to mind his own business, aloof and important, in his office. Mr. Wittman must have felt the same way because he stepped—almost jumped— quickly aside.

Mrs. Larson, the school secretary, took one look at Ramona, sprang from her desk, and said, "Well, you need a little help, don't you?"

Ramona nodded, grateful to Mrs. Larson for behaving as if eggy third graders walked into her office every day. The secretary led her into a tiny room equipped with a cot, washbasin, and toilet that adjoined the office.

"Let's see," said Mrs. Larson, "how shall we go about this? I guess the best way is to wash your hands, then dunk your head. You've heard of egg shampoos, haven't you? They are supposed to be wonderful for the hair."

"Yow!" yelped Ramona, when she dipped her head into the washbasin. "The water's cold."

"It's probably a good thing we don't have warmer water," said Mrs. Larson. "You wouldn't want to cook the egg in your hair, would you?" She rubbed and Ramona snuffled. She rinsed and Ramona sniffed. Finally Mrs. Larson said, "That's the best I can do," and handed Ramona a wad of paper towels. "Dry yourself off the best you can," she said.

"You can wash your hair when you get home."

Ramona accepted the towels. As she sat on the cot, rubbing and blotting and seething in humiliation and anger, she listened to sounds from the office, the click of the type-writer, the ring of the telephone, Mrs. Larson's voice answering.

Ramona began to calm down and feel a little better. Maybe Mrs. Kemp would let her wash her hair after school. She could let Willa Jean pretend to be working in a beauty shop and not say anything about her Sustained Silent Reading. One of these days Willa Jean was sure to catch on that she was just reading a book, and Ramona wanted to postpone that time as long as possible.

Toward the end of lunch period, Ramona heard teachers drift into the office to leave papers or pick up messages from their boxes. Then Ramona made an interesting discovery.

Teachers talked about their classes.

"My class has been so good today," said one teacher. "I can hardly believe it. They're little angels."

"I don't know what's the matter with my class today," said another. "Yesterday they knew how to subtract, and today none of them seems able to remember."

"Perhaps it's the weather," suggested another teacher.

Ramona found all this conversation most interesting. She had blotted her hair as best she could when she heard Mrs. Whaley's big cheerful voice speaking to Mrs. Larson. "Here are those tests I was supposed to hand in yesterday," she said. "Sorry I'm late." Mrs. Larson murmured an answer.

Then Mrs. Whaley said, "I hear my little show-off came in with egg in her hair." She laughed and added, "What a nuisance."

Ramona was so stunned she did not try

to hear Mrs. Larson's answer. Show-off! Nuisance! Did Mrs. Whaley think she had broken a raw egg into her hair on purpose to show off? And to be called a nuisance by her teacher when she was not a nuisance. Or was she? Ramona did not mean to break an egg in her hair. Her mother was to blame. Did this accident make her a nuisance?

Ramona did not see why Mrs. Whaley could think she was a nuisance when Mrs. Whaley was not the one to get her hands all eggy. Yet Ramona had heard her say right out loud that she was a show-off and a nuisance. That hurt, really hurt.

Ramona sat as still as she could with the damp paper towels in her hands. She did not want to risk even the softest noise by throwing them into the wastebasket. Lunch period came to an end, and still she sat. Her body felt numb and so did her heart. She could never, never face Mrs. Whaley again. Never.

Mrs. Larson's typewriter clicked cheerfully away. Ramona was forgotten, which was the way she wanted it. She even wanted to forget herself and her horrible hair, now drying into stiff spikes. She no longer felt like a real person.

The next voice Ramona heard was that of Yard Ape. "Mrs. Larson," he said, as if he had been running in the hall, "Mrs. Whaley said to tell you Ramona didn't come back after lunch."

The typing stopped. "Oh, my goodness," said Mrs. Larson, as she appeared in the doorway. "Why, Ramona, are you still here?"

How was Ramona supposed to answer?

"Run along back to class with Danny," said the secretary. "I'm sorry I forgot all about you."

"Do I have to?" asked Ramona.

"Of course," said Mrs. Larson. "Your hair is almost dry. You don't want to miss class."

Ramona did want to miss class. Forever. The third grade was spoiled forever.

"Aw, come on, Ramona," said Yard Ape, for once not teasing.

Surprised by sympathy from Yard Ape, Ramona reluctantly left the office. She expected him to go on ahead of her, but instead he walked beside her, as if they were friends instead of rivals. Ramona felt strange walking down the hall alone with a boy. As she trudged along beside him, she felt she had to tell someone the terrible news. "Mrs. Whaley doesn't like me," she said in a flat voice.

"Don't let old Whaley get you down," he answered. "She likes you OK. You're a good kid."

Ramona was a little shocked at hearing her teacher called "old Whaley." However, she squeezed comfort from Yard Ape's opinion. She began to like him, really like him.

When they reached their classroom, Yard Ape, perhaps thinking he had been *too* nice to Ramona, turned and said to her with his old grin, "Egghead!"

Oh! There was nothing for Ramona to do but follow him into the room. Sustained Silent Reading, or DEAR, as Mrs. Whaley called it, was over, and the class was practicing writing cursive capital letters. Mrs. Whaley was describing capital *M* as she wrote it on the board. "Swoop down, swoop up, down, up again, and down." Ramona avoided looking at her teacher as she got out paper and pencil and began to write the capital letters of the alphabet in careful, even script. She enjoyed the work, and it soothed her hurt feelings until she came to the letter Q.

Ramona sat looking at the cursive capital Q, the first letter of her last name. Ramona had always been fond of Q, the only letter of the alphabet with a neat little tail. She enjoyed printing Q, but she did not like her written Q. She had made it right, but it looked like a big floppy 2, which Ramona felt was a dumb way to make such a nice letter.

Ramona decided right then and there that she would never again write a cursive Q. She would write the rest of her last name, *uimby*, in cursive, but she would always, no matter what Mrs. Whaley said, print her capital Q's.

So there, Mrs. Whaley, thought Ramona. You can't make me write a cursive Q if I don't want to. She began to feel like a real person again.

4

The Quimbys' Quarrel

"But Ramona," said Mrs. Quimby on Saturday, "I've already told you that I boiled several eggs so I wouldn't have to boil an egg for you every morning. I put the boiled eggs on one shelf in the refrigerator and the raw eggs on another. In my hurry, I took an egg from the wrong shelf. I am sorry. There is nothing more I can say."

Ramona remained silent. She felt mean

and unhappy because she wanted to forgive her mother, but something in that dark, deep-down place inside her would not let her. Hearing her teacher call her a show-off and a nuisance hurt so much she could not stop being angry at almost everyone.

Mrs. Quimby sighed in a tired sort of way as she gathered up sheets and towels to feed into the washing machine in the basement. Ramona stared out the window and wished the misty rain, which fell softly and endlessly, would go away so she could go outdoors and roller-skate away her bad feelings.

Beezus was no help. She had spent the night at Mary Jane's house with several other girls, and they had stayed up late watching a horror movie on television and eating popcorn. Afterward they stayed awake talking, too scared to go to sleep. That morning Beezus had come home tired and grouchy and had fallen asleep almost immediately.

Ramona wandered around the house looking for something to do, when she discovered her father sitting on the couch, pencil in hand, drawing pad on his knee, frowning at one bare foot.

"Daddy, what are you doing that for?" Ramona wanted to know.

"That's what I keep asking myself," her father answered, as he wiggled his toes. "I have to draw a picture of my foot for my art class."

"I wish we got to do things like that in my school," said Ramona. She found pencil and paper, pulled off one shoe and sock, and climbed on the couch beside her father. Both studied their feet and began to sketch. Ramona soon found that drawing a foot was more difficult than she had expected. Like her father, she stared, frowned, drew, erased, stared, frowned, and drew. For a little while she forgot she was cross. She was enjoying herself.

"There," said Ramona at last. She had
drawn a good, not an excellent, foot. She
looked at her father's paper and was disappointed in what she saw. It was the kind of
picture a teacher would pin up off in the
corner where no one but the artist would
notice it. Her father's foot looked like a
flipper. For the first time, Ramona began to
doubt that her father was the best artist in

the whole world. This thought made her feel sad in addition to reminding her she was cross at that world.

Mr. Quimby studied Ramona's picture. "That's not bad," he said. "Not bad at all."

"My foot is easier to draw." Ramona felt as if she should apologize for drawing a better foot than her grown-up father. "My foot is sort of—neater," she explained. "Your foot is kind of bony and your toes are hairy. That makes your foot harder to draw."

Mr. Quimby crumpled his drawing and threw it into the fireplace. "You make me sound like Bigfoot," he said with a rueful laugh, as he threw a cushion at Ramona.

The day dragged on. By dinner time Ramona still had not been able to forgive her mother, who looked even more tired. Mr. Quimby had crumpled several more unsatisfactory drawings of his foot, and Beezus had emerged from her room sleepy-eyed and half-awake, when her mother called the family to supper.

"I wish we could have corn bread again," Ramona said, not because she particularly liked corn bread, but because she felt so cross she wanted to complain about something. Corn bread was a pretty shade of yellow, which would have looked cheerful on a misty day. She leaned forward to sniff the plate of food set before her.

"Ramona." Even though her father did not speak the words, his voice said, "We do not sniff our food in this house."

Ramona sat up. Broccoli and baked potato, both easy to eat. Pot roast. Ramona leaned closer to examine her meat. She could not find one bit of fat, and there was only a bit of gravy poured over her serving. Good. Ramona refused even the tiniest bit of fat. She did not like the slippery squishy feeling in her mouth.

"Delicious," remarked Mr. Quimby, who did not feel he had to inspect his food before eating.

"Nice and tender," said Beezus, beginning to cheer up after her hard night.

Ramona seized her fork, speared her meat to her plate, and began to saw with her knife.

"Ramona, try to hold your fork properly," said her father. "Don't grip it with your fist. A fork is not a dagger."

With a small sigh, Ramona changed her hold on her fork. Grown-ups never remembered the difficulty of cutting meat when one's elbows were so far below the tabletop. She succeeded in cutting a bite of meat the way her parents thought proper. It was unusually tender and not the least bit stringy like some pot roasts her mother had prepared. It tasted good, too. "Yummy," said Ramona, forgetting her anger.

The family ate in contented silence until

Beezus pushed aside her gravy with the side of her fork. Gravy was fattening, and although Beezus was slender, even skinny, she was taking no chances.

"Mother!" Beezus's voice was accusing. *"This meat has a rough surface!"*

"It does?" answered Mrs. Quimby innocently.

Ramona understood her mother was trying to hide something when she saw her parents exchange their secret-sharing glance. She too scraped aside her gravy. Beezus was right. One edge of her meat was covered with tiny bumps.

"This meat is tongue." Beezus pushed her serving aside with her fork. "I don't like tongue."

Tongue! Like Beezus, Ramona pushed her meat aside. "Yuck," she said.

"Girls, stop being silly." Mrs. Quimby's voice was sharp.

"What do you mean you don't like tongue?" demanded Mr. Quimby. "You were just eating it and enjoying it."

"But I didn't know it was tongue then," said Beezus. "I hate tongue."

"Me too," said Ramona. "All those yucky

little bumps. Why can't we have plain meat?"

Mrs. Quimby was losing patience. "Because tongue is cheaper. That's why. It's cheaper and it's nutritious."

"You know what I think," said Mr. Quimby. "I think this whole thing is a lot of nonsense. You liked tongue when you didn't know it was tongue, so there is no reason why you can't eat it now."

"Yes, this whole thing is ridiculous," said Mrs. Quimby.

"Tongue is disgusting," said Beezus. "Picky-picky can have mine."

"Mine, too," echoed Ramona, knowing she should eat what was set before her, but tongue— Her parents were asking too much.

The meal continued in silence, the girls guilty but defiant, the parents unrelenting. When Mr. Quimby finished his serving of tongue, he helped himself from Ramona's plate. Picky-picky, purring like a rusty motor, walked into the dining room and rubbed against legs to remind the family that he should eat too.

"I wonder," said Mrs. Quimby, "why we named the *cat* Picky-picky." She and Mr. Quimby looked at one another and only partly suppressed their laughter. The girls exchanged sulky glances. Parents should not laugh at their children.

Beezus silently cleared the table. Mrs. Quimby served applesauce and oatmeal cookies while Mr. Quimby talked about his work as Santa's Little Helper in the frozen-food warehouse. He told how snow fell inside the warehouse door when someone opened it and let in warm air. He told about a man who had to break icicles from his moustache when he left the warehouse.

Snow indoors, icicles on a moustache—Ramona was full of questions that she would not let herself ask. Maybe working as Santa's

Little Helper wasn't as much fun as she had thought.

"I'll tell you what," said Mr. Quimby to Mrs. Quimby, when the last cookie crumb had been eaten. "You need a rest. Tomorrow the girls can get dinner and you can take it easy."

"Good idea," said Mrs. Quimby. "Sometimes I do get tired of cooking."

"But I'm supposed to go to Mary Jane's tomorrow," protested Beezus.

"Call her up and tell her you can't come." Mr. Quimby was both cheerful and heartless.

"That's not fair," said Beezus.

"Tell me why it isn't fair," said Mr. Quimby.

When Beezus had no answer, Ramona understood their plight was serious. When their father behaved this way, he never changed his mind. "But I don't know how to cook," Ramona protested. "Except Jell-O and French toast."

"Nonsense," said Mrs. Quimby. "You are in the third grade, and you can read. Anyone who can read can cook."

"What'll we cook?" Beezus had to accept the fact that she and Ramona had no way out.

"The same things I cook," said her mother. "Whatever I have bought on special that you can find in the refrigerator."

"And corn bread." Mr. Quimby, his face serious but his eyes amused, looked at Ramona. "I expect to be served corn bread."

That evening, after the dishes had been put away, Picky-picky was polishing gravy from his whiskers and their parents were watching the evening news on television. Ramona marched into Beezus's room and shut the door. "It's all your fault," she informed her sister, who was lying on the bed with a book. "Why didn't you keep still?"

"It's just as much your fault," said Beezus.

"You and your yucks."

Both girls recognized nothing would be gained by arguing over blame.

"But you like to cook," said Ramona.

"And you like to make Jell-O and French toast," said Beezus.

The sisters looked at one another. What had gone wrong? Why didn't they want to prepare dinner?

"I think they're mean," said Ramona.

"They're punishing us," said Beezus. "That's what they're doing."

The sisters scowled. They liked to cook; they did not like to be punished. They sat in silence, thinking cross thoughts about parents, especially their parents, their unfair, unkind parents who did not appreciate what nice daughters they had. Lots of parents would be happy to have nice daughters like Beezus and Ramona.

"If I ever have a little girl, I won't ever

make her eat tongue," said Ramona. "I'll give her good things to eat. Things like stuffed olives and whipped cream."

"Me too," agreed Beezus. "I wonder what there is for us to cook."

"Let's go look in the refrigerator," suggested Ramona.

Beezus objected. "If they hear us open the refrigerator, Mom and Dad will think we're hungry, and we'll get a lecture on not eating our dinner."

"But I *am* hungry," said Ramona, although she understood the truth of Beezus's words. Oh well, she wouldn't actually starve to death before breakfast. She found herself thinking of French toast, golden with egg under a snowfall of powdered sugar.

"Maybe. . . ." Beezus was thoughtful. "Maybe if we're extra good, they'll forget about the whole thing."

Ramona now felt sad as well as angry.

Here she had worked so hard to do her part by getting along at the Kemps', and now her family was not pulling together. Something had gone wrong. Beezus was probably right. The only way to escape punishment was to try being extra good.

"OK." Ramona agreed, but her voice was gloomy. What a dismal thought, being extra good, but it was better than allowing their parents to punish them.

Ramona went to her own room, where she curled up on her bed with a book. She wished something nice would happen to her mother and father, something that would help them forget the scene at the dinner table. She wished her father would succeed in drawing a perfect foot, the sort of foot his teacher would want to hang in the front of the room above the middle of the blackboard. Maybe a perfect foot would make him happy.

And her mother? Maybe if Ramona could

forgive her for not boiling the egg she would be happy. In her heart Ramona had forgiven her, and she was sorry she had been so cross with her mother. She longed to go tell her, but now she could not, not when she was being punished.

5

The Extra-good Sunday

Sunday morning Ramona and Beezus were still resolved to be perfect until dinner time. They got up without being called, avoided arguing over who should read Dear Abby's advice first in the paper, complimented their mother on her French toast, and went off through the drizzly rain to Sunday school neat, combed, and bravely smiling.

Later they cleaned up their rooms without being told. At lunchtime they ate without complaint the sandwiches they knew were made of ground-up tongue. A little added pickle relish did not fool them, but it did help. They dried the dishes and carefully avoided looking in the direction of the refrigerator lest their mother be reminded they were supposed to cook the evening meal.

Mr. and Mrs. Quimby were good-humored. In fact, everyone was so unnaturally pleasant that Ramona almost wished someone would say something cross. By early afternoon the question was still hanging in the air. Would the girls really have to prepare dinner?

Why doesn't somebody say something? Ramona thought, weary of being so good, weary of longing to forgive her mother for the raw egg in her lunch.

"Well, back to the old foot," said Mr.

Quimby, as he once more settled himself on the couch with drawing pad and pencil and pulled off his shoe and sock.

The rain finally stopped. Ramona watched for dry spots to appear on the sidewalk and thought of her roller skates in the closet. She looked into Beezus's room and found her sister reading. Ramona knew Beezus wanted to telephone Mary Jane but had decided to wait until Mary Jane called to ask why she had not come over. Mary Jane did not call. The day dragged on.

When dry spots on the concrete in front of the Quimbys' house widened until moisture remained only in the cracks of the sidewalk, Ramona pulled her skates out of her closet. To her father, who was holding a drawing of his foot at arm's length to study it, she said, "Well, I guess I'll go out and skate."

"Aren't you forgetting something?" he asked.

"What?" asked Ramona, knowing very well what.

"Dinner," he said.

The question that had hung in the air all day was answered. The matter was settled.

"We're stuck," Ramona told Beezus. "Now we can stop being so good."

The sisters went into the kitchen, shut the door, and opened the refrigerator.

"A package of chicken thighs," said Beezus with a groan. "And a package of frozen peas. And yoghurt, one carton of plain and one of banana. There must have been a special on yoghurt." She closed the refrigerator and reached for a cookbook.

"I could make place cards," said Ramona, as Beezus frantically flipped pages.

"We can't eat place cards," said Beezus. "Besides, corn bread is your job because you brought it up." Both girls spoke in whispers. There was no need to let their parents, their mean old parents, know what was going on in the kitchen.

In her mother's recipe file, Ramona found the card for corn bread written in Mr. Quimby's grandmother's shaky handwriting, which Ramona found difficult to read.

"I can't find a recipe for chicken thighs," said Beezus, "just whole chicken. All I know is that Mother bakes thighs in the flat glass dish with some kind of sauce."

"Mushroom soup mixed with something and with some kind of little specks stirred in." Ramona remembered that much from watching her mother.

Beezus opened the cupboard of canned goods. "But there isn't any mushroom soup," she said. "What are we going to do?"

"Mix up something wet," suggested Ramona. "It would serve them right if it tasted awful."

"Why don't we make something awful?"

asked Beezus. "So they will know how we feel when we have to eat tongue."

"What tastes really awful?" Ramona was eager to go along with the suggestion, united with her sister against their enemy—for the moment, their parents.

Beezus, always practical, changed her mind. "It wouldn't work. We have to eat it too, and they're so mean we'll probably have to do the dishes besides. Anyway, I guess you might say our honor is at stake, because they think we can't cook a good meal."

Ramona was ready with another solution. "Throw everything in one dish."

Beezus opened the package of chicken thighs and stared at them with distaste. "I can't stand touching raw meat," she said, as she picked up a thigh between two forks.

"Do we have to eat the skin?" asked Ramona. "All those yucky little bumps."

Beezus found a pair of kitchen tongs. She

tried holding down a thigh with a fork and pulling off the skin with the tongs.

"Here, let me hold it," said Ramona, who was not squeamish about touching such things as worms or raw meat. She took a firm hold on the thigh while Beezus grasped the skin with the tongs. Both pulled, and the skin peeled away. They played tug-of-war with each thigh, leaving a sad-looking heap of skins on the counter and a layer of chicken thighs in the glass dish.

"Can't you remember what little specks Mother uses?" asked Beezus. Ramona could not. The girls studied the spice shelf, unscrewed jar lids and sniffed. Nutmeg? No. Cloves? Terrible. Cinnamon? Uh-uh. Chili powder? Well. . . . Yes, that must be it. Ramona remembered that the specks were red. Beezus stirred half a teaspoon of the dark red powder into the yoghurt, which she poured over the chicken. She slid the

dish into the oven set at 350 degrees, the temperature for chicken recommended by the cookbook.

From the living room came the sound of their parents' conversation, sometimes serious and sometimes highlighted by laughter. While we're slaving out here, thought Ramona, as she climbed up on the counter to reach the box of cornmeal. After she climbed down, she discovered she had to climb up again for baking powder and soda. She finally knelt on the counter to save time and asked Beezus to bring her an egg.

"It's a good thing Mother can't see you up there," remarked Beezus, as she handed Ramona an egg.

"How else am I supposed to reach things?" Ramona successfully broke the egg and tossed the shell onto the counter. "Now I need buttermilk."

Beezus broke the news. There was no

buttermilk in the refrigerator. "What'll I do?" whispered Ramona in a panic.

"Here. Use this." Beezus thrust the carton of banana yoghurt at her sister. "Yoghurt is sort of sour, so it might work."

The kitchen door opened a crack. "What's going on in there?" inquired Mr. Quimby.

Beezus hurled herself against the door. "You stay out!" she ordered. "Dinner is going to be a—surprise!"

For a moment Ramona thought Beezus had been going to say a mess. She stirred egg and yoghurt together, measured flour, spilling some on the floor, and then discovered she was short of cornmeal. More panic.

"My cooking teacher says you should always check to see if you have all the ingredients before you start to cook," said Beezus.

"Oh, shut up." Ramona reached for a package of Cream of Wheat, because its grains were about the same size as cornmeal.

She scattered only a little on the floor.

Something was needed to sop up the sauce with little red specks when the chicken was served. Rice! The spilled Cream of Wheat gritted underneath Beezus's feet as she measured rice and boiled water according to the directions on the package. When the rice was cooking, she slipped into the dining room to set the table and then remembered they had forgotten salad. Salad! Carrot sticks were quickest. Beezus began to scrape carrots into the sink.

"Yipe!" yelped Ramona from the counter. "The rice!" The lid of the pan was chittering. Beezus snatched a larger pan from the cupboard and transferred the rice.

"Do you girls need any help?" Mrs. Quimby called from the living room.

"No!" answered her daughters.

Another calamity. The corn bread should bake at 400 degrees, a higher temperature than that needed for the chicken. What was Ramona to do?

"Stick it in the oven anyway." Beezus's face was flushed.

In went the corn bread beside the chicken.

"Dessert!" whispered Beezus. All she could find was a can of boring pear halves. Back to the cookbook. "Heat with a little butter and serve with jelly in each half," she read. Jelly. Half a jar of apricot jam would have to do. The pears and butter went into the saucepan. Never mind the syrup spilled on the floor.

"Beezus!" Ramona held up the package of peas.

Beezus groaned. Out came the partially cooked chicken while she stirred the thawing peas into the yoghurt and shoved the dish back into the oven.

The rice! They had forgotten the rice, which was only beginning to stick to the pan. Quick! Take it off the burner. How did their mother manage to get everything cooked at the right time? Put the carrot sticks on a dish. Pour the milk. "Candles!" Beezus whispered. "Dinner might look better if we have candles."

Ramona found two candle holders and two partly melted candles of uneven length. One of them had been used in a Halloween jack-o'-lantern. Beezus struck the match to light them, because although Ramona was brave about touching raw meat, she was skittish about lighting matches.

Was the chicken done? The girls anxiously examined their main dish, bubbling and brown around the edges. Beezus stabbed a thigh with a fork, and when it did not bleed, she decided it must be done. A toothpick pricked into the corn bread came out clean. The corn bread was done—flat, but done.

Grit, grit, grit sounded under the girls' feet. It was amazing how a tiny bit of spilled

Cream of Wheat could make the entire kitchen floor gritty. At last their dinner was served, the dining-room light turned off, dinner announced, and the cooks, tense with anxiety that was hidden by candlelight, fell into their chairs as their parents seated themselves. Was this dinner going to be edible?

"Candles!" exclaimed Mrs. Quimby. "What a festive meal!"

"Let's taste it before we decide," said Mr. Quimby with his most wicked grin.

The girls watched anxiously as their father took his first bite of chicken. He chewed thoughtfully and said with more surprise than necessary, "Why this is good!"

"It really is," agreed Mrs. Quimby, and took a bit of corn bread. "Very good, Ramona," she said.

Mr. Quimby tasted the corn bread. "Just like Grandmother used to make," he pronounced.

The girls exchanged suppressed smiles. They could not taste the banana yoghurt, and by candlelight no one could tell that the corn bread was a little pale. The chicken, Ramona decided, was not as good as her parents thought—or pretended to think— but she could eat it without gagging.

Everyone relaxed, and Mrs. Quimby said chili powder was more interesting than paprika and asked which recipe they had used for the chicken.

Ramona answered, "Our own," as she exchanged another look with Beezus. Paprika! Those little specks in the sauce should have been paprika.

"We wanted to be creative," said Beezus.

Conversation was more comfortable than it had been the previous evening. Mr. Quimby said he was finally satisfied with his drawing, which looked like a real foot. Beezus said her cooking class was studying the food groups everyone should eat every day. Ramona said there was this boy at school who called her Egghead. Mr. Quimby explained that Egghead was slang for a very smart person. Ramona began to feel better about Yard Ape.

The meal was a success. If the chicken did not taste as good as the girls had hoped and the corn bread did not rise like their mother's, both were edible. Beezus and Ramona were silently grateful to their parents for enjoying—or pretending to enjoy—their cooking. The whole family cheered up. When they had finished their pears with apricot jam, Ramona gave her mother a shy smile.

Mrs. Quimby smiled back and patted Ramona's hand. Ramona felt much lighter. Without using words, she had forgiven her mother for the unfortunate egg, and her mother had understood. Ramona could be happy again.

"You cooks have worked so hard," said Mr. Quimby, "that I'm going to wash the dishes. I'll even finish clearing the table."

"I'll help," volunteered Mrs. Quimby.

The girls exchanged another secret smile as they excused themselves and skipped off to their rooms before their parents discovered the pile of chicken skins and the broken eggshell on the counter, the carrot scrapings in the sink, and the Cream of Wheat, flour, and pear syrup on the floor.

6

Supernuisance

Once more the Quimbys were comfortable with one another—or reasonably so. Yet Mr. and Mrs. Quimby often had long, serious discussions at night behind their closed bedroom door. The sober sound of their voices worried Ramona, who longed to hear them laugh. However, by breakfast they were usually cheerful—cheerful but hurried.

Ramona was less comfortable at school. In fact, she was most uncomfortable because she was so anxious not to be a nuisance to her teacher. She stopped volunteering answers, and except for the bus ride and Sustained Silent Reading she dreaded school.

One morning, when Ramona was wishing she could get out of going to school, she dug a hole in the middle of her oatmeal with her spoon and watched it fill with milk as she listened to the noise from the garage, the grinding growl of a car that was reluctant to start. "Grr-rrr-rrr," she said, imitating the sound of the motor.

"Ramona, don't dawdle." Mrs. Quimby was whisking about the living room, picking up newspapers, straightening cushions, running a dustcloth over the windowsills and coffee table. Light housekeeping, she called it. Mrs. Quimby did not like to come home to an untidy house.

Ramona ate a few spoonfuls of oatmeal, but somehow her spoon felt heavy this morning.

"And drink your milk," said her mother. "Remember, you can't do good work in school if you don't eat a good breakfast."

Ramona paid scant attention to this little speech that she heard almost every morning. Out of habit, she drank her milk and managed most of her toast. In the garage the car stopped growling and started to throb.

Ramona had left the table and was brushing her teeth when she heard her father call in through the back door to her mother, "Dorothy, can you come and steer the car while I push it into the street? I can't get it to go into reverse."

Ramona rinsed her mouth and rushed to the front window in time to see her father put all his strength into pushing the now silent car slowly down the driveway and into the street while her mother steered. At the foot of the driveway, Mrs. Quimby started the motor and drove the car forward beside the curb.

"Now try it in reverse," Mr. Quimby directed.

In a moment Mrs. Quimby called out, "It won't go."

Ramona put on her coat, picked up her lunch box, and hurried out to see what happened when a car would go forward but not backward. She soon discovered her parents found nothing funny about this state of affairs.

"I'll have to take it to the mechanic." Mr. Quimby looked cross. "And then take a bus, which means missing my first class."

"Let me take it, and you hurry and catch a bus now," said Mrs. Quimby. "The answering service can take the doctor's messages a few minutes longer until I get to the office." Then, noticing Ramona standing on the sidewalk, she said, "Run along or you'll miss your bus," and blew Ramona a kiss.

"What if you have to back up?" asked Ramona.

"With luck I won't have to," her mother answered. "Hurry along now."

"So long, Ramona," said Mr. Quimby. Ramona could see that he was more concerned with the car than with her. Perhaps this knowledge made her feet seem heavier than usual as she plodded off to her bus stop. The ride to school seemed longer than usual. When Yard Ape said, "Hi, Egghead," she did

not bother to answer, "Deviled Egghead to you," as she had planned.

When school started, Ramona sat quietly filling spaces in her workbook, trying to insert the right numbers into the right spaces but not much caring if she failed. Her head felt heavy, and her fingers did not want to move. She thought of telling Mrs. Whaley that she did not feel good, but her teacher was busy writing a list of words on the blackboard and would probably think anyone who interrupted was a nuisance.

Ramona propped her head on her fist, looking at twenty-six glass jars of blue oatmeal. *Oh-h-h.* She did not want to think about blue oatmeal or white oatmeal or any oatmeal at all. She sat motionless, hoping the terrible feeling would go away. She knew she should tell her teacher, but by now Ramona was too miserable even to raise her hand. If she did not move, not even her little finger or an eyelash, she might feel better.

Go away, blue oatmeal, thought Ramona, and then she knew that the most terrible, horrible, dreadful, awful thing that could happen was going to happen. Please, God, don't let me. . . . Ramona prayed too late.

The terrible, horrible, dreadful, awful thing happened. Ramona threw up. She threw up right there on the floor in front of everyone. One second her breakfast was where it belonged. Then everything in her middle seemed to go into reverse, and there was her breakfast on the floor.

Ramona had never felt worse in her whole life. Tears of shame welled in her eyes as she was aware of the shock and horror of everyone around her. She heard Mrs. Whaley say, "Oh, dear—Marsha, take Ramona to the office. Danny, run and tell Mr. Watts that someone threw up. Children, you may hold your noses and file into the hall until Mr. Watts comes and cleans up."

Her instructions made Ramona feel even worse. Tears streamed down her face, and she longed for Beezus, now far away in junior high school, to come and help her. She let Marsha guide her down the steps and through the hall as the rest of her class, noses pinched between thumbs and forefingers, hurried out of the classroom.

"It's all right, Ramona," Marsha said gently, while keeping her distance as if she expected Ramona to explode.

Ramona was crying too hard to answer. Nobody, nobody in the whole world, was a bigger nuisance than someone who threw up in school. Until now she thought Mrs. Whaley had been unfair when she called her a nuisance, but now—there was no escaping the truth—she really *was* a nuisance, a horrible runny-nosed nuisance with nothing to blow her nose on.

When Ramona and Marsha entered the office, Marsha was eager to break the news. "Oh, Mrs. Larson," she said, "Ramona threw up." Even the principal, sitting at his desk in the inner office, heard the news. Ramona knew he would not come out and start being her pal, because nobody wanted to be a pal to someone who threw up.

Mrs. Larson, seizing a Kleenex from a box on her desk, sprang from her typewriter. "Too bad," she said calmly, as if throwers–up came into the office every day. "Blow," she directed, as she held the Kleenex to Ramona's nose. Ramona blew. The principal, of course, stayed in his office where he was safe.

Mrs. Larson then took Ramona into the little room off the office, the same room in which she had washed egg out of Ramona's hair. She handed Ramona a paper cup of water. "You want to rinse your mouth, don't you?" Ramona nodded, rinsed, and felt better. Mrs. Larson did not behave as if she were a nuisance.

The school secretary laid a sheet of clean paper on the pillow on the cot, motioned Ramona to lie down, and then covered her with a blanket. "I'll phone your mother and ask her to come and take you home," she said.

"But she's at work," Ramona whispered, because speaking aloud might send her stomach into reverse again. "And Daddy is at school."

"I see," said Mrs. Larson. "Where do you go after school?"

"To Howie Kemp's house," said Ramona, closing her eyes and wishing she could go to sleep and not wake up until all this misery was over. She was aware that Mrs. Larson dialed a number and after a few moments replaced the receiver. Howie's grandmother was not home.

Then the terrible, horrible, dreadful, awful feeling returned. "Mrs. L-Larson," quavered Ramona. "I'm going to throw up."

In an instant, Mrs. Larson was holding Ramona's head in front of the toilet. "It's a good thing I have three children of my own so I'm used to this sort of thing," she said. When Ramona had finished, she handed her another cup of water and said cheerfully, "You must feel as if you've just thrown up your toenails."

Ramona managed a weak and wavery smile. "Who's going to take care of me?" she asked, as Mrs. Larson covered her with the blanket once more.

"Don't worry," said Mrs. Larson. "We'll find someone, and until we do, you rest right here."

Ramona felt feeble, exhausted, and grateful to Mrs. Larson. Closing her eyes had never felt so good, and the next thing she knew she heard her mother whispering, "Ramona." She lifted heavy lids to see her mother standing over her.

"Do you feel like going home?" Mrs. Quimby asked gently. She was already holding Ramona's coat.

Tears filled Ramona's eyes. She was not sure her legs would stand up, and how would they get home without a car? And what was her mother doing here when she was supposed to be at work? Would she lose her job?

Mrs. Quimby helped Ramona to her feet and draped her coat over her shoulders. "I have a taxi waiting," she said, as she guided Ramona toward the door.

Mrs. Larson looked up from her typewriter. "'Bye, Ramona. We'll miss you," she said. "I hope you'll feel better soon."

Ramona had forgotten what it was like to feel better. Outside a yellow taxicab was chugging at the curb. A taxi! Ramona had never ridden in a taxicab, and now she was too sick to enjoy it. Any other time she would have felt important to be leaving school in a taxi in the middle of the morning.

As Ramona climbed in, she saw the driver look her over as if he were doubtful about something. I will not throw up in a taxi, Ramona willed herself. I will not. A taxi is too expensive to throw up in. She added

silent words to God, Don't let me throw up in a taxi.

Carefully Ramona laid her head in her mother's lap and with every click of the meter thought, I will not throw up in a taxi. And she did not. She managed to wait until she was home and in the bathroom.

How good Ramona's bed felt with its clean white sheets. She let her mother wipe her face and hands with a cool washcloth and later take her temperature. Afterward, Ramona did not care about much of anything.

Late in the afternoon she awoke when Beezus whispered, "Hi," from the doorway.

When Mr. Quimby came home, he too paused in the doorway. "How's my girl?" he inquired softly.

"Sick," answered Ramona, feeling pitiful. "How's the car?"

"Still sick," answered her father. "The

mechanic was so busy he couldn't work on it today."

In a while Ramona was aware that her family was eating dinner without her, but she did not care. Later Mrs. Quimby took Ramona's temperature again, propped her up, and held a glass of fizzy drink to her lips, which surprised Ramona. Her mother did not approve of junk foods.

"I talked to the pediatrician," Mrs. Quimby explained, "and she said to give you this because you need fluids."

The drink gave Ramona a sneezy feeling in her nose. She waited anxiously. Would it stay down? Yes. She sipped again, and in a moment again.

"Good girl," whispered her mother.

Ramona fell back and turned her face into her pillow. Remembering what had happened at school, she began to cry.

"Dear heart," said her mother. "Don't cry.

You just have a touch of stomach flu. You'll feel better in a day or so."

Ramona's voice was muffled. "No, I won't."

"Yes, you will." Mrs. Quimby patted Ramona through the bedclothes.

Ramona turned enough to look at her mother with one teary eye. "You don't know what happened," she said.

Mrs. Quimby looked concerned. "What happened?"

"I threw up on the floor in front of the whole class," sobbed Ramona.

Her mother was reassuring. "Everybody knows you didn't throw up on purpose, and you certainly aren't the first child to do so." She thought a moment and said, "But you should have told Mrs. Whaley you didn't feel good."

Ramona could not bring herself to admit her teacher thought she was a nuisance. She let out a long, quavery sob.

Mrs. Quimby patted Ramona again and turned out the light. "Now go to sleep," she said, "and you'll feel better in the morning."

Ramona was sure that, although her stomach might feel better in the morning, the rest of her would still feel terrible. She wondered what nickname Yard Ape would give her this time and what Mrs. Whaley said to the school secretary about her at lunchtime. As she fell asleep, she decided she was a supernuisance, and a sick one at that.

7

The Patient

During the night Ramona was half awakened when her mother wiped her face with a cool washcloth and lifted her head from the pillow to help her sip something cold. Later, as the shadows of the room were fading, Ramona had to hold a thermometer under her tongue for what seemed like a long time. She felt safe, knowing her mother was watching over her. Safe but sick.

No sooner did she find a cool place on her pillow than it became too hot for comfort, and Ramona turned again.

As her room grew light, Ramona dozed off, faintly aware that her family was moving quietly so they would not disturb her. One tiny corner of her mind was pleased by this consideration. She heard breakfast sounds, and then she must have fallen completely asleep, because the next thing she knew she was awake and the house was silent. Had they all gone off and left her? No, someone was moving quietly in the kitchen. Howie's grandmother must have come to stay with her.

Ramona's eyes blurred. Her family had all gone off and left her when she was sick. She blinked away the tears and discovered on her bedside table a cartoon her father had drawn for her. It showed Ramona leaning against one tree and the family car leaning against another. He had drawn her with crossed eyes and a turned-down mouth. The car's headlights were crossed and its front bumper turned down like Ramona's mouth. They both looked sick. Ramona discovered she remembered how to smile. She also discovered she felt hot and sweaty instead of hot and dry. For a moment she struggled to sit up and then fell back on her pillow. Sitting up was too much work. She longed for her

mother, and suddenly, as if her wish were granted, her mother was entering the bedroom with a basin of water and a towel.

"Mother!" croaked Ramona. "Why aren't you at work?"

"Because I stayed home to take care of you," Mrs. Quimby answered, as she gently washed Ramona's face and hands. "Feeling better?"

"Sort of." In some ways Ramona felt better, but she also felt sweaty, weak, and worried. "Are you going to lose your job?" she asked, remembering the time her father had been out of work.

"No. The receptionist who retired was glad to come in for a few days to take my place." Mrs. Quimby gave Ramona a sponge bath and helped her into cool, dry pajamas. "There," she said. "How about some tea and toast?"

"Grown-up tea?" asked Ramona, relieved

that her mother's job was safe so that her father wouldn't have to drop out of school.

"Grown-up tea," answered her mother, as she propped Ramona up with an extra pillow. In a few minutes she brought a tray that held a slice of dry toast and a cup of weak tea.

Nibbling and sipping left Ramona tired and gloomy.

"Cheer up," said Mrs. Quimby, when she came to remove the tray. "Your temperature is down, and you're going to be all right."

Ramona did feel a little better. Her mother was right. She had not thrown up on purpose. Other children had done the same thing. There was that boy in kindergarten and the girl in first grade. . . .

Ramona dozed off, and when she awoke, she was bored and cranky. She wanted butter on the toast her mother brought her and scowled when her mother said people with stomach flu should not eat butter.

Mrs. Quimby smiled and said, "I can tell you're beginning to get well when you act like a wounded tiger."

Ramona scowled. "I am *not* acting like a wounded tiger," she informed her mother. When Mrs. Quimby made her a bed on the living-room couch so she could watch television, she was cross with the television set because she found daytime programs dumb, stupid, and boring. Commercials were much more interesting than the programs. She lay back and hoped for a cat-food commercial because she liked to look at nice cats. As she waited, she brooded about her teacher.

"Of course I didn't throw up on purpose," Ramona told herself. Mrs. Whaley should know that. And deep down inside I am really a nice person, she comforted herself. Mrs. Whaley should know that, too.

"Who pays teachers?" Ramona suddenly

asked, when her mother came into the room.

"Why, we all do." Mrs. Quimby seemed surprised by the question. "We pay taxes, and teachers' salaries come out of tax money."

Ramona knew that taxes were something unpleasant that worried parents. "I think you should stop paying taxes," Ramona informed her mother.

Mrs. Quimby looked amused. "I wish we could—at least until we finish paying for the room we added to the house. Whatever put such an idea into your head?"

"Mrs. Whaley doesn't like me," Ramona answered. "She is supposed to like me. It's her job to like me."

All Mrs. Quimby had to say was, "If you're this grouchy at school, liking you could be hard work."

Ramona was indignant. Her mother was supposed to feel sorry for her poor, weak little girl.

Picky-picky strolled into the living room and stared at Ramona as if he felt she did not belong on the couch. With an arthritic leap, he jumped up beside her on the blanket, washed himself from his ears to the tip of his tail, kneaded the blanket, and, purring, curled up beside Ramona, who lay very still so he would not go away. When he was asleep, she petted him gently. Picky-picky usually avoided her because she was noisy, or so her mother said.

A funny man appeared on the television screen. He had eaten a pizza, which had given him indigestion. He groaned. "I can't believe I ate the *whole* thing." Ramona smiled.

The next commercial showed a cat stepping back and forth in a little dance. "Do you think we could train Picky-picky to do that?" Ramona asked her mother.

Mrs. Quimby was amused at the idea of old Picky-picky dancing. "I doubt it," she said.

"That cat isn't really dancing. They just turn the film back and forth so it looks as if he's dancing."

How disappointing. Ramona dozed while another cat-food commercial appeared. She awoke enough to watch a big yellow cat ignore several brands of cat food before he settled down to eat a bowl of dry food silently. That's funny, thought Ramona. When Picky-picky ate dry cat food, he ground and crunched so noisily she could hear him from any room in the house, but television cats never made any sound at all when they ate. The commercials lied. That's what they did. Ramona was cross with cat-food commercials. Cheaters! She was angry with the whole world.

Late that afternoon Ramona was aroused once more by the doorbell. Was it someone interesting? She hoped so, for she was bored. The visitor turned out to be Sara.

Ramona lay back on her pillow and tried to look pale and weak as her mother said, "Why, hello, Sara. I'm glad to see you, but I don't think you should come in until Ramona is feeling better."

"That's all right," said Sara. "I just brought some letters the class wrote to Ramona, and Mrs. Whaley sent a book for her to read."

"Hi, Sara," said Ramona with the weakest smile she could manage.

"Mrs. Whaley said to tell you this book is not for DEAR. This one is for a book report," Sara explained from the doorway.

Ramona groaned.

"She said to tell you," Sara continued, "that she wants us to stand up in front of the class and pretend we are selling the book. She doesn't want us to tell the whole story. She says she has already heard all the stories quite a few times."

Ramona felt worse. Not only would she

have to give a book report, she would have to listen to twenty-five book reports given by other people, another reason for wanting to stay home.

When Sara left, Ramona examined the big envelope she had brought. Mrs. Whaley had written Ramona's name on the front with a floppy cursive capital Q and beneath it in her big handwriting, "Miss you!" followed by a picture of a whale and y.

I bet she doesn't mean it, thought Ramona. She opened the envelope of the first letters anyone had ever written to her. "Mother, they wrote in cursive!" she cried, delighted. Although all the letters said much the same thing—we are sorry you are sick and hope you get well soon—they made Ramona feel good. She knew they were written to teach letter writing and handwriting at the same time, but she didn't care.

One letter was different. Yard Ape had

written, "Dear Superfoot, Get well or I will eat your eraser." Ramona smiled because his letter showed he liked her. She looked forward to the return of her father and sister so she could show off her mail.

Bored with television and cramped from lying still so she would not disturb Picky-picky, Ramona waited. How sorry they would be to see her so pale and thin. Surely her father would bring her a little present, something to entertain her while she had to stay in bed. A paperback book because she could now read books with chapters? New crayons? Her father understood the importance of sharp-pointed crayons to someone who liked to draw.

Beezus arrived first with an armload of books that she dropped on a chair. "Homework!" she said and groaned. Now that she was in junior high school, she was always talking about all the work she had to do, as if Ramona did nothing in school. "How do you feel?" she finally got around to asking.

"Sick," said Ramona in a faint voice, "but my whole class wrote to me."

Beezus glanced at the sheaf of letters. "They copied them off the blackboard," she said.

"Writing a whole letter in cursive is hard work for lots of people when they are in the third grade." Ramona was hurt at having her letters belittled. She pushed Picky-picky off the couch so she could stretch her legs. The television droned on and on.

"I wonder what's keeping your father," remarked Mrs. Quimby, looking out the front window.

Ramona knew why her father was late, but she did not say so. He was buying her a little present because she was sick. She could hardly wait. "My class is giving book reports," she informed Beezus, so her sister would know she had schoolwork to do too. "We have to pretend to sell a book to someone."

"We did that a couple of times," said Beezus. "Teachers always tell you not to tell the whole story, and half the kids finish by saying, 'If you want to know what happens next, read the book,' and somebody always says, 'Read this book, or I'll punch you in the nose.'"

Ramona knew who would say that in her

class. Yard Ape, that was who.

"Here he comes now," said Mrs. Quimby, and she hurried to open the door for Ramona's father, who kissed her as he entered.

"Where's the car?" she asked.

"Bad news." Mr. Quimby sounded tired. "It has to have a new transmission."

"Oh, no!" Mrs. Quimby was shocked. "How much is that going to cost?"

Mr. Quimby looked grim. "Plenty. More than we can afford."

"We'll have to afford it somehow," said Mrs. Quimby. "We can't manage without a car."

"The transmission people are letting us pay it off in installments," he explained, "and I'll manage to get in some more hours as Santa's Little Helper at the warehouse."

"I wish there were some other way. . . ." Mrs. Quimby looked sad as she went into the kitchen to attend to supper.

Only then did Mr. Quimby turn his attention to Ramona. "How's my little punkin?" he asked.

"Sick." Ramona forgot to look pitiful, she was so disappointed that her father had not brought her a present.

"Cheer up," Mr. Quimby half smiled. "At least you don't need a new transmission, and you'll feel better tomorrow."

"What's a transmission?" asked Ramona.

"That's what makes the car go," explained her father.

"Oh," said Ramona. Then to show her father that her life was not so easy, she added, "I have to give a book report at school."

"Well, make it interesting," said Mr. Quimby, as he went off to wash for supper.

Ramona knew her father was worried, but she could not help thinking he might have felt sorrier for his sick little girl. Anyone would think he loved the car more. She lay back genuinely weak, exhausted by television, and sorry her father would have to work more hours in the frozen-food warehouse where, no matter how many pairs of woolen socks he wore, his feet were always cold and he sometimes had to go outside until feeling came back into his cheeks.

When her mother, after serving the rest of the family, said the time had come for Ramona to get into her own bed and have a little supper on a tray, she was ready to go. The thought that her mother did not think she was a nuisance comforted her.

8

Ramona's Book Report

The Quimby family was full of worries. The parents were worried about managing without a car while a new transmission was installed and even more worried about paying for it. Beezus was worried about a party she had been invited to, because boys had also been invited. She was afraid it would turn out to be a dancing party, and she felt silly trying to dance. Besides, eighth-grade boys acted like a bunch of little kids at parties. Ramona, still feeling weak, moped around the house for another day worrying about her book report. If she made it interesting, Mrs. Whaley would think she was showing off. If she did not make it interesting, her teacher would not like it.

On top of everything, Beezus happened to look at her father's head as he bent over his books at the dining-room table that evening. "Daddy, you're getting thin on top!" she cried out, shocked.

Ramona rushed to look. "Just a little thin," she said, because she did not want her father's feelings hurt. "You aren't bald yet."

Mrs. Quimby also examined the top of her husband's head. "It *is* a little thin," she agreed, and kissed the spot. "Never mind. I found a gray hair last week."

"What is this? A conference about my hair?" asked Mr. Quimby, and he grabbed his wife around the waist. "Don't worry," he told

her. "I'll still love you when you're old and
gray."

"Thanks a lot," said Mrs. Quimby, not
wanting to think of herself as old and gray.
They both laughed. Mr. Quimby released
his wife and gave her a playful slap on the
bottom, an act that amused and shocked his
daughters.

Ramona had two feelings about this conversation. She did not want her father's hair to grow thin or her mother's hair to grow gray. She wanted her parents to stay exactly as they were for ever and ever. But oh, how good it was to see them be so affectionate with one another. She knew her mother and father loved one another, but sometimes, when they were tired and hurried, or when they had long, serious conversations after the girls had gone to bed, she wondered and worried, because she knew children whose parents had stopped loving one another. Now she knew everything was all right.

Suddenly Ramona felt so happy that a book report did not seem so difficult after all—if she could think of a way to make it interesting.

The book, *The Left-Behind Cat*, which Mrs. Whaley had sent home for Ramona to read for her report, was divided into chapters but used babyish words. The story was about a cat that was left behind when a family moved away and about its adventures with a dog, another cat, and some children before it finally found a home with a nice old couple who gave it a saucer of cream and named it Lefty because its left paw was white and because it had been left behind. Medium-boring, thought Ramona, good enough to pass the time on the bus, but not good enough to read during Sustained Silent Reading. Besides, cream cost too much to give to a cat. The most the old people would give a cat was half-and-half, she thought. Ramona required accuracy from books as well as from people.

"Daddy, how do you sell something?" Ramona interrupted her father, who was studying, even though she knew she should not. However, her need for an answer was urgent.

Mr. Quimby did not look up from his book. "You ought to know. You see enough commercials on television."

Ramona considered his answer. She had always looked upon commercials as entertainment, but now she thought about some of her favorites—the cats that danced back and forth, the dog that pushed away brand-X dog food with his paw, the man who ate a pizza, got indigestion, and groaned that he couldn't believe he ate the *whole* thing, the six horses that pulled the Wells Fargo bank's stagecoach across deserts and over mountains.

"Do you mean I should do a book report like a TV commercial?" Ramona asked.

"Why not?" Mr. Quimby answered in an absentminded way.

"I don't want my teacher to say I'm a nuisance," said Ramona, needing assurance from a grown-up.

This time Mr. Quimby lifted his eyes

from his book. "Look," he said, "she told you to pretend you're selling the book, so sell it. What better way than a TV commercial? You aren't being a nuisance if you do what your teacher asks." He looked at Ramona a moment and said, "Why do you worry she'd think you're a nuisance?"

Ramona stared at the carpet, wiggled her toes inside her shoes, and finally said, "I squeaked my shoes the first day of school."

"That's not being much of a nuisance," said Mr. Quimby.

"And when I got egg in my hair, Mrs. Whaley said I was a nuisance," confessed Ramona, "and then I threw up in school."

"But you didn't do those things on purpose," her father pointed out. "Now run along. I have studying to do."

Ramona thought this answer over and decided that since her parents agreed, they must be right. Well, Mrs. Whaley could just go jump in a lake, even though her teacher had written, without wasting words, that she missed her. Ramona was going to give her book report any way she wanted. So there, Mrs. Whaley.

Ramona went to her room and looked at her table, which the family called "Ramona's studio," because it was a clutter of crayons, different kinds of paper, Scotch tape, bits of yarn, and odds and ends that Ramona used for amusing herself. Then Ramona thought a moment, and suddenly, filled with inspiration, she went to work. She knew exactly what she wanted to do and set about doing it. She worked with paper, crayons, Scotch tape, and rubber bands. She worked so hard and with such pleasure that her cheeks grew pink. Nothing in the whole world felt as good as being able to make something from a sudden idea.

Finally, with a big sigh of relief, Ramona

leaned back in her chair to admire her work: three cat masks with holes for eyes and mouths, masks that could be worn by hooking rubber bands over ears. But Ramona did not stop there. With pencil and paper, she began to write out what she would say. She was so full of ideas that she printed rather

than waste time in cursive writing. Next she phoned Sara and Janet, keeping her voice low and trying not to giggle so she wouldn't disturb her father any more than necessary, and explained her plan to them. Both her friends giggled and agreed to take part in the book report. Ramona spent the rest of the evening memorizing what she was going to say.

The next morning on the bus and at school, no one even mentioned Ramona's throwing up. She had braced herself for some remark from Yard Ape, but all he said was, "Hi, Superfoot." When school started, Ramona slipped cat masks to Sara and Janet, handed her written excuse for her absence to Mrs. Whaley, and waited, fanning away escaped fruit flies, for book reports to begin.

After arithmetic, Mrs. Whaley called on several people to come to the front of the room to pretend they were selling books to the class. Most of the reports began, "This is a book about . . ." and many, as Beezus had predicted, ended with ". . . if you want to find out what happens next, read the book."

Then Mrs. Whaley said, "We have time for one more report before lunch. Who wants to be next?"

Ramona waved her hand, and Mrs. Whaley nodded.

Ramona beckoned to Sara and Janet, who giggled in an embarrassed way but joined Ramona, standing behind her and off to one side. All three girls slipped on their cat masks and giggled again. Ramona took a deep breath as Sara and Janet began to chant, "*Meow*, meow, meow, meow. *Meow*, meow, meow, meow," and danced back and forth like the cats they had seen in the cat-food commercial on television.

"*Left-Behind Cat* gives kids something to smile about," said Ramona in a loud clear voice, while her chorus meowed softly behind her. She wasn't sure that what she said was exactly true, but neither were the commercials that showed cats eating dry cat food without making any noise. "Kids who have tried *Left-Behind Cat* are all smiles, smiles, smiles. *Left-Behind Cat* is the book kids ask for by name. Kids can read it every day and thrive on it. The happiest kids read *Left-Behind Cat*. *Left-Behind Cat* contains cats, dogs, people—" Here Ramona caught sight of Yard Ape leaning back in his seat, grinning in the way that always flustered her. She could not help interrupting herself with a giggle, and after suppressing it she tried not to look at Yard Ape and to take up where she had left off. ". . . cats, dogs, people—" The giggle came back, and Ramona was lost. She could not remember what came next. ". . . cats, dogs, people," she repeated, trying to start and failing.

Mrs. Whaley and the class waited. Yard Ape

grinned. Ramona's loyal chorus meowed and danced. This performance could not go on all morning. Ramona had to say something, anything to end the waiting, the meowing, her book report. She tried desperately to recall a cat-food commercial, any cat-food commercial, and could not. All she could remember was the man on television who ate the pizza, and so she blurted out the only sentence she could think of, "I can't believe I read the *whole* thing!"

Mrs. Whaley's laugh rang out above the laughter of the class. Ramona felt her face turn red behind her mask, and her ears, visible to the class, turned red as well.

"Thank you, Ramona," said Mrs. Whaley. "That was most entertaining. Class, you are excused for lunch."

Ramona felt brave behind her cat mask. "Mrs. Whaley," she said, as the class pushed back chairs and gathered up lunch boxes, "that wasn't the way my report was supposed to end."

"Did you like the book?" asked Mrs. Whaley.

"Not really," confessed Ramona.

"Then I think it was a good way to end your report," said the teacher. "Asking the class to sell books they really don't like isn't fair, now that I stop to think about it. I was only trying to make book reports a little livelier."

Encouraged by this confession and still safe behind her mask, Ramona had the boldness to speak up. "Mrs. Whaley," she said with her heart pounding, "you told Mrs. Larson that I'm a nuisance, and I don't think I am."

Mrs. Whaley looked astonished. "When did I say that?"

"The day I got egg in my hair," said Ramona. "You called me a show-off and said I was a nuisance."

Mrs. Whaley frowned, thinking. "Why, Ramona, I can recall saying something about my little show-off, but I meant it affectionately, and I'm sure I never called you a nuisance."

"Yes, you did," insisted Ramona. "You said I was a show-off, and then you said, 'What a nuisance.'" Ramona could never forget those exact words.

Mrs. Whaley, who had looked worried, smiled in relief. "Oh, Ramona, you misunderstood," she said. "I meant that trying to wash egg out of your hair was a nuisance for Mrs. Larson. I didn't mean that you personally were a nuisance."

Ramona felt a little better, enough to come out from under her mask to say, "I wasn't showing off. I was just trying to crack an egg on my head like everyone else."

Mrs. Whaley's smile was mischievous. "Tell me, Ramona," she said, "don't you ever try to show off?"

Ramona was embarrassed. "Well . . . maybe . . . sometimes, a little," she admitted. Then she added positively, "But I wasn't showing off that day. How could I be showing off when I was doing what everyone else was doing?"

"You've convinced me," said Mrs. Whaley with a big smile. "Now run along and eat your lunch."

Ramona snatched up her lunch box and went jumping down the stairs to the cafeteria. She laughed to herself because she knew exactly what all the boys and girls from her class would say when they finished their lunches. She knew because she planned to say it herself. "I can't believe I ate the *whole* thing!"

9
Rainy Sunday

Rainy Sunday afternoons in November were always dismal, but Ramona felt this Sunday was the most dismal of all. She pressed her nose against the living-room window, watching the ceaseless rain pelting down as bare black branches clawed at the electric wires in front of the house. Even lunch, leftovers Mrs. Quimby had wanted to clear out of the refrigerator, had been dreary,

with her parents, who seemed tired or dis-
couraged or both, having little to say and
Beezus mysteriously moody. Ramona longed
for sunshine, sidewalks dry enough for roller-
skating, a smiling, happy family.

"Ramona, you haven't cleaned up your
room this weekend," said Mrs. Quimby, who
was sitting on the couch, sorting through
a stack of bills. "And don't press your nose
against the window. It leaves a smudge."

Ramona felt as if everything she did was
wrong. The whole family seemed cross today,
even Picky-picky who meowed at the front
door. With a sigh, Mrs. Quimby got up to let
him out. Beezus, carrying a towel and sham-
poo, stalked through the living room into
the kitchen, where she began to wash her
hair at the sink. Mr. Quimby, studying at the
dining-room table as usual, made his pencil
scratch angrily across a pad of paper. The
television set sat blank and mute, and in the

fireplace a log sullenly refused to burn.

Mrs. Quimby sat down and then got up again as Picky-picky, indignant at the wet world outdoors, yowled to come in. "Ramona, clean up your room," she ordered, as she let the cat and a gust of cold air into the house.

"Beezus hasn't cleaned up her room." Ramona could not resist pointing this omission out to her mother.

"I'm not talking about Beezus," said Mrs. Quimby. "I'm talking about you."

Still Ramona did not move from the window. Cleaning up her room seemed such a boring thing to do, no fun at all on a rainy afternoon. She thought vaguely of all the exciting things she would like to do—learn to twirl a lariat, play a musical saw, flip around and over bars in a gymnastic competition while crowds cheered.

"Ramona, *clean up your room!*" Mrs. Quimby raised her voice.

"Well, you don't have to yell at me." Ramona's feelings were hurt by the tone of her mother's voice. The log in the fireplace settled, sending a puff of smoke into the living room.

"Then do it," snapped Mrs. Quimby. "Your room is a disaster area."

Mr. Quimby threw down his pencil. "Young lady, you do what your mother says, and you do it now. She shouldn't have to tell you three times."

"Well, all right, but you don't have to be so cross," said Ramona. To herself she thought, Nag, nag, nag.

Sulkily Ramona took her hurt feelings off to her room, where she pulled a week's collection of dirty socks from under her bed. On her way to the bathroom hamper, she looked down the hall and saw her sister standing in the living room, rubbing her hair with a towel.

"Mother, I think you're mean," said Beezus

from under the towel.

Ramona stopped to listen.

"I don't care how mean you think I am," answered Mrs. Quimby. "You are not going to go, and that is that."

"But all the other girls are going," protested Beezus.

"I don't care if they are," said Mrs. Quimby. "You are not."

Ramona heard the sound of a pencil being slammed on the table and her father saying, "Your mother is right. Now would you kindly give me a little peace and quiet so I can get on with my work."

Beezus flounced past Ramona into her room and slammed the door. Sobs were heard, loud, angry sobs.

Where can't she go? Ramona wondered, as she dumped her socks into the hamper. Then, because she had been so good about picking up her room, Ramona returned to

the living room, where Picky-picky, as cross and bored as the rest of the family, was once again meowing at the front door. "Where can't Beezus go?" she asked.

Mrs. Quimby opened the front door, and when Picky-picky hesitated, vexed by the cold wind that swept into the room, assisted him out with her toe. "She can't sleep over at Mary Jane's house with a bunch of girls from her class."

A year ago Ramona would have agreed with her mother so that her mother would love her more than Beezus, but this year she knew that she too might want to spend the night at someone's house someday. "Why can't Beezus sleep at Mary Jane's?" she asked.

"Because she comes home exhausted and grouchy." Mrs. Quimby stood by the door, waiting. Picky-picky's yowl was twisted by the wind, and when she opened the door, another cold gust swept through the house.

"With the price of fuel oil being what it is, we can't afford to let the cat out," remarked Mr. Quimby.

"Would you like to take the responsibility

if I don't let him out?" asked Mrs. Quimby, before she continued with her answer to Ramona. "There are four people in the family, and she has no right to make the whole day disagreeable for the rest of us because she has been up half the night giggling with a bunch of silly girls. Besides, a growing girl needs her rest."

Ramona silently agreed with her mother about Beezus's coming home cross after such a party. At the same time, she wanted to make things easier for herself when she was in junior high school. "Maybe this time they would go to sleep earlier," she suggested.

"Fat chance," said Mrs. Quimby, who rarely spoke so rudely. "And furthermore, Ramona, Mrs. Kemp did not come right out and say so, but she did drop a hint that you are not playing as nicely with Willa Jean as you might."

Ramona heaved a sigh that seemed to

come from the soles of her feet. In the bedroom, Beezus, who had run out of real sobs, was working hard to force out fake sobs to show her parents how mean they were to her.

Mrs. Quimby ignored the sighs and the sobs and continued. "Ramona, you know that getting along at the Kemps' is your job in this family. I've told you that before."

How could Ramona explain to her mother that Willa Jean had finally caught on that Sustained Silent Reading was just plain reading a book? For a while, Willa Jean wanted Ramona to read aloud a few boring books the Kemps owned, the sort of books people who did not know anything about children so often gave them. Willa Jean listened to them several times, grew bored, and now insisted on playing beauty shop. Ramona did not want her fingernails painted by Willa Jean and knew she would be blamed if Willa Jean spilled nail polish. Instead of Mrs. Kemp's taking care of Ramona, Ramona was taking care of Willa Jean.

Ramona looked at the carpet, sighed again, and said, "I try." She felt sorry for herself, misunderstood and unappreciated. Nobody in the whole world understood how hard it was to go to the Kemps' house after school when she did not have a bicycle.

Mrs. Quimby relented. "I know it isn't easy," she said with a half smile, "but don't give up." She gathered up the bills and checkbook and went into the kitchen, where she began to write checks at the kitchen table.

Ramona wandered into the dining room to seek comfort from her father. She laid her cheek against the sleeve of his plaid shirt and asked, "Daddy, what are you studying?"

Once again Mr. Quimby threw down his pencil. "I am studying the cognitive processes of children," he answered.

Ramona raised her head to look at him.

159

"What does that mean?" she asked.

"How kids think," her father told her.

Ramona did not like the sound of this subject at all. "Why are you studying *that*?" she demanded. Some things should be private, and how children thought was one of them. She did not like the idea of grown-ups snooping around in thick books trying to find out.

"That is exactly what I have been asking myself." Mr. Quimby was serious. "Why am I studying this stuff when we have bills to pay?"

"Well, I don't think you should," said Ramona. "It's none of your business how kids think." Then she quickly added, because she did not want her father to drop out of school and be a checker again, "There are lots of other things you could study. Things like fruit flies."

Mr. Quimby smiled at Ramona and rumpled her hair. "I doubt if anyone could figure

out how you think," he said, which made Ramona feel better, as if her secret thoughts were still safe.

Mr. Quimby sat gnawing his pencil and staring out the window at the rain. Beezus, who had run out of fake sobs, emerged from her room, red-eyed and damp-haired, to stalk about the house not speaking to anyone.

Ramona flopped down on the couch. She

hated rainy Sundays, especially this one, and longed for Monday when she could escape to school. The Quimbys' house seemed to have grown smaller during the day until it was no longer big enough to hold her family and all its problems. She tried not to think of the half-overheard conversations of her parents after the girls had gone to bed, grown-up talk that Ramona understood just enough to know her parents were concerned about their future.

Ramona had deep, secret worries of her own. She worried that her father might accidentally be locked in the frozen-food warehouse, where it was so cold it sometimes snowed indoors. What if he was filling a big order, and the men who were lucky enough to get small orders to fill left work ahead of him and forgot and locked the warehouse, and he couldn't get out and froze to death? Of course that wouldn't happen. "But it might," insisted a tiny voice in the back of her mind. Don't be silly, she told the little voice. "Yes, but—" began the little voice. And despite the worry that would not go away Ramona wanted her father to go on working so he could stay in school and someday get a job he liked.

While Ramona worried, the house was silent except for the sound of rain and the scratch of her father's pencil. The smoking log settled in the fireplace, sending up a few feeble sparks. The day grew darker, Ramona was beginning to feel hungry, but there was no comfortable bustle of cooking in the kitchen.

Suddenly Mr. Quimby slammed shut his book and threw down his pencil so hard it bounced onto the floor. Ramona sat up. Now what was wrong?

"Come on, everybody," said her father. "Get cleaned up. Let's stop this grumping around. We are going out for dinner, and we are going to smile and be pleasant if it kills us. That's an order!"

The girls stared at their father and then at one another. What was going on? They had not gone out to dinner for months, so how could they afford to go now?

"To the Whopperburger?" asked Ramona.

"Sure," said Mr. Quimby, who appeared cheerful for the first time that day. "Why not? The sky's the limit."

Mrs. Quimby came into the living room with a handful of stamped envelopes. "But Bob——" she began.

"Now don't worry," her husband said. "We'll manage. During Thanksgiving I'll be putting in more hours in the warehouse and getting more overtime. There's no reason why we can't have a treat once in a while. And the Whopperburger isn't exactly your four-star gourmet restaurant."

Ramona was afraid her mother might give a lecture on the evils of junk food, but she did not. Gloom and anger were forgotten. Clothes were changed, hair combed, Picky-picky was shut in the basement, and the family was on its way in the old car with the new transmission that never balked at backing down the driveway. Off the Quimbys sped to the nearest Whopperburger, where they discovered other families must have wanted to get out of the house on a rainy day, for the restaurant was crowded, and they had to wait for a table.

There were enough chairs for the grown-ups and Beezus, but Ramona, who had the youngest legs, had to stand up. She amused herself by punching the buttons on the cigarette machine in time to the Muzak, which was playing "Tie a Yellow Ribbon 'Round the Old Oak Tree." She even danced a little to the music, and, when the tune came to an end, she turned around and found herself face to face with an old man with neatly trimmed gray hair and a moustache that turned up at the ends. He was dressed as if everything he wore—a flowered shirt, striped tie, tweed coat and plaid slacks—had come from different stores or from a rummage sale, except that the crease in his trousers was sharp and his shoes were shined.

The old man, whose back was very straight, saluted Ramona as if she were a soldier and said, "Well, young lady, have you been good to your mother?"

Ramona was stunned. She felt her face turn red to the tips of her ears. She did not know how to answer such a question. Had she been good to her mother? Well . . . not always, but why was this stranger asking? It was none of his business. He had no right to ask such a question.

Ramona looked to her parents for help

and discovered they were waiting with amusement for her answer. So were the rest of the people who were waiting for tables. Ramona scowled at the man. She did not have to answer him if she did not want to.

The hostess saved Ramona by calling out, "Quimby, party of four," and leading the family to a plastic-upholstered booth.

"Why didn't you answer the man?" Beezus was as amused as everyone else.

"I'm not supposed to talk to strangers," was Ramona's dignified answer.

"But Mother and Daddy are with us," Beezus pointed out, rather meanly, Ramona thought.

"Remember," said Mr. Quimby, as he opened his menu, "we are all going to smile and enjoy ourselves if it kills us."

As Ramona picked up her menu, she was still seething inside. Maybe she hadn't always been good to her mother, but that man had no right to pry. When she discovered he was seated in a single booth across the aisle, she gave him an indignant look, which he answered with a merry wink. So he had been teasing. Well, Ramona didn't like it.

When Ramona opened her menu, she made an exciting discovery. She no longer had to depend on colored pictures of hamburgers, French fries, chili, and steak to help her make up her mind. She could now read what was offered. She studied carefully, and when she came to the bottom of the menu, she read the dreaded words, "Child's Plate for Children Under Twelve." Then came the list of choices: fish sticks, chicken drumsticks, hot dogs. None of them, to Ramona, food for a treat. They were food for a school cafeteria.

"Daddy," Ramona whispered, "do I have to have a child's plate?"

"Not if you don't want to." Her father's smile was understanding. Ramona ordered the smallest adult item on the menu.

Whopperburger was noted for fast service, and in a few minutes the waitress set down the Quimbys' dinners: a hamburger and French fries for Ramona, a cheeseburger and French fries for Beezus and her mother, and hamburgers with chili for her father.

Ramona bit into her hamburger. Bliss. Warm, soft, juicy, tart with relish. Juice dribbled down her chin. She noticed her mother start to say something and change her mind. Ramona caught the dribble with her paper napkin before it reached her collar. The French fries—crisp on the outside, mealy on the inside—tasted better than anything Ramona had ever eaten.

The family ate in companionable silence for a few moments until the edge was taken off their hunger. "A little change once in a

while does make a difference," said Mrs. Quimby. "It does us all good."

"Especially after the way—" Ramona stopped herself from finishing with, "—after the way Beezus acted this afternoon." Instead she sat up straight and smiled.

"Well, I wasn't the only one who—" Beezus also stopped in midsentence and smiled. The parents looked stern, but they managed to smile. Suddenly everyone relaxed and laughed.

The old man, Ramona noticed, was eating a steak. She wished her father could afford a steak.

As much as she enjoyed her hamburger, Ramona was unable to finish. It was too much. She was happy when her mother did not say, "Someone's eyes are bigger than her stomach." Her father, without commenting on the unfinished hamburger, included her in the orders of apple pie with hot cinnamon sauce and ice cream.

Ramona ate what she could, and after watching the ice cream melt into the cinnamon sauce, she glanced over at the old man, who was having a serious discussion with the waitress. She seemed surprised and upset about something. The Muzak, conversation of other customers, and rattle of dishes made eavesdropping impossible. The waitress left. Ramona saw her speak to the manager, who listened and then nodded. For a moment Ramona thought the man might not have enough money to pay for the steak he had eaten. Apparently he did, however, for after listening to what the waitress had to say, he left a tip under the edge of his plate and picked up his check. To Ramona's embarrassment, he stood up, winked, and saluted her again. Then he left. Ramona did not know what to make of him.

She turned back to her family, whose smiles were now genuine rather than determined. The sight of them gave her courage to ask the question that had been nibbling at the back of her mind, "Daddy, you aren't going to be a college dropout, are you?"

Mr. Quimby finished a mouthful of pie

before he answered, "Nope."

Ramona wanted to make sure. "And you won't ever be a checker and come home cross again?"

"Well," said her father, "I can't promise I won't come home cross, but if I do, it won't be from standing at the cash register trying to remember forty-two price changes in the produce section while a long line of customers, all in a hurry, wait to pay for their groceries."

Ramona was reassured.

When the waitress descended on the Quimbys to offer the grown-ups a second cup of coffee, Mr. Quimby said, "Check, please."

The waitress looked embarrassed. "Well . . . a . . ." She hesitated. "This has never happened before, but your meals have already been paid for."

The Quimbys looked at her in astonishment. "But who paid for them?" demanded Mr. Quimby.

"A lonely gentleman who left a little while ago," answered the waitress.

"He must have been the man who sat across the aisle," said Mrs. Quimby. "But why would he pay for our dinners? We never saw him before in our lives."

The waitress smiled. "Because he said you are such a nice family, and because he misses his children and grandchildren." She dashed off with her pot of coffee, leaving the Quimbys in surprised, even shocked, silence. A nice family? After the way they had behaved on a rainy Sunday.

"A mysterious stranger just like in a book," said Beezus. "I never thought I'd meet one."

"Poor lonely man," said Mrs. Quimby at last, as Mr. Quimby shoved a tip under his saucer. Still stunned into silence, the family struggled into their wraps and splashed across the parking lot to their car, which started promptly and backed obediently out of its parking space. As the windshield wipers began their rhythmic exercise, the family rode in silence, each thinking of the events of the day.

"You know," said Mrs. Quimby thoughtfully, as the car left the parking lot and headed down the street, "I think he was right. We are a nice family."

"Not all the time," said Ramona, as usual demanding accuracy.

"Nobody is nice all the time," answered her father. "Or if they are, they are boring."

"Not even your parents are nice all the time," added Mrs. Quimby.

Ramona secretly agreed, but she had not expected her parents to admit it. Deep down inside, she felt she herself was nice all the time, but sometimes on the outside her niceness sort of—well, curdled. Then people did not understand how nice she really was. Maybe other people curdled too.

"We have our ups and downs," said Mrs. Quimby, "but we manage to get along, and we stick together."

"We are nicer than some families I know," said Beezus. "Some families don't even eat dinner together." After a moment she made a confession. "I don't really like sleeping on someone's floor in a sleeping bag."

"I didn't think you did." Mrs. Quimby reached back and patted Beezus on the knee. "That's one reason I said you couldn't go. You didn't want to go, but didn't want to admit it."

Ramona snuggled inside her car coat, feeling cozy enclosed in the car with the heater breathing warm air on her nice family. She was a member of a nice sticking-together family, and she was old enough to be depended upon, so she could ignore—or at

least try to ignore—a lot of things. Willa
Jean—she would try reading her Sustained
Silent Reading books aloud because Willa
Jean was old enough to understand most of
them. That should work for a little while.
Mrs. Whaley—some things were nice about

her and some were not. Ramona could get along.

"That man paying for our dinner was sort of like a happy ending," remarked Beezus, as the family, snug in their car, drove through the rain and the dark toward Klickitat Street.

"A happy ending for today," corrected Ramona. Tomorrow they would begin all over again.

BEVERLY CLEARY is one of America's most popular authors. Born in McMinnville, Oregon, she lived on a farm in Yamhill until she was six and then moved to Portland. After college, as the children's librarian in Yakima, Washington, she was challenged to find stories for non-readers. She wrote her first book, HENRY HUGGINS, in response to a boy's question, "Where are the books about kids like us?"

Mrs. Cleary's books have earned her many prestigious awards, including the American Library Association's Laura Ingalls Wilder Award, presented in recognition of her lasting contribution to children's literature. Her DEAR MR. HENSHAW was awarded the 1984 John Newbery Medal, and both RAMONA QUIMBY, AGE 8 and RAMONA AND HER FATHER have been named Newbery Honor Books. In addition, her books have won more than thirty-five statewide awards based on the votes of her young readers. Her characters, including Henry Huggins, Ellen Tebbits, Otis Spofford, and Beezus and Ramona Quimby, as well as Ribsy, Socks, and Ralph S. Mouse, have delighted children for generations. Mrs. Cleary lives in coastal California.

Visit Beverly Cleary on the World Wide Web at www.beverlycleary.com.

1

The Rich Uncle

"Guess what?" Ramona Quimby asked one Friday evening when her Aunt Beatrice dropped by to show off her new ski clothes and to stay for supper. Ramona's mother, father, and big sister Beezus, whose real name was Beatrice, paid no attention and went on eating. Picky-picky, the cat, meowed through the basement door, asking to share the meal.

Aunt Beatrice, who taught third grade, knew how to behave toward her third-grade niece. "What?" she asked, laying down her fork as if she expected to be astounded by Ramona's news.

Ramona took a deep breath and announced, "Howie Kemp's rich uncle is coming to visit." Except for Aunt Bea, her family was not as curious as Ramona had hoped. She plunged on anyway because she was happy for her friend. "Howie's grandmother is really excited, and so are Howie and Willa Jean." And so, to be truthful, was Ramona, who disliked having to go to the Kemps' house after school, where Howie's grandmother looked after her grandchildren and Ramona while the two mothers were at work. A rich uncle, even someone else's rich uncle, should make those long after-school hours more interesting.

"I didn't know Howie had a rich uncle," said Mrs. Quimby.

"He's Howie's father's little brother, only now he's big," explained Ramona.

"Why, that must be Hobart Kemp," said Aunt Beatrice. "He was in my class in high school."

"Oh, yes. I remember. That boy with the blond curly hair who played baseball." Mrs. Quimby motioned to her daughters to clear

3

away the plates. "All the girls said he was cute."

"That's the one," said Aunt Bea. "He used to chew licorice and spit on the grass to make the principal think he was chewing tobacco like a professional baseball player, which was what he wanted to be."

"Where's this cute licorice-chewing uncle coming from, and how did he get so rich?" asked Ramona's father, beginning to be interested. "Playing baseball?"

"He's coming from—" Ramona frowned. "I can't remember the name, but it sounds like a fairy tale and has camels." Narnia? Never-never-land? No, those names weren't right.

"Saudi Arabia," said Beezus, who also went to the Kemps' after school. Being in junior high school, she could take her time getting there.

"Yes, that's it!" Ramona wished she had remembered first. "Howie says he's bringing the whole family presents." She imagined bags of gold like those in *The Arabian Nights*, which Beezus had read to her. Of course, nobody carried around bags of gold today, but she enjoyed imagining them.

"What's Howie's uncle doing in Saudi Arabia?" asked Mr. Quimby. "Besides spitting licorice in the sand?"

"Daddy, don't be silly," said Ramona. "I don't know exactly." Now that she was the center of attention, she wished she had more information. "Something about oil. Drills or rigs or something. Howie understands all about it. His uncle earned a lot of money." The Quimbys were a family who had to worry about money.

"Oh, that kind of rich," said Mr. Quimby. "I thought maybe a long-lost uncle had died and left him a castle full of servants, jewels, and rare old wines."

"Daddy, that's so old-fashioned," said

5

Ramona. "That's only in books."

The conversation drifted off, leaving Ramona behind. Her father, who would earn his teaching credential in June, said he was inquiring around for schools that needed an art teacher, and he also told about the problems of the men who worked in the same frozen-food warehouse where he worked on weekends at below-freezing temperatures. Mrs. Quimby told about two people who got into an argument over a parking space at the doctor's office where she worked. Aunt Bea talked about a man named Michael who had invited her to go skiing and was the reason she had bought new ski clothes. Beezus wondered aloud if Michael would ask Aunt Bea to marry him. Aunt Bea laughed at that, saying she had known him only two weeks, but since this was January, there were several months of skiing left and there was no telling what might happen.

No more was said about Howie's uncle that evening. Days went by. Uncle Hobart didn't come and didn't come. Every evening Mr. Quimby asked, "Has Old Moneybags arrived?" And Ramona had to say no.

Finally one morning, as Ramona and Howie were waiting for the school bus, Ramona said, "I don't think you have a rich uncle at all. I think you made him up."

Howie said he did too have a rich uncle. Even little Willa Jean, when Ramona went to the Kemps' after school, talked about Uncle Hobart and the presents he was bringing. Ramona informed Howie and Willa Jean rather crossly that her mother said it wasn't nice to talk about other people's money. They paid no attention—after all, he was their very own uncle, not Ramona's—and went right on talking about Uncle Hobart this and Uncle Hobart that. Uncle Hobart had landed in New York. He had actually telephoned, live and in person. Uncle Hobart was driving across the country. Uncle Hobart was delayed by a storm in the Rockies. Ramona wished she had never heard of Uncle Hobart.

Then, one day after school, Ramona and Howie saw a muddy van parked on the Kemps' driveway.

"It's Uncle Hobart!" Howie shouted, and began to run.

Ramona took her time. Somehow she had expected Uncle Hobart to arrive in a long black limousine, not a muddy van. She followed Howie into the house, where the famous uncle turned out to be a medium-young man who had not shaved for several days and who was wearing old jeans and a faded T-shirt. He was holding Willa Jean on his lap. The warm, sweet smell of apple pie filled the air.

"Down you go, Doll," said Uncle Hobart, lifting Willa Jean to the floor and grabbing

Howie in a bear hug. "How's my favorite nephew?" he asked, and held Howie off to look at him while Mrs. Kemp hovered and Willa Jean embraced her Uncle Hobart's knee.

Ramona was embarrassed. She felt she was in the way because she was not related. She sat down on a chair, opened a book, but did not read. She studied Uncle Hobart, who didn't look rich to her. He looked like a plain man—a big disappointment.

Willa Jean let go of her uncle's knee. "See what Uncle Hobart brought us," she said, and pointed to a pair of objects that looked like two small sawhorses, each holding a red leather cushion. Willa Jean sat astride one. "Giddyup, you old camel," she said and informed Ramona, "This is my camel saddle."

"Hey, a camel saddle!" said Howie when he saw his present. He imitated Willa Jean. After a few more giddyups, there was nothing

9

more to do with a camel saddle except sit on it.

Pooh, who wants a boring old camel saddle, Ramona wanted to say, at the same time wishing she had a saddle to sit on these winter days when she liked to read by the furnace outlet.

Finally Uncle Hobart noticed Ramona. "Well, who's this young lady?" he asked. "Howie, you didn't tell me you had a girl-friend."

Both Ramona and Howie turned red and somehow felt ashamed.

"Aw, that's just old Ramona," Howie muttered.

To Ramona's horror, Uncle Hobart began to strum an imaginary guitar and sing:

"Ramona, I hear the mission bells above.
Ramona, they're ringing out our song of love.
I press you, caress you,
And bless the day you taught me to care."

Ramona knew right then that she did not like Uncle Hobart and never would. She had heard that song before. When Grandpa Day lived in Portland, he used to sing it to tease her, too. "I'm not Howie's girlfriend," she said in her most grown-up manner. "I have to stay here until my mother is through work. It is"—could she get the words out right?—"strictly a business arrangement."

Uncle Hobart found this very funny, which made Ramona dislike him even more.

"Cut it out, Uncle Hobart," said Howie, a remark much appreciated by Ramona, who pretended to read her book while inside she churned with anger. She was *glad* she didn't have an Uncle Hobart. She was *glad* she didn't have any uncles at all, just Aunt Beatrice, who never embarrassed children and who always came when the family needed her.

"Did you bring us any more presents?" asked Willa Jean.

"Willa Jean, that isn't nice," said Mrs. Kemp, smiling because she was so happy to have her youngest son home at last.

"Willa Jean, how did you guess?" asked Uncle Hobart. "Come on out to the van, and I'll show you."

"Me, too?" Howie quickly forgot his annoyance.

"Sure." As he went out the door, Uncle Hobart said, "It's great to be back in a country full of green grass and trees."

Ramona heard Howie ask, "What do camels eat if there isn't any grass?"

When they returned, Ramona lost her struggle to be interested in her book. Uncle Hobart was carrying a small accordion.

"Grandma, look!" Howie was wheeling what appeared to be part of a bicycle. "It's a real unicycle!"

"Is it broken?" asked Willa Jean. "It has only one wheel."

"Hobart, whatever were you thinking of?" Mrs. Kemp frowned at the unicycle.

"I was thinking of the unicycle you wouldn't let me have when I was Howie's age," said Uncle Hobart. "Now, Mom, don't you worry about a thing. I'll help him. He's not going to break any bones." He set the accordion on the floor by Willa Jean. "And this is for you," he said.

Willa Jean eyed the accordion. "What does it do?" she asked.

"You can play music on it," answered her uncle. "It's a Viennese accordion. I bought it from one of the men I worked with and even learned to play it a little."

"Isn't that lovely, Willa Jean?" said Mrs. Kemp. "Your very own musical instrument. We'll put it away until you're old enough to learn to play it."

"No!" Willa Jean put on her stubborn look. "I want to play it now!"

Uncle Hobart took the accordion and began to play and sing:

"Ramona, I hear the mission bells above,
Ramona, they're ringing out our song of love."

Ramona stared at her book as she thought mean, dark thoughts about Uncle Hobart. He stopped playing and said, "What's the matter, Ramona? Don't you like my music?"

"No." Ramona looked the uncle in the eye. "You're teasing. I don't like grown-ups who tease."

"Why, Ramona!" Mrs. Kemp was most disapproving. "That's no way to talk to Howie's uncle."

"Now, Mom, don't get excited," said Uncle Hobart. "Ramona has a point. I was teasing, but I'll reform. Okay, Ramona?"

"Okay," agreed Ramona, suspecting he might still be teasing.

"Uncle Hobart, Uncle Hobart, let me play it," begged Willa Jean.

The uncle placed Willa Jean's hands through the straps at each end of the accordion. "You squeeze in and pull out while you press the little buttons," he explained.

Before he could give any more instructions, Howie grabbed his uncle by the hand and dragged him outdoors. Mrs. Kemp, sure that bones were about to be broken, followed. Ramona watched through the window. Uncle Hobart hopped on the unicycle and, waving to his audience, pedaled to the corner and back. "See, nothing to it," he said. "Once you know how."

"Hobart, where on earth did you learn to ride that thing?" his mother called out from the front steps.

"In college," answered her son. "Come on, Howie, it's your turn." Holding the unicycle upright with one hand, he helped Howie

15

mount the seat over the single wheel. "Now pedal," he directed. Howie pedaled; the unicycle tipped forward, setting Howie on the sidewalk.

Indoors, Willa Jean struggled with the accordion, too heavy for her, and made it give out a loud groan, as if it were in pain.

"No, not that way," Ramona heard Uncle Hobart say. "It's like riding a bicycle, only instead of balancing sideways, you have to balance back and forth at the same time."

With a flushed and determined face, Howie mounted the unicycle again. If he learns to ride it, maybe he'll let me ride his bicycle, thought Ramona, who longed for a bicycle, even a secondhand, three-speed bicycle. Howie tipped over backward into his uncle's arms. The accordion squawked. Ramona felt rather lonely, left out and in the way.

"Hobart, do be careful," shouted Mrs.

Kemp above the squawk and screech of Willa Jean's playing.

Ramona could see that learning to ride a unicycle was going to take time, so she turned her attention to Willa Jean and the accordion.

Willa Jean set her gift on the floor and sat down on her camel saddle with a scowl. "It's too big and it won't play music."

"Let me try." Ramona was sure she could make music come out of the accordion. It looked so easy. She slipped her hands through the straps. The only song she could think of was, unfortunately, "Ramona." She pumped and pushed the buttons, only to produce the cry of a suffering accordion. She tried pushing different buttons while she pushed the bellows in and out. *Hee-haw, hee-haw.* This was not the music Ramona had in mind.

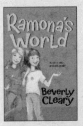